1980

THE BEST SHORT PLAYS 1975

BOOKS AND PLAYS *by Stanley Richards*

BOOKS:

The Best Short Plays 1974
The Best Short Plays 1973
The Best Short Plays 1972
The Best Short Plays 1971
The Best Short Plays 1970
The Best Short Plays 1969
The Best Short Plays 1968
Ten Great Musicals of the American Theatre
Best Mystery and Suspense Plays of the Modern Theatre
10 Classic Mystery and Suspense Plays of the Modern Theatre
Best Plays of the Sixties
Modern Short Comedies from Broadway and London
Best Short Plays of the World Theatre: 1968—1973
Best Short Plays of the World Theatre: 1958—1967
Canada on Stage

PLAYS:

Through a Glass, Darkly
August Heat
Sun Deck
Tunnel of Love
Journey to Bahia
O Distant Land
Mood Piece
Mr. Bell's Creation
The Proud Age
Once to Every Boy
Half-Hour, Please
Know Your Neighbor
Gin and Bitterness
The Hills of Bataan
District of Columbia

Chilton Book Company
RADNOR, PENNSYLVANIA

THE BEST SHORT PLAYS 1975

edited and with an introduction by

S T A N L E Y   R I C H A R D S

Best Short Plays Series

Copyright © 1975 by Stanley Richards
First Edition
All Rights Reserved
Published in Radnor, Pa., by Chilton Book Company
and simultaneously in Don Mills, Ont., Canada
by Thomas Nelson & Sons, Ltd.

Designed by Adrienne Onderdonk Dudden
Manufactured in the United States of America

ISBN 0-8019-5887-3
Library of Congress Catalog Card No. 38-806

for Roberta Kent

CONTENTS

INTRODUCTION

As editor of *The Best Short Plays* series, I have been asked
often whether there was a definite theme to each volume.
That theme is quality and diversity. And in this volume, as
with those in the past, we have a varied and eclectic collection of plays that I hope will appeal to and entertain a vast
majority of readers. To impress one sector, say that of the
theatre of the absurd or the vastly experimental, and neglect
that faction which prefers and enjoys the theatre of realism
and tangible thought would be tantamount to stuffing dinner
guests with twelve courses of the same cut of beef. Thus, it
is a creative editor's obligation to select as varied and bal-
anced a collection of plays as possible; but in whatever form
they may have been written (drama, comedy, experimental,
absurdist), they must have those essential and common com-
ponents: quality and dramatic style.

Since, in general, it is only the author or editor of a
book and his publishers who are treated to a compendium of
notices from reviewers, I hope it will not be too impertinent
of me to share with you some recent newspaper and magazine quotes; for in essence and in most cases, the reviewers
have put down quite succinctly what I have attempted to do
in *The Best Short Plays* series.

To begin with there is George Oppenheimer, one of
the theatre's most respected critics who upon covering one of
the volumes in the series commented: "I was again made
aware of the variety in our theatre. Mr. Richards has done an
exemplary job in picking what he considers the best short
plays of the past year from America and England, and his
selection exhibits vividly the virtues and the vices of the
contemporary scene."

In his coverage of the succeeding volume, drama critic Emory Lewis wrote: "Every once in a long while a splendid summer book comes along that must be read. Such a volume is *The Best Short Plays 1972*, edited by Stanley Richards who has selected dramatists representing both the styles of today and tomorrow. The book is a healthy, glowing statement about the superb state of contemporary playwriting...It makes me feel much better about the current state of writing for the theatre."

Going farther afield, the British magazine *Drama* observed: "Nowadays the structure of plays is something so loose that any attempt to arrive at a formula of any kind may be regarded as almost quaint. And yet the best of plays once written and published assume the proportions of authority in a way that at once gives them 'class' and even 'style.'

"Look at any published page of [Harold] Pinter and the precision is immediate; it has a quality that is unique and this is certainly one of the things any anthologist must be looking for when compiling a volume under the auspicious title of *The Best Short Plays*.

"Stanley Richards who has edited this book shows a real understanding of what is meant by the best of something and manages a selection of short plays which is truly astonishing in that each and every one may be described as a winner. It is seldom that one can say much about the assembly of work drawn from so many quarters, but this book is without doubt important theatre reading both from the practical and academic point of view.

"Perhaps the best feature is that there is no attempt to be fashionable. There is no snob value in this: one is simply aware that all the writers included by Mr. Richards are truly writers—not apprentices."

Finally, and in order not to bore the reader with such extravagant (though, admittedly, most welcome) praise, I would just like to conclude with one more critical quote: "Theatrically speaking, this collection seems to have everything—drama, tension, pathos, humor and absurdity.

Mr. Richards has selected short plays that are representative of the life blood, the response, and the creative power of the international theatre at its best. Also selecting them to give the reader a cross section of themes, subject matter, styles and types...He has singlehandedly given the short play form new life, luster and dimension and has brought to *The Best Short Plays* series not only the most eminent names in the theatre of the western world, but the most exciting of the new breed of playwright as well."

I do hope that all of the above does not indicate a voyage into self-indulgence. But as stated earlier, I did want to share with you the fact that the press has eloquently pinpointed my aims in compiling each year's collection of *The Best Short Plays.*

As every dramatist and theatrical management knows, publication of a play prolongs its life. Once published, it not only is read but brought to the attention of myriad producing groups who otherwise might be unaware of the existence of some of these meritorious plays. And that is where both the play and the author reach complete fulfillment: in production.

There is equal gratification for an editor to discover that the plays he has selected suddenly and successfully take to life on the stage or in television. As a point of fact, when I chose Terence Rattigan's moving drama *After Lydia (In Praise of Love)* for inclusion in this anthology, I hadn't the slightest awareness that it would evolve into a major Broadway production with two of the theatre's most luminous stars, Rex Harrison and Julie Harris. Nor for that matter, when I contracted for the inclusion of Terrence McNally's delightful comedy, *Ravenswood* (then being performed Off-Broadway as part of a double bill, *Bad Habits),* did I have any indication that it would later make a successful transference to Broadway's Booth Theatre.

It also is equally heartening to hear from authors and their representatives that plays in this series are so widely produced in regional theatres, colleges and universities.

From the printed page to the stage is the goal of every writer and I am indeed proud and privileged to provide a forum for their theatrical acceptance.

STANLEY RICHARDS
New York, N.Y.

Terrence McNally

RAVENSWOOD

Terrence McNally

When Terrence McNally's double bill, *Bad Habits,* opened at the Off-Broadway Astor Place Theatre on February 4, 1974, it was greeted with joyous praise by the press. The evening's entertainment was comprised of two thematically related short plays, both set in curative homes founded on opposing philosophies: *Ravenswood* (which appears in an anthology for the first time in *The Best Short Plays 1975)* and *Dunelawn.*

Clive Barnes of *The New York Times* called it "a continuous obbligato of laughter," while *Variety* hailed it as "the best comedy so far this season." Douglas Watt in the *New York Daily News* thought it "funny enough for two theatres" and his colleague on the *New York Post,* Richard Watts, Jr., found it "genuinely funny... Terrence McNally is undeniably a writer with a gift for laughter." The critical verdict was unanimous: *Bad Habits* was a howling success and after a sellout engagement at the Astor Place Theatre, it was transferred on May 5, 1974, to Broadway's Booth Theatre where, as of this writing, it continues to delight audiences. The recipient of two "Obie" awards, it also was chosen as one of the "ten best plays of the New York theatre season, 1973-74" by Otis L. Guernsey, Jr., editor of the theatre yearbook.

In *Ravenswood,* Dr. Pepper offers permissiveness as a cure for embattled couples of all sexes. The daffy doctor (and his equally eccentric servant with a mania for giving rubdowns) advises his clients to enjoy themselves as the quickest road to emotional adjustment. It is satire of a high order on America's craze for adjustment.

Born in 1939 and raised in Corpus Christi, Texas, the author came to New York to attend Columbia University, where he earned a B.A. degree in English in 1960. On graduation he was awarded the Harry Evans Traveling Fellowship for work in creative writing and in 1967 he received a Guggenheim Fellowship.

On March 20, 1963, Mr. McNally made his Broadway debut as playwright with a new adaptation of *The Lady of the Camellias,* designed and directed by Franco Zeffirelli. Two years later, the author again was represented on Broadway, this time with an original work that had had its premiere (1964) at the Tyrone Guthrie Theatre, Minneapolis—*And Things That Go Bump in the Night.* The New York presentation (1965) was directed by Michael Cacoyannis and starred Eileen Heckart.

Few of his contemporaries would contest the fact that Terrence McNally was one of the most reviewed young dramatists of the 1968-69 season when six of his short plays occupied Manhattan stages: the double bill *Sweet Eros* and *Witness,* Gramercy Arts; *¡Cuba Si!,* with Viveca Lindfors, Theatre de Lys; *Tour,* a highlight of *Collision Course,* Café au Go Go; and *Noon,* included in the tripartite *Morning, Noon and Night,* Henry Miller's Theatre.

His most outstanding success during that period was *Next* (included in *The Best Short Plays 1970)* which opened at the Greenwich Mews Theatre on February 10, 1969. Paired with Elaine May's *Adaptation,* and starring James Coco, *Next* ran for 707 performances.

The author also enjoyed wide praise for his 1968 television production, *Apple Pie. The New York Times* lauded the three short plays in the overall work as "a bitingly original look at some American attitudes toward the war in Vietnam." Mr. McNally continued his exploration of the same theme in *Bringing It All Back Home* which was introduced in *The Best Short Plays 1969.*

In October, 1971, his full-length play *Where Has Tommy Flowers Gone?* was produced at the Eastside Playhouse and in 1973 his *Whiskey* was performed at Theatre at St. Clement's, New York City, and was welcomed as an "hilarious commentary on contemporary society and its standards."

Another recent McNally work, *The Tubs,* was given its premiere by the Yale Repertory Theatre, New Haven, and his plays have been staged in many regional theatres as well as in Europe and South America.

Characters:

APRIL PITT
ROY PITT
OTTO
JASON PEPPER, M.D.
DOLLY SCUPP —wife.
HIRAM SPANE
FRANCIS TEAR
HARRY SCUPP — husband

Scene:

The setting is outdoors. Bare stage. Bright sunlight. Birds chirping. Huge flowers, lush foliage. Heaven on earth.

April and Roy Pitt enter.

APRIL: So this is Ravenswood! Nice. Very nice.

ROY: Look at that clay court, honey. Real clay. Can you stand it?

(Otto enters with their luggage)

APRIL: That's Vuitton, buddy.

OTTO: Ja, fraulein.

APRIL: Just thought I'd mention it.

OTTO: Ja, fraulein.

APRIL: Jesus, Roy, it's the Gestapo. I just hope this Pepper fellow's all he's cracked up to be.

ROY: Hey, April, the ol' elbow's working!

APRIL: Christ knows we've been through analysis!

ROY: I told you: he's just gonna have us talk to each other.

APRIL: We talk to each other all the time. What's he gonna do?

ROY: Listen.

APRIL: Just listen? A hundred and forty-five clams a

day and he just listens? I knew I should have checked this guy out first.

ROY: Look what he did for Sandy and Reg.

APRIL: Sandy and Reg are lesbians and they're not in show business. They run a pet shop in Montauk for Christ's sake!

ROY: But they're happy.

APRIL: Sure, they're in dyke heaven those two. I'm talking about us, Roy.

ROY: So am I, April.

APRIL: I'm beginning not to like the smell of this whole set-up. When's our first session? This Pepper character doesn't deliver, we're gonna blow this nickel joint and head straight for the Cape. Right, Roy? *(But Roy is following Otto and his luggage)* I said easy with the Vuitton, schmuck!

(She goes. The stage is empty a beat. The birds chirp. Jason Pepper, M.D. enters with Dolly Scupp. He is in a wheelchair and drinking a martini. Dolly is pushing him. Her right foot is bandaged. She is limping and using a cane)

DR. PEPPER: Over there's our lake. A pond you might call it but I like to think of it as a lake. After all, it's the only body of water for miles and miles. When your husband was admitted to Ravenswood it was frozen over and quite covered with snow. And now look at it. Ah, the seasons, the seasons! I do love the seasons, Mrs. Scupp.

DOLLY: Me, too.

DR. PEPPER: Harry didn't tell me you were coming.

DOLLY: He didn't know. I woke up this morning and said to myself "I'm driving up to Ravenswood today." Don't ask me why. I just had this sudden urge to see you.

DR. PEPPER: It's a delightful surprise.

DOLLY: I hope so.

DR. PEPPER: Your absence has made his rehabilitation somewhat more difficult, you understand. I prefer to treat couples who are having difficulties *as* couples.

DOLLY: There's nothing wrong with me, if that's what you're driving at.

DR. PEPPER: Should I be?

DOLLY: Is my husband getting any better, Dr. Pepper?

DR. PEPPER: It's Jason, Mrs. Scupp. Please, I insist on it. And you're right: it's high time we had a little chat.

DOLLY: You look different on your book jacket.

DR. PEPPER: I know. Taller. May I? *(Dolly gives him the book she has been carrying under her arm) Marriage for the Fun of It!* Oh God, are people still reading this old tome?

DOLLY: Everybody who's still married.

DR. PEPPER: I thought I knew something in those days.

DOLLY: You're being too modest.

DR. PEPPER: Possibly. It's one of my virtues. This was taken years ago at a garden party for Hannah Tod-Laarsen in Sneden's Landing. I was sloshed. Thank God I'm not a surgeon. Cigarette?

DOLLY: No, thank you.

DR. PEPPER: It's a special tobacco, imported from Panama, that's been fertilized with hen feces. I don't think you'll find them at your A&P in Scarsdale.

DOLLY: I wouldn't think so.

DR. PEPPER: They've an extraordinarily...*pungent* taste!

DOLLY: I don't smoke.

DR. PEPPER: You're joking!

DOLLY: I gave it up years ago.

DR. PEPPER: During the big scare, huh?

(He is lighting his cigarette)

DOLLY: I thought the majority of doctors had, too.

DR. PEPPER: *(Exhaling)* And doesn't that just *sound* like something the majority of doctors would do? Fortunately, there remain a few of us who refuse to be stampeded along with the common herd. I'm referring to men like Otis Strunk of the Merton Institute, Guernsey Nethercott out at Las Palmetas?

DOLLY: I'm sorry, but I'm not familiar with them.

DR. PEPPER: Who is? I can't discuss colors with a blind person, Mrs. Scupp.

DOLLY: Actually, I wanted to give them up.

DR. PEPPER: Wanted to?

DOLLY: Well, I had this terrible cough and then my electrocardiogram turned out poorly. Our doctor insisted.

DR. PEPPER: And who might that be?

DOLLY: Dr. Fernald.

DR. PEPPER: Helmut Fernald up at Grassyview? I should've guessed he'd jump on the bandwagon.

DOLLY: No, George Fernald in White Plains, the County Medical Center.

DR. PEPPER: He wouldn't drive in a white Buick station wagon, usually there's a couple of dalmations yapping around in the back, and be married to one of the McIntyre sisters, would he?

DOLLY: I don't think so. Our Dr. Fernald's married to a Korean girl and I'm pretty sure they have a dachschund. I don't know what he drives. He's just our family doctor.

DR. PEPPER: Well, that explains it. The curse of modern medicine, that lot.

DOLLY: Dr. Fernald?

DR. PEPPER: Your friendly neighborhood, family G.P. Now don't get me started on *that*, Mrs. Scupp.

DOLLY: But surely, doctor, you're not suggesting that smoking is good for you?

DR. PEPPER: Of course not.

DOLLY: I didn't think so.

DR. PEPPER: What I *am* suggesting is that *not* smoking is conceivably worse.

DOLLY: I don't follow.

DR. PEPPER: Do you want to talk turkey, or not, Mrs. Scupp?

DOLLY: Of course I do! And please, call me Dolly.

DR. PEPPER: Dolly, is it?

DOLLY: I'm afraid so.

DR. PEPPER: Hello, Dolly.

DOLLY: Hello.

DR. PEPPER: Well, hello, Dolly.

DOLLY: It's my curse.

DR. PEPPER: You think Dr. Pepper's easy? Now let's start at the beginning and I'll try to keep it in layman's terms.

DOLLY: Thank you.

DR. PEPPER: Everything in life is bad for you. The air, the sun, the force of gravity, butter, eggs, coffee, this cigarette....

DOLLY: That drink.

DR. PEPPER: Canned tuna fish.

DOLLY: No!

DR. PEPPER: It's true! It's loaded with dolphin meat. There's an article on canned tuna fish in this month's *Food Facts* that will stand your hair on end. Peter Pan Peanut Butter, too, the chunky style. Though don't tell anyone but I've got a big jar of it in my bottom desk drawer.

DOLLY: Dolphin meat, you say?

DR. PEPPER: Ammoniacal nitrogen. The dolphin meat's in the tuna fish.

DOLLY: I love tuna fish.

DR. PEPPER: Don't we all, Mrs. Scupp? Right now, this very moment, as I speak these words, you're ten seconds closer to death than when I started. Eleven seconds, twelve seconds, thirteen. Have I made my point? Now how would an ice-cold, extra-dry, straight-up Gordon's gin martini grab you? *(He rings a service bell)*

DOLLY: I'm afraid it wouldn't.

DR. PEPPER: Ah, vodka is the lovely lady from Scarsdale's poison. *(He rings again)*

DOLLY: I don't drink anymore.

DR. PEPPER: You don't smoke, you don't drink...

DOLLY: And it's Larchmont.

(Otto appears)

OTTO: Das newly-weds est arriven.

DR. PEPPER: Das newly-weds Pitts?

OTTO: Ja, herr doktor. Ich putten zem in das kleine honeymoon cabin.

DR. PEPPER: Good, Otto, good. Tell them we'll have our first session after lunch. Show them the lake, the stables, the tennis court. The grand tour, Otto.

OTTO: I could give Mrs. Pitt a rubdown maybe?

DR. PEPPER: No, Otto.

OTTO: Whirlpool?

DR. PEPPER: Nothing, Otto. Just the tour.

OTTO: Das usual?

DR. PEPPER: Last call, Mrs. Scupp.

DOLLY: I'll have a Tab maybe.

OTTO: Nein Tab.

DOLLY: A Fresca?

OTTO: Nein Fresca.

DOLLY: Anything dietetic.

OTTO: Nichts dietetic, nichts!

DOLLY: Water then.

OTTO: Wasser?

DR. PEPPER: Wasser fur das frau!

OTTO: Jawohl.

DR. PEPPER:

(Otto has turned to go)

Und Otto! Dry-lich!

(Otto goes)

It's an extraordinary race. Is Scupp German?

DOLLY: We don't know what it is.

DR. PEPPER: Then I can say it: I can't stand them. It was a German who incapacitated me.

DOLLY: The war?

DR. PEPPER: My first wife. She pushed me down a short but lethal flight of stairs backstage at the Academy of Music in Philadelphia.

DOLLY: How horrible!

DR. PEPPER: It was the single most electrifying experience of my life.

DOLLY: But why would anyone do such a thing?

DR. PEPPER: You should be able to answer that, Mrs. Scupp.

DOLLY: My husband should, you mean!

DR. PEPPER: With my wife it was self-defense.

DOLLY: You mean you tried to kill her?

DR. PEPPER: Symbolically. I was just thinking: it's

funny how no one ever asks why it was a flight of stairs back-stage at the Academy of Music; you must admit, it's not your usual place for an attempted homicide. My wife was a lieder singer. She'd just given an all-Hugo Wolf recital. She asked me how I thought it went and I said, "Maybe the only thing in the world more boring than an all-Hugo Wolf recital is your singing of an all-Hugo Wolf recital." *(Dolly chuckles)* The remark just kind of popped out of me. And when it popped, she pushed and down I went. Four short steps and here I am. Don't look so tragic, Mrs. Scupp. No Anita Wertmuller and her all-Hugo Wolf recital and no Ravens-wood. Having been unhappy in marriage, hopefully I can help others to solve their problems. Look for the silver lining, yes?

DOLLY: Harry told you about trying to run me over with the lawn mower?

DR. PEPPER: The third and fourth toes of your left foot, wasn't it?

DOLLY: The second and third of the right.

DR. PEPPER: Accidents will happen.

DOLLY: Not with a remote control power lawn mower, doctor!

DR. PEPPER: Those things are devils.

DOLLY: Harry was controlling it. I was sunbathing.

DR. PEPPER: Harry didn't go into it in much detail.

DOLLY: Of course he didn't. That's why he's here.

DR. PEPPER: He said there'd been an accident and that was why you hadn't come with him.

DOLLY: I wouldn't have come with him even if it hadn't happened. I'm sorry, but I can't afford to take any more chances like that with him.

DR. PEPPER: That's what marriage is, Mrs. Scupp.

DOLLY: Not with a husband who tried to kill you it isn't! Two toes, doctor.

DR. PEPPER: Two legs, Dolly.

DOLLY: You don't understand. My husband tried to kill me and I want to know is he getting any better yet, doctor?

DR. PEPPER: He'll be along shortly. You can see for yourself.

DOLLY: Where is he?

DR. PEPPER: Still in bed if I know Harry.

DOLLY: It must be the medication you're using.

DR. PEPPER: He's not on medication. I hope we're talking about the same man.

DOLLY: I hope we are, too.

(Hiram Spane enters. He is wearing a sun hat, bath-robe and beach sandals).

DR. PEPPER: Good morning, Hiram!

HIRAM: Morning? I was hoping it was late after-noon. I haven't been up this early since the opening of the World's Fair.

DR. PEPPER: What were you doing at a World's Fair, Hiram?

HIRAM: I don't know! Some pavilion or something mother was opening or closing or whatever she did at or to pavilions.

DOLLY: Which World's Fair was that?

HIRAM: The last one. I don't believe we've been in-troduced. Bitch.

DR. PEPPER: This is Mrs. Scupp.

HIRAM: Harry's wife! How do you do? I'm sorry, you're not a bitch and I'm only a bitch when I've got a head on me, like this one. I thought *I* mixed a wicked vodka stinger! What did your husband do? Study alchemy?

DOLLY: Harry? Drinking? My Harry? Harry Scupp?

DR. PEPPER: Why don't you take that dip now, Hiram?

HIRAM: You like to swim?

DOLLY: I love to, but—

HIRAM: Come on. I believe in the buddy system. You start to drown, I'll save you. I start to drown, forget it.

DOLLY: I didn't bring a suit.

HIRAM: That never stopped anyone around this place. What do you think I've got on under here?

DOLLY: I blush to think.

HIRAM: *You blush to think?* I've got to live with it! If that goddamn snapping turtle doesn't attack me again, doctor, you can tell Otto I'll be joining you here shortly for my Bullshot!

(He goes)

DR. PEPPER: Hiram Spane of the Newport Spanes. They own everything.

DOLLY: He seems...

DR. PEPPER: He is.

DOLLY: Is he a patient here?

DR. PEPPER: Hiram's been a patient here since I founded Ravenswood.

DOLLY: What's his problem?

DR. PEPPER: You're looking at him.

DOLLY: Oh, my God!

(Francis Tear has appeared. He is wearing a bathing cap, a bathrobe and rubber bathing shoes)

DR. PEPPER: Francis Tear of the Baltimore Tears. They made their fortune in plumbing. Good morning, Francis! You just missed each other.

FRANCIS: We're not speaking today.

DR. PEPPER: You and I?

FRANCIS: Hiram and me. He said something very cutting to me last night. Hurt me to the quick, he did. I don't think I'm ready to forgive him yet.

DR. PEPPER: Fine, fine, there's no point in rushing it.

FRANCIS: Do you think I look like an embryo, madam?

DOLLY: Not at all.

FRANCIS: Thank you.

DR. PEPPER: This is Mrs. Scupp, Francis.

FRANCIS: Hello.

DR. PEPPER: Harry Scupp's wife.

FRANCIS: Well, I didn't think it was his mother. I'm Francis Tear of the Baltimore Tears. We made our fortune in plumbing!

DOLLY: Yes, I know.

FRANCIS: Somebody had to do it.

DOLLY: I suppose so.

FRANCIS: What are you in?

DOLLY: I'm just a housewife.

FRANCIS: So's Hiram. He's also in distress. Psychic distress, doctor!

DR. PEPPER: Not now, Francis. I like your new bathing slippers.

FRANCIS: There may be fairies at the bottom of somebody's garden but there are very sharp rocks at the bottom of *his* lake. Hiram's mother had them sent. It was a pleasure, Mrs. Scupp. It must be Jewish, Scupp.

DOLLY: I was just telling Jason, we don't know what it is.

FRANCIS: It's Jewish. *(He turns to go)* Oh, no! I get the raft today, Hiram! You had it yesterday! And this doesn't mean I'm speaking to you yet! *(He is gone)*

DR. PEPPER: Eighteen years they've been together.

DOLLY: Are they homosexuals?

DR. PEPPER: Good God, I hope not. Although, I'd like to be a fly on that wall, if they are. I think they're just old, old friends.

DOLLY: Then what are they doing here?

DR. PEPPER: I think they want to stay that way. Let's face it, Mrs. Scupp, love is where you find it.

DOLLY: That's true.

DR. PEPPER: Don't be blind, it's all around you.

DOLLY: I just didn't know you treated male couples at Ravenswood.

DR. PEPPER: A male couple is better than no couple at all, don't you think, Mrs. Scupp?

DOLLY: Harry is so intolerant of people like that.

DR. PEPPER: He seems quite fond of those two.

DOLLY: Harry has a lot of problems but one thing he's not is queer! Of course at this point any change in him would have to be one for the better. *(She is still laughing when Otto returns with the martini and glass of water. Otto barks out a gruff laugh, which of course makes Dolly wonder how much of their conversation he has overheard)*

DOLLY: Thank you, Otto.

DR. PEPPER: Danke, Otto.

OTTO: Das frau wole ein rubdown?

DOLLY: I don't think so.

OTTO: *(Shrugging)* Okay. *(He takes a magazine out of his back pocket, opens it, sits and reads. The magazine has a startling cover. Otto chuckles. Dolly fidgets)*

DR. PEPPER: Cheers!

DOLLY: Doctor—

DR. PEPPER: Dont't mind Otto. It would take a lot more than your lawn mower to get his nose out of that magazine.

DOLLY: Why would Harry want to kill me?

DR. PEPPER: I've never been more fond of a patient.

DOLLY: Doctor, why would he want to kill me? You haven't answered my question.

DR. PEPPER: Do you still want to talk turkey or not, Mrs. Scupp?

DOLLY: About Harry? Of course I do.

DR. PEPPER: About you.

DOLLY: What do you mean?

DR. PEPPER: Does Labor Day weekend, 1963, the parking lot outside Benny's Clam Box in Rockport, Maine, do anything for you?

DOLLY: I don't know. Should it?

DR. PEPPER: Harry was loading the car trunk and you put the car into reverse.

DOLLY: Benny's Clam Box?

DR. PEPPER: We have very complete files on our guests here, Mrs. Scupp. Ravenswood is a long way from the Westchester County Medical Center and your quack G.P. with his Korean war bride and dachschund.

DOLLY: *(Impressed)* You mean Dr. Fernald?

DR. PEPPER: Now: eight months later you tried to run him over with a golf cart at the Westchester Country Club.

DOLLY: It was an accident. My foot got stuck on the accelerator.

DR. PEPPER: A year later he asked you if there was water in the swimming pool before diving in.

DOLLY: I thought he'd asked me something about our puli.

DR. PEPPER: Your puli didn't end up in White Plains Hospital with a broken leg! *(Dolly is starting to go to pieces)* And what about your safari to East Africa last winter?

DOLLY: He didn't tell you about that, too!

DR. PEPPER: Harry's just lucky he's not the one who's stuffed and mounted over the fireplace, Mrs. Scupp.

DOLLY: I was delirious. A touch of malaria, I remember. I mistook him for something else!

DR. PEPPER: No, you didn't.

DOLLY: I don't want to hear those things.

DR. PEPPER: You said you wanted to talk turkey. All right, here's the real turkey, Mrs. Scupp: You and your husband have been trying to kill one another since Labor Day weekend of 1963. Why?

(Dolly has broken down now. There is a long pause as she sobs and sobs. Dr. Pepper regards her compassionately)

DOLLY: Has he been neat, doctor?

DR. PEPPER: Neat?

DOLLY: Neat!

DR. PEPPER: Oh, neat! A little over-fastidious when he got here, perhaps ...

DOLLY: Did you ever hear of a man who went around straightening license plates in a public parking lot?

DR. PEPPER: He was that bad?

DOLLY: The worst! And if they're dirty he dusts them.

DR. PEPPER: Really?

DOLLY: And what about a man who gets up at seven A.M. and vacuums before he goes to work?

DR. PEPPER: That's pretty neat.

DOLLY: And the coasters, doctor.

DR. PEPPER: Coasters?

DOLLY: Those things you put under glasses so they don't leave a ring. I can be downstairs in the den watching television late at night and he'll come in with a coaster for my glass.

DR. PEPPER: I thought you said he went to bed early?

DOLLY: He wakes up worrying I'm making rings!

DR. PEPPER: This is a whole other side of him, of course.

DOLLY: The same with the cigarettes when I smoked. As soon as I'd put one out, he'd take the ashtray in the kitchen and wash it. He said it was a filthy habit.

DR. PEPPER: It is.

DOLLY: But washing out an ashtray after each cigarette?

DR. PEPPER: Don't you have a housekeeper?

DOLLY: With a husband like that who can keep one? Doctor, he goes into my closets and straightens my shoes.

DR. PEPPER: Usually they wear them.

DOLLY: I wish he would put them on some time and break his leg. No, he just straightens them. But it's the coasters, the coasters that are the worst. He's got them in the bathroom. He's worried about water rings *on* the bathtub.

DR. PEPPER: What about in bed?

DOLLY: He sleeps with a flashlight on the bed table.

DR. PEPPER: Because of burglars!

DOLLY: No, water rings! In case of burglars he'd send me down! His hobby is tropical fish, Doctor. What kind of a hobby are guppies for a man? I hate tropical fish. You can't even eat them. And you know something else I hate? Stereo equipment! I hate woofers, weefers, baffles, pre-amps. I hate his black Volvo station wagon with the snow tires on it in August. I hate his bay rum cologne. I hate his baggy boxer shorts. I hate his big clumpy cordovans. I hate his Bermuda shorts with the knee socks. I hate his "Genius at work" barbecue apron. I hate the way he reads road signs on a trip. "Soft shoulders, Dolly" "Falling rock, Dolly." I mean *I* can read. "Oh, oh, Dolly, slippery when wet." I hate his friends: especially Fred Plummer who comes over once a week to play rummy with him and vacuum up afterwards. I'd even say I hate his voice, Doctor, but I haven't heard it in years. Only Paco, our dog can. So don't make too much out of that incident with the lawn mower. That was just the straw that broke the camel's back.

DR. PEPPER: And a very attractive camel she is, too.

DOLLY: Thank you.

OTTO: *(Looking up from his magazine)* Das frau wole ein rubdown now?

(Dr. Pepper silences him with a gesture. Otto resumes reading)

DR. PEPPER: Mrs. Scupp! Dolly! Look at me. *(Dolly raises her head)* I'm not famous for saving marriages, Mrs. Scupp. I'm not even certain I believe in them. I'm famous for successful marriages for people who want to be married. I think I can help you but you have to want me to help you.

(Harry is heard calling "Otto! Otto! off)

Harry's coming. I'll leave you two alone. Otto.

DOLLY: But—!

DR. PEPPER: I've done all I can for him. It's up to you now.

DOLLY: I'm frightened.

DR. PEPPER: Given your track record I think Harry is the one with cause for alarm, Mrs. Scupp. I'll be right over there. Behind the hedges.

(Otto wheels Dr. Pepper off. Dolly composes herself. Harry Scupp enters. He, too, is dressed for swimming. He is carrying a small cardboard box)

HARRY: Otto? Otto?

(Otto appears)

OTTO: Morgen, herr Scupp. Das usual?

HARRY: Thanks, Otto.

(Otto clicks his heels and goes. Harry looks at the box in his hand and is about to throw it away)

DOLLY: Hello, Harry.

HARRY: Hello, Dolly.

DOLLY: Surprised to see me?

HARRY: Wow!

DOLLY: How are you?

HARRY: Fine. How are you?

DOLLY: Fine.

HARRY: How are the kids?
DOLLY: Fine.
HARRY: You look well.
DOLLY: I've lost weight.
HARRY: I haven't.
DOLLY: I've got your *Stereo Reviews* and *Popular Aquariums* in the car.
HARRY: Thank you.
DOLLY: And your summer pajamas you wrote for.
HARRY: The blue cottons?
DOLLY: I thought you meant the yellow drip-drys.
HARRY: That's okay.
DOLLY: I'm sorry.
HARRY: Really, it doesn't matter.
DOLLY: It's a pleasant drive up here.
HARRY: I hope you took it easy on the cloverleaf outside of Inglenook.
DOLLY: Oh, I did. I thought of you when I read the sign.
HARRY: Thirteen and a half people have been killed on it so far this year.
DOLLY: I'll be extra careful on the way back.
HARRY: When are you leaving?
DOLLY: That depends. What's in the box?
HARRY: Otis.
DOLLY: Otis?
HARRY: My angel fish.
DOLLY: What happened?
HARRY: Douglas killed him.
DOLLY: Who's Douglas?
HARRY: My blue beta.
DOLLY: That's awful.
HARRY: It's just a fish.
(He throws the box into the bushes)
DOLLY: You always used to give them such nice burials.
HARRY: I guess I'm getting cynical in my old age. *(He is taking out a cigarette)* So what's new?

DOLLY: Nothing much.

HARRY: I guess you sold the lawn mower.

DOLLY: No. It's in the garage waiting for you.

HARRY: Thanks.

DOLLY: It's broken, of course.

HARRY: I wasn't really trying to get you with it.

DOLLY: Yes, you were. *Why,* Harry?

HARRY: There were a million reasons. The aquarium filter you forgot to pick up. The refrigerator needed defrosting. That bridge party you had the night before. Paco needed his booster shots; the vet had sent you three warning cards already. You'd let my subscription to *Fortune* run out.

DOLLY: *Forbes.*

HARRY: The car keys were upstairs when they should have been downstairs. You'd let Billy play with my stereo. There were new rings on the coffee table. It was hot. Things like that. What was it with *me?*

DOLLY: The coasters.

HARRY: Not the fish?

DOLLY: The coasters.

HARRY: I wasn't going to mention it, but...

(He motions toward Dolly's glass. She puts it on a coaster)

DOLLY: I'm sorry.

HARRY: That's okay.

DOLLY: Dr. Pepper seems to think you're ready to leave now.

HARRY: He's done wonders for me, Dolly.

DOLLY: When did you take that up?

HARRY: A couple of months ago. You want one?

DOLLY: No, thank you.

HARRY: They're fertilized with chicken shit, honey.

DOLLY: I know!

(Otto has returned with a Bloody Mary)

HARRY: You're still on the wagon, too, I see.

DOLLY: Please, don't mention it.

HARRY: Poor Dolly, I remember how you loved your Chesterfields, Manhattans.

DOLLY: Whiskey sours.

HARRY: Whiskey sours were they? In those days I thought anything brown in a glass was a Manhattan. Thanks, Otto.

OTTO: Rubdown, herr Scupp?

HARRY: Not just now, Otto. Maybe later.

OTTO: Jawohl.

(Otto sits and opens his magazine)

DOLLY: You look terrible, Harry.

HARRY: I'm a little hungover.

DOLLY: On what?

HARRY: Margaritas. They're vicious, Dolly. Stay away from them.

DOLLY: What were you doing drinking margaritas?

HARRY: The Plungs.

DOLLY: Who?

HARRY: The Plungs.

DOLLY: What are the Plungs?

HARRY: Jeanine and Billy Plung. This young couple from Roanoke I got friendly with while they were up here. We had a farewell party for them last night. Jeanine had me doing the rhumba with her until nearly three.

DOLLY: You can't rhumba, Harry. You can't even fox trot.

HARRY: Jeanine said I'm a natural.

DOLLY: I thought they were taking care of you up here.

HARRY: They are. I never felt better in my life.

DOLLY: I don't know why you started smoking at your age.

HARRY: I like to smoke now.

DOLLY: That's not a good enough reason.

HARRY: I can't think of a better one.

DOLLY: Margaritas! And the rhumba, Harry! I mean, really!

HARRY: It's true.

DOLLY: How old was this woman?

HARRY: Twenty-two, twenty-three.

DOLLY: Harry, what's gotten into you?

HARRY: I'm my old self again. It's me, Harry Scupp with the De Soto roadster with the rumble seat and the good hooch and let's have a good time and "Beat Port Chester, Larchmont!" and Glen Island Casino and Dolly Veasey is my number one date. It's gonna be like the old times again, Doll.

DOLLY: We never had old times like that.

HARRY: It's never too late.

DOLLY: And what do you mean? Your old self?

HARRY: I love you. I don't want to kill you anymore.

DOLLY: You never had a De Soto roadster. We took the bus.

HARRY: I'm talking about life, Dolly. *Joie de vivre.* You want to see what I've been doing since I've been up here? Close your eyes. I'm not going to hit you. *(Dolly closes her eyes. He takes something out of his bathrobe pocket)* It's incredible you should be here today. I just finished this last night. Okay, Doll, open.

DOLLY: What is it?

HARRY: An ashtray.

DOLLY: An ashtray?

HARRY: It's a nude study of Jeanine.

DOLLY: Jeanine Plung?

HARRY: Isn't that pretty?

DOLLY: You sure it's Jeanine, Harry?

HARRY: Of course it's Jeanine. Who else could it be?

DOLLY: She posed for this?

HARRY: Eight sessions we had.

DOLLY: Nude?

HARRY: How else do you sculpt a nude? I did one of Billy I'm thinking of turning into a lamp.

DOLLY: What you're suggesting, Harry, is that you were somewhat more than just friendly with these people.

HARRY: Oh, I was! You'd go crazy over them and vice versa.

DOLLY: I wouldn't count on it.

HARRY: Now wait right here. There's something else I want to show you. Don't move.

(He runs off)

DOLLY: Doctor!

DR. PEPPER: *(Emerging)* Do you find any change in him?

DOLLY: What have you done to him?

DR. PEPPER: He's called you "honey" several times at least.

DOLLY: They're loaded with chicken shit, honey, is what he said. You mean Harry and these Plung people...?

DR. PEPPER: Just Mrs. Plung.

DOLLY: Where was Mr. Plung while all this was going on?

DR. PEPPER: Rumor has it with Otto.

DOLLY: I'm not surprised. And you just allowed all this to happen?

DR. PEPPER: There are no rules at Ravenswood, Mrs. Scupp.

DOLLY: Which means that you let my husband go off into the woods with that horrid Plung woman!

DR. PEPPER: How did you know she was horrid? That's one secret I thought I'd kept to myself. Dreadful woman. I don't know what your husband ever saw in her. He would've been better off with Otto.

DOLLY: I'm beginning to think you made my husband do all these terrible things.

DR. PEPPER: I've never made anyone do anything, Mrs. Scupp, which is the secret of my success here, such as it is. I allow everyone to do exactly as he pleases.

DOLLY: At your rates that's hardly what I'd call a bargain.

DR. PEPPER: You'd be surprised how few people know what it is they want.

DOLLY: I know what I want.

DR. PEPPER: Do you, Mrs. Scupp?

DOLLY: I thought I did until I saw him like this.

HARRY: *(Off)* You didn't know I was a frustrated song and dance man, did you?

DOLLY: I'm getting a headache. Do you have an aspirin?

DR. PEPPER: No.

DOLLY: Anything for it?

DR. PEPPER: This is Ravenswood, Mrs. Scupp. *(He hides as Harry rushes back in. He has a ukulele)*

HARRY: Now you're really gonna get a kick out of this, Dolly. It turns out I've got a singing voice. And feet, too. I've got rhythm, Dolly. You ready? Now listen to this. *(He launches into "Aba Daba Honeymoon." It's obvious he's been practicing. He's still pretty terrible, but he's having fun. He will tap dance, too)*

DOLLY: Stop it! I can't stand seeing you like this!

HARRY: Like what?

DOLLY: Smoking, drinking, singing, dancing! Making ashtrays!

HARRY: I told you it was a new me. Wait'll they see this at the country club. *(He launches into "Oceana Roll." Finally, Dolly smashes the ashtray. He stops)* You broke my ashtray.

DOLLY: I'm taking you home.

HARRY: You broke my ashtray.

DOLLY: I thought you came here to get better.

HARRY: You broke my ashtray! *(Harry is advancing on her)*

DOLLY: Harry? Keep away from me, Harry!

(Dolly is trying to get something out of her purse. Harry has started to strangle her. Dr. Pepper emerges)

DR. PEPPER: Harry!

(Harry takes his hands from Dolly's throat. Dolly has taken a can out of her purse and is pointing it. Hiram and Francis are heard calling to Harry from the lakeside. "Harry!" "Harry!")

HARRY: I promised I'd race them out to the raft. They're like kids that way. They'll keep it up all morning until I do.

(He goes. Dolly is trembling)

DR. PEPPER: What is it?

DOLLY: Mace!

DR. PEPPER: It's too bad my first wife didn't carry one of those. Too bad for me, that is.

DOLLY: You said he was better!

DR. PEPPER: You don't see the change?

DOLLY: Not the change I wanted!

DR. PEPPER: He loved that piece of sculpture.

DOLLY: What have you done to him?

DR. PEPPER: Harry's done himself. Maybe it's your turn now.

DOLLY: Maybe it isn't!

DR. PEPPER: Know what you want, Mrs. Scupp. That's the first step.

DOLLY: I want a good marriage.

DR. PEPPER: Give me three months.

DOLLY: And I want to be happy.

DR. PEPPER: Make it three and a half.

DOLLY: That's not much, is it?

DR. PEPPER: Sometimes it's everything. Now: it's a beautiful summer's day. God's in his heaven and all's right with the world. Harry will be waiting for you down by the lake. I'd go to him if I were you.

DOLLY: I'm still a little frightened of Harry! I can't go swimming with this foot. Maybe I could get him to take me boating.

DR. PEPPER: I wouldn't push my luck. Try skimming stones or the volleyball court maybe, Mrs. Scupp.

DOLLY: It's Dolly. Please, it's Dolly.

DR. PEPPER: Okay, Dolly.

DOLLY: It always happens.

DR. PEPPER: I know what you're going to say.

DOLLY: I always get a crush on doctors!

(Dolly rushes off. Dr. Pepper sits sipping his martini and smoking. There is more thunder. He looks up at the heavens and starts singing "Wien, du Stadt Meiner Traume"—"Vienna, City of My Dreams")

OTTO: Herr doktor is singing the song I love so much.

DR. PEPPER: I can't seem to get it out of my head this morning.

OTTO: My mother used to sing that song.

DR. PEPPER: It's a beauty.

OTTO: My mother was a pig! Herr doktor would like a nice rubdown now maybe? *(Dr. Pepper shakes his head)* I put him in the whirlpool bath? *(Dr. Pepper shakes his head)* He take a little nap then?

DR. PEPPER: Herr doktor just wants everyone to be happy.

OTTO: Happy?

DR. PEPPER: Du bist happy, Otto?

OTTO: Was ist happy?

DR. PEPPER: That's a good question, Otto.

(Otto grunts, goes back to reading his magazine. Just then a tennis ball bounces across the stage and hits Dr. Pepper in the head. He spills his martini)

ROY PITT: *(Off)* Hey, mac, you want to send that back?

DR. PEPPER: Otto! *(He points to the tennis ball)*

APRIL PITT: *(Off)* What's the matter with you? Send the ball back, you creep!

(Otto returns the ball)

ROY: *(Off)* Thanks a lot!

APRIL: *(Off)* Yeah, thanks loads!

DR. PEPPER: Das ists das newly-weds Pitts?

OTTO: Ja, das ists das Pitts.

DR. PEPPER: *(Holds out his empty glass)* Bitte, Otto.

(Hiram and Francis are returning)

Better make that three. Mach dad drei cocktails. Das usuals!

OTTO: Jawohl.

(He goes)

DR. PEPPER: Who won?

FRANCIS: *(Singing, skipping almost)* Harry and me! Harry and me! Harry and Me!

HIRAM: They ganged up on me as usual.

FRANCIS: We beat you! We beat you! Da da da we beat you!

HIRAM: Well, Harry beat you.

FRANCIS: And we both beat you!

HIRAM: I was worried about that turtle.

FRANCIS: Even with these on, I beat him. *(Indeed, water is sloshing out of his rubber bathing slippers)* I beat you! I beat you!

HIRAM: I am going to beat you black and blue if you keep that up, Francis!

DR. PEPPER: Boys, boys!

FRANCIS: I'm still not speaking to you!

HIRAM: That's a blessing!

FRANCIS: But—*(Very softly)* I beat you! I beat you!

DR. PEPPER: Did you tell Francis he looked like an embryo, Hiram?

HIRAM: If I'd seen him in that bathing cap, I would've said he looked like a prophylactic.

FRANCIS: Hiram is a poor sport! Hiram is a poor sport!

HIRAM: If there's anything more vulgar than swimming it's a swimming race.

FRANCIS: It was his idea.

HIRAM: Does that sound like me, Jason?

FRANCIS: It was, too!

HIRAM: You see what I have to put up with?

FRANCIS: Last night after dinner you said "Let's challenge Harry Scupp to a swimming race tomorrow."

HIRAM: You sure you can't do anything for him, doctor?

FRANCIS: You did, you did!

HIRAM: I'd suggest a lobotomy but obviously he's already had one.

FRANCIS: I cross my heart he did!

HIRAM: Several, from the look of it!

FRANCIS: *(Getting quite hysterical)* He lies, Doctor, he lies! He did suggest a swimming race after dinner with Harry Scupp last night! He did! He did!

DR. PEPPER: Don't hold it back, Francis.

FRANCIS: *(A real tantrum now: feet and fists pounding*

the ground) Tell him it was your idea, Hiram! Tell him, tell him, tell him, tell him, tell him! *(He exhausts himself)*

HIRAM: All right, so it *was* my idea. I don't like to lose. It's the Spane in me. A Baltimore Tear wouldn't understand that. *(Genuinely)* I'm sorry, Francis. *(Francis sulks)* Now get up. You know I can't stand to see you grovel like that.

FRANCIS: I'm not groveling, Hiram. I'm letting it all out for once. Right, Doctor?

DR. PEPPER: Just keep going. I think we're getting somewhere.

FRANCIS: He always wants to compete with me. I can't help it if I always win. I don't even want to win. I just do. Backgammon, bridge, Chinese checkers, mah-jongg....

HIRAM: You never beat me in mah-jongg.

FRANCIS: Yes, I did. That time in Morocco.

HIRAM: I don't count that.

FRANCIS: Why not?

HIRAM: I had dysentery.

FRANCIS: So did I!

HIRAM: I said I was sorry!

FRANCIS: I always win! At anything! Anagrams, parcheesi, tennis...!

HIRAM: You playing tennis? That'll be the day!

FRANCIS: That game we play with the paddles and the little net!

HIRAM: That's table tennis, Francis!

FRANCIS: Well I win, don't I? Like I always do? I can't lose to him at anything! And he hates me for it! Hates me to death!

HIRAM: While you're down there crowing, Francis, why don't you tell the doctor the *real* story?

FRANCIS: What real story?

HIRAM: What real story!

FRANCIS: I don't know what you're talking about.

HIRAM: Tell him about Celine. *(Short pause)* I didn't think so.

DR. PEPPER: Who's Celine?

HIRAM: A Welsh corgi we had when we lived on Sixty-Ninth Street.

DR. PEPPER: It's a lovely breed.

HIRAM: Francis killed her.

FRANCIS: It was an accident.

HIRAM: He threw her out the window.

FRANCIS: I didn't throw her out the window. She jumped.

HIRAM: Of course he did!

FRANCIS: You weren't there. She jumped out!

HIRAM: Celine hadn't jumped *anywhere* since mummy's car backed over her in New Hope three years before! You threw that dog!

FRANCIS: She'd been trying to catch this big fly in her mouth when suddenly she just sailed out the window right after it.

DR. PEPPER: What floor were you on?

FRANCIS: The fourteenth.

HIRAM: The fatal fourteenth.

FRANCIS: I didn't throw her.

HIRAM: Well, who left the window open?

FRANCIS: You couldn't breathe that night.

HIRAM: And you were thinking of yourself first, as usual!

DR. PEPPER: No air conditioning?

FRANCIS: This was years ago.

HIRAM: When dog-killers could still get away with something as simple as an open window. God knows what he'd come up with today.

DR. PEPPER: What a ghastly story.

HIRAM: Most crimes of passion are. Francis was jealous of her. Celine adored me, couldn't stand him. She used to pee in his closet out of spite. So he killed her.

FRANCIS: If you say that again I'm going to smack your face for you!

HIRAM: Say what? You dog murderer!

(Francis flies at him. They struggle. They do minor violence to each other)

DR. PEPPER: That's right, boys, let it out. Let it out! No holding back now. That's right, that's right. Just let everything out now.
(During the struggle Otto will return with the drinks. He looks to Dr. Pepper. Dr. Pepper motions him to let the combatants be. Otto shrugs, sits down with his magazine. Eventually, Hiram and Francis will collapse with exhaustion)
DR. PEPPER: All right now?
FRANCIS: I don't think Ravenswood is working out for us.
HIRAM: Of course Ravenswood isn't working out for us! Why should it?
DR. PEPPER: Did you ever think of getting another dog?
HIRAM: No more dogs. Celine was a terrible shedder.
FRANCIS: Another one would probably just pee in my closet, too.
HIRAM: Or maybe mine next time.
FRANCIS: No more dogs, Hiram? Promise?
HIRAM: The only reason we stay together is because no one else in the world would put up with us.
DR. PEPPER: If you can leave here having realized that much, I'll be satisfied.
HIRAM: *You'll* be satisfied?
DR. PEPPER: So should you.
HIRAM: We are, I suppose, we are.
DR. PEPPER: In a funny way, it's too bad you're *not* that way.
FRANCIS: What way?
HIRAM: Even if we were, I wouldn't go near that one with a ten-foot pole.
FRANCIS: What way, Hiram?
HIRAM: We're queer enough without getting into that, wouldn't you say, Francis?
FRANCIS: Oh, that way! Likewise, a ten-foot pole! You're the only real friend I've ever had.

HIRAM: And I'm sure Dr. Pepper can see why. Help me up, will you? I think I twisted something.

DR. PEPPER: Otto.

(Otto picks up Hiram. Francis struggles to his feet)

FRANCIS: Are we dressing for lunch?

HIRAM: I don't know about the end of the Baltimore Tear line but the last remaining Newport Spane is. Otto, where's my Bullshot?

(Otto is carrying Hiram in his arms like a doll. As they move toward the drinks, another tennis ball will bound across the stage, hitting Dr. Pepper again)

ROY: *(Off)* Ball! Ball!

HIRAM: Thank you, Doctor. It was a wonderful session. *(He drinks)*

ROY: *(Off)* Ball! Ball!

HIRAM: Who are those dreadful people?

(Francis is scrambling for tennis ball)

DR. PEPPER: The Pitts.

ROY: *(Off)* Hey, you, mac, you wanna return that for Christ's sake?

HIRAM: My name is not Mac and I'm not your ball boy! Put that down, Francis!

(Francis drops the ball)

APRIL: *(Off)* Just throw us the goddamn ball, will you?

HIRAM: Why don't you try fucking yourself, madam!

ROY: *(Off)* Hey, you can't talk to my wife like that!

HIRAM: I don't think I want to talk to your wife, period!

FRANCIS: Pitts? What kind of name is Pitts?

HIRAM: Appropriate! Come on, Francis. I want to catch the Julia Child re-run.

FRANCIS: It sounds Armenian.

(They are gone, Otto carrying Hiram and Francis following. Dr. Pepper is alone with the tennis ball)

ROY: *(Off)* Will you please go back there? We'll lose our place on the court!

APRIL: *(Off)* I'll get the court back! I want to see you handle something for once!

ROY: *(Off)* I told you: I'm gonna flatten that S.O.B.! Keep the court!

APRIL: *(Off)* We've got the court!

(Roy and April enter. They are dressed for tennis and carrying racquets)

ROY: Where'd he go?

DR. PEPPER: Good morning.

ROY: We saw you talking to him! Now where is he?

DR. PEPPER: Who?

ROY: That guy who insulted my wife!

DR. PEPPER: Your wife?

APRIL: What do I look like? His dog?

DR. PEPPER: You must be Mr. and Mrs. Pitt.

ROY: Yeah, as a matter of fact, we *are.*

APRIL: And they got some nice class of people up at this place!

ROY: *(Cautioning her)* Honey! I think we've been recognized.

DR. PEPPER: I'm afraid so.

ROY: Celebrity-time!

APRIL: Oh, Christ!

ROY: *(Taking off his sun glasses and shaking Dr. Pepper's hand)* Hi, Roy Pitt. Nice to see you. We were hoping to be a little incognito up here! It's just as well. I think people who wear big sunglasses are big phonies. This is my wife, April James.

APRIL: Hi, April James. Nice to see you.   `

DR. PEPPER: April James?

APRIL: It's my professional name.

DR. PEPPER: I see!

ROY: You see that, honey? Even with these things on he recognized us.

DR. PEPPER: And what do *you* do, Mrs. Pitt?

APRIL: Thanks a lot, buddy.

ROY: She's an actress.

APRIL: I don't even know you but I really needed
that little ego boost.

ROY: Honey, my movie was on the Late Show last
night. *Cold Fingers.* He probably caught it.

APRIL: God knows, you did!

ROY: It's the power of the medium, you know that
kind of exposure.

APRIL: *Cold Fingers* should have *opened* on the Late
Show.

ROY: Now don't start with me.

APRIL: Boy, I really needed that little zap.

ROY: He's a dummy.

APRIL: *Journey Through Hell* for Christ's sake! You
didn't see me in *Journey Through Hell?*

DR. PEPPER: Were you in that?

ROY: That was my beautiful April all right!

APRIL: You bet your sweet ass it was!

DR. PEPPER: That was a wonderful movie, Mrs. Pitt.

APRIL: You see that? Another zap?

ROY: April wasn't in the movie. She created the role
Off-Broadway, but she didn't get the film version.

APRIL: This is really my day!

ROY: She was brilliant in that part.

APRIL: I know. Too bad the play didn't support me.

DR. PEPPER: I enjoyed the film, too.

ROY: Try to cool it with her, will you?

APRIL: Try *Random Thoughts and Vaguer Notions,*
why don't you?

ROY: That one was on Broadway.

DR. PEPPER: I wasn't able to catch it.

APRIL: It ran nearly eighty performances. You
didn't exactly have to be a jack rabbit.

ROY: April!

APRIL: Before you zap me again, I didn't do the
movie of that one either.

ROY: You never read notices like she got for that
one. Show 'em to him, honey.

APRIL: They're in the car. I break my balls trying to

make that piece of garbage work and they sign some WASP starlet for the movie thinking she's going to appeal to that goddamn Middle American drive-in audience.

ROY: I don't really think you can call Googie Gomez a WASP starlet.

APRIL: White bread! That's all she is, white bread!

ROY: *(Calling off)* Hey, that court's taken, buddy! We got it reserved!

APRIL: You heard him!

DR. PEPPER: I think that's the ground keeper.

ROY: That's okay, mac! Sorry! Hang in there!

APRIL: Hi! April James! Nice to see you!

ROY: Hi! Roy Pitt! Nice to see you! Ssh!

APRIL: What is it?

ROY: I thought I heard our phone.

APRIL: Way out here? What are you? The big ear?

ROY: You told the service where I'd be?

APRIL: Of course I did. I might be getting a call, too, you know.

ROY: I'm expecting an important call from the coast. I'm not usually this tense.

APRIL: Hah!

ROY: This could be the big one, April.

APRIL: Almost anything would be bigger than *Cold Fingers!*

(Otto has appeared)

ROY: You got one hell of a thirsty star out here, waiter.

APRIL: Two thirsty stars.

ROY: What are you having, honey?

APRIL: A screwdriver.

ROY: I'll have some Dom Perignon. The champagne.

APRIL: Roy!

ROY: It's included.

APRIL: Eighty-six the screwdriver! I'll have the same.

OTTO: The fraulein would like a nice rubdown maybe?

APRIL: From you?

ROY: Just bring the Dom Perignon, will you?

DR. PEPPER: And Otto! *(He holds up his glass. Otto goes)*

APRIL: *(Looking at Dr. Pepper's legs)* We do a lot of benefits, you know.

ROY: April's been asked to do the Muscular Dystrophy and Multiple Sclerosis Telethons two years straight.

APRIL: Retarded Children wanted me last month but they weren't paying expenses.

ROY: Nobody's blaming you, honey.

APRIL: I mean there's charity and then there's charity. I mean you gotta draw the line somewhere, right? What am I? Chopped Liver?

ROY: Retarded Children wouldn't even send a limousine for her! Our agent told 'em they could take their telethon and shove it! *(He is opening up a sun reflector)*

APRIL: What are you doing?

ROY: I want to get some of the benefits.

APRIL: There's not enough sun for a tan.

ROY: That's what you think. It's a day like this you can really bake yourself. Just because the sky's grey doesn't mean those rays aren't coming through.

(April is sitting near Dr. Pepper. Roy is sprawled out on a lounger. He just loves being in the sun with his reflector like this)

APRIL: *(Short pause)* What are you in for?

DR. PEPPER: The usual.

APRIL: A bad marriage, huh? That's too bad. You're probably wondering what we're doing up here. I know on the surface it must look like we got a model marriage. Believe me, we got our little problems, too. Right, honey?

ROY: Right.

APRIL: Have you had a session with Dr. Pepper yet?

DR. PEPPER: Many. *(He opens a book)*

APRIL: Is he all he's cracked up to be?

DR. PEPPER: I think so, but of course I'm prejudiced. *(He smiles at April, begins to read)*

APRIL: He's gonna have his hands full with that one!

DR. PEPPER: *(Looking up from his book)* I'm sorry.

APRIL: Skip it.

(Dr. Pepper returns to his book. April silently mouths an obscenity at him and turns her attention to Roy)

ROY: You're blocking my sun.

APRIL: You're just gonna lie there like that?

ROY: Uh-huh.

APRIL: So where's *my* reflector?

ROY: I told you to pack it if you wanted it.

APRIL: I want it.

ROY: You said you didn't want to get any darker.

APRIL: I'm starting to fade.

ROY: No, you're not.

APRIL: It's practically all gone. Look at you. You're twice as dark!

ROY: It's not a contest, honey.

APRIL: I mean what's the point of getting a tan if you don't maintain it? Roy!

ROY: *(For Dr. Pepper's benefit, but without looking up from the reflector)* Do you believe this? I was with my agents all day and I'm supposed to be worried about a goddamn reflector!

APRIL: Just give me a couple of minutes with it.

ROY: It's the best sun time now.

APRIL: You know I've got that audition Wednesday.

ROY: No. N-O. April's up for another new musical. They were interested in us both actually but I've got these film commitments.

APRIL: Tentative film commitments.

ROY: You're getting hostile, honey.

APRIL: What's hostile is you not packing my reflector.

ROY: *I* was busy with my agents. *You* are getting hostile.

APRIL: I've got a career, too, you know.

ROY: *(Sitting up)* Sshh!

APRIL: Hello? Yes, we're checking on the availability of Roy Pitt for an Alpo commercial!

ROY: Shut up, April! *(He listens)* Shit! *(He lies back)*

APRIL: Roy?

ROY: After that? You've gotta be kidding!

APRIL: I didn't—

ROY: I wouldn't give you this reflector if you whistled "Swanee River" out of your ass!

APRIL: I can, too!

ROY: I know. I've heard you.

APRIL: Just lie there and turn into leather.

ROY: I will.

APRIL: There are other things in the world more important than your sun tan, you know.

ROY: Like yours?

APRIL: For openers.

ROY: Like your career?

APRIL: Yes, as a matter of fact!

ROY: Will you stop competing with me, April? That's one of the reasons we came here. I can't help it if I'm hotter than you right now.

APRIL: That could change, Roy. Don't forget *Star Is Born.*

ROY: Well, until it does, love me for what I am: Roy Pitt, the man. But don't resent me for my career.

APRIL: I know, Roy.

ROY: I love you for what you are: April James, the best little actress in New York City.

APRIL: What do you mean, "best little actress?"

ROY: I'm trying to make a point, honey!

APRIL: As opposed to what? A dwarf one?

ROY: If we're going to have a good marriage and, April, I want that more than anything...!

APRIL: More than you wanted *Lenny?*

ROY: I didn't want *Lenny.*

APRIL: He would've crawled through broken glass for that part!

ROY: I didn't want *Lenny.* Now goddamnit, shut up!

APRIL: I can't talk to you when you get like that.

ROY: Get like what? You haven't laid off me since we got in the car.

APRIL: You know I'm upset.

ROY: Are you still harping on *The Seagull?*

APRIL: I'm thinking of slitting the two wrists this time, Roy!

ROY: We've all been fired from shows.

APRIL: Before they went into rehearsal?

ROY: You told me they decided to go black.

APRIL: With Heather MacNamara? They fired me!

ROY: Actually Heather isn't a bad choice for that part.

APRIL: She's the pits!

ROY: *(Breaking himself up)* We're the Pitts! We liked her in *The Harpist.*

APRIL: *You* liked her in *The Harpist.* I'd like her in her coffin.

ROY: Obviously they're going ethnic with it.

APRIL: Heather MacNamara isn't even ethnic. She's white bread. I'm ethnic. I want a hit, Roy. I need a hit. I'm going crazy for a hit. I mean, when's it my turn?

ROY: Honey, you're making a shadow.

APRIL: I'm sorry.

ROY: That's okay. Just stick with me, kid. We're headed straight for the top.

APRIL: Roy?

ROY: What, angel?

APRIL: Your tapes are showing. *(Roy clutches at his hairpiece)* Roy wears a piece.

ROY: It's no secret. I've never pretended. It's not like your nose job!

APRIL: Don't speak to me. Just lie there and turn into Naugahyde like your mother!

ROY: Why don't you go call your agent? They're casting bus and truck understudies. *(Pause)* You want the reflector?

APRIL: Give him skin cancer, God, give him skin cancer, please!

DR. PEPPER: Excuse me, I know it's none of my business, but how long have you two been married?

APRIL: Three months.

ROY: And you were right the first time, it's none of your business.

APRIL: But we lived together a long time before we did.

ROY: Not long enough.

APRIL: Eight *centuries* it felt like!

ROY: Do you have to cry on the world's shoulder, April?

APRIL: I want us to work, Roy! I love you.

(Pause)

ROY: I know. I love you, too, April.

APRIL: You're the best.

ROY: *We're* the best.

APRIL: You really think this Pepper fellow can help us?

DR. PEPPER: I'm no miracle worker.

ROY: You?

DR. PEPPER: Jason Pepper. Welcome to Ravenswood.

ROY: You're Dr. Pepper?

DR. PEPPER: Only to my worst enemies. Let's try Jason, shall we?

APRIL: Oh, Roy!

ROY: The least you could've done was told us!

APRIL: I'm so ashamed!

ROY: Talk about seeing people at their worst!

DR. PEPPER: I'm used to it.

ROY: Yeah, but you haven't heard the other side of the story.

DR. PEPPER: And I'm sure it's a good one, too.

APRIL: Roy, I want to leave. I could just die!

ROY: *(Comforting her)* Anything you say, honey.

(Hiram and Francis enter. They wear striped blazers, ascots, straw boaters and white summer flannels)

HIRAM: You know what they say about white flannels, don't you Jason? The devil's invention. Never out of the cleaners.

FRANCIS: I put mine on first, of course, and then he decided he was going to wear his!

HIRAM: Don't be ridiculous.

FRANCIS: We *look* ridiculous.

DR. PEPPER: I think you both look rather dashing.

HIRAM: Thank you, Jason.

FRANCIS: Monkey see, monkey do.

DR. PEPPER: This is Mr. and Mrs. Pitt.

ROY: And you owe my wife an apology.

HIRAM: I don't recall speaking to you, mac.

ROY: Now, look, you...!

APRIL: It doesn't matter.

ROY: To me it does. You're my wife!

APRIL: Not in front of...*(She motions toward Dr. Pepper)*...please?

HIRAM: *(Bowing)* Hiram Spane of the Newport Spanes, Mrs. Pitt. I've got a foul temper and a vicious tongue. Someone yells "ball" at me and they start working overtime. And that's about as much of an apology as you're going to get out of me.

APRIL: Thank you.

HIRAM: This is Francis Tear of the Baltimore Tears.

FRANCIS: We're in plumbing.

APRIL: Pleased to meet you. This is my husband, Roy.

HIRAM: *(Not extending his hand)* Charmed, I'm sure.

ROY: *(Pumping Francis')* Hi, Roy Pitt. Nice to see you.

FRANCIS: Do you like to swim?

HIRAM: Francis!

FRANCIS: I just asked!

ROY: Sshh!

HIRAM: I beg your pardon?

ROY: Shut up! *(He listens, hears something)* There it is! *(Crossing his fingers)* Baby, baby, baby! *(He runs off)*

HIRAM: Is your husband insane, Mrs. Pitt?

APRIL: He's been expecting that call.

HIRAM: That wasn't my question.

APRIL: He's an actor. It might be a job. Normal people wouldn't understand. How long have you two been married?

FRANCIS: We're not married, Mrs. Pitt.

APRIL: Oh!

HIRAM: Oh?

APRIL: How nice.

FRANCIS: That's what you think.

APRIL: We have lots of friends like that in the city.

HIRAM: Like what?

APRIL: Like you two. We're both in show business. We have to practically!

HIRAM: We're not in show business, Mrs. Pitt, and we certainly don't have to have friends like you.

APRIL: Did I say something wrong?

HIRAM: And I'm sure you're just getting started. Excuse me.

APRIL: I was just trying to make small talk. I got better things to do than yak it up with a couple of aunties, you know!

DR. PEPPER: Children, children!

HIRAM: Looks to me like Ravenswood is going to the dogs, Jason. Well the pits anyway.

APRIL: Look, mouth!

(Otto and Harry have appeared. Otto is carrying a suitcase. Harry is dressed for traveling)

HARRY: It's a black Volvo station wagon, Otto. It's the one with snow tires. You can't miss it. And then how about a round for everyone!

OTTO: Jawohl, herr Scupp. *(He goes)*

HARRY: He understood. Now that I'm leaving he understood.

DR. PEPPER: Otto always understood.

FRANCIS: Harry's leaving, Hiram!

HIRAM: I can see that, Francis.

DR. PEPPER: I haven't officially released you yet, Harry.

HARRY: I'll save you the trouble. I'm officially releasing myself. What were you planning on, Jason? Keeping me here till Doomsday?

DR. PEPPER: Where's Dolly?

HARRY: Changing.

DR. PEPPER: Changing?

HARRY: She's decided to stay. Try to help her, Jason.

(Dolly has entered, dressed in Harry's bathrobe)

DR. PEPPER: What happened down at the lake?

HARRY: What didn't happen, you mean!

DOLLY: It was like our honeymoon.

HARRY: Don't make it sound too dramatic, Dolly. We decided that our marriage was better than no marriage at all.

DOLLY: You don't throw twenty-five years away because of two toes. The toes I can get along without. But without Harry...!

HARRY: I think we're doing the right thing, Jason.

DOLLY: I know we are, Harry.

DR. PEPPER: Just so long as it makes you both happy! *(Dolly is lighting a cigarette)* How is it?

DOLLY: Like honey. It's like someone just poured ten years of honey down my throat.

DR. PEPPER: This is Mrs. Pitt. She and her husband have just arrived.

(Roy returns)

ROY: Hi, Roy Pitt. Nice to see you. Hi, Roy Pitt, nice to see you.

APRIL: Did you get it?

ROY: It looks good but nothing definite.

APRIL: When would you leave?

ROY: We'll talk about it later. Hi, Roy Pitt. Nice to see you.

DOLLY: Wait a minute! Wait a minute! The Retarded Children Telethon, right? That's her, honey! The girl we were so crazy about. You sang "Do, Do, Do What You Done, Done, Done Before, Baby."

APRIL: That was for Leukemia, actually, the Leukemia Telethon.

DOLLY: Oh, we think you're just terrific!

APRIL: Thank you.

DOLLY: I mean she's just terrific.

ROY: I know.

DOLLY: You're headed straight for the top. A voice like that, a face and figure like yours. I hope *your* line of work keeps you busy, Mr. Pitt. You're in for a lot of lonely days and nights.

APRIL: Roy's an actor, too.

DOLLY: Are you? I'll tell you something: I don't think Harry and I would've run into so many problems if we'd had more in common.

APRIL: Dr. Pepper's really helped you then?

DOLLY: Helped *him.* We'll see about me. Did you hear that, Harry? Mr. Pitt is an actor, too!

(Harry lets out a sudden, urgent scream)

DR. PEPPER: How was it?

HARRY: Fantastic.

DOLLY: Is he going to be doing that often, doctor?

DR. PEPPER: That depends on you.

DOLLY: If he pulls that in the middle of a board meeting he's going to be looking for a new job.

DR. PEPPER: You might try it yourself sometime.

DOLLY: Me? I'm as cool as a cucumber.

DR. PEPPER: What brought that one on, Harry?

HARRY: The truth?

DR. PEPPER: You're still at Ravenswood, Harry.

HARRY: I want to shtup Mrs. Pitt.

ROY: Hey!

HARRY: You see how her tennis outfit's all slit up the side? There's no tan line. You know how women who are tan all over drive me crazy, Jason.

ROY: What did you say?

APRIL: It's okay, Roy. He just said he *wanted* to shtup me. He didn't *do* it.

(Dolly lets out a sudden, urgent scream)

DR. PEPPER: How do you feel?

DOLLY: Hoarse.

HARRY: You'll get used to it.

(Otto has returned with a tray of drinks. He passes it around. Everyone will take one)

I'm really gonna miss you two, you know. Take good care of her.

HIRAM: When you come back for her, God knows, we'll still be here. I think we're probably permanent.

FRANCIS: We're just lucky Hiram's mother can afford it.

HIRAM: *You're* just lucky Hiram's mother can afford it.

FRANCIS: Old Bingo money, that's all she is! Goodbye, Harry. I'll miss you.

DOLLY: No! No farewell toasts. I propose a welcome toast to the new arrivals.

HARRY: You can't drink to yourself.

DOLLY: All right! Here's to new marriage and the Pitts.

HARRY: Here's to our old one, honey.

HIRAM: Here's to friendship.

FRANCIS: Here's to Hiram.

HIRAM: Why thank you, Francis.

ROY: Here's to April James.

FRANCIS: April who, Hiram?

HIRAM: Some RKO starlet obviously.

APRIL: Here's to Hollywood and Mr. and Mrs. Roy Pitt.

DOLLY: Doctor?

DR. PEPPER: Here's to... all of you.

OTTO: Here's to Ravenswood.

(They drink, applaud, hug, laugh, etc.)

OTTO: Das lunchen ist served.

(They break apart and start making their exits)

HARRY: Goodbye, Jason. And thank you. She's all yours now.

DR. PEPPER: *(Warmly)* Dolly!

DOLLY: About that crush. It's strictly platonic.

DR. PEPPER: Are you sure?

DOLLY: When's my first session?

HARRY: *(To Roy)* I know where I've seen you! *Lenny!* You were in *Lenny!* (*Roy lets out a sudden, urgent scream*) What did I say?

APRIL: Nothing. It's all right. Goodbye.

DOLLY: Come on, Harry. I'll walk you to the car.

(April is comforting Roy. Dolly and Harry are gone)

FRANCIS: Hiram?

HIRAM: Will somebody just look at these flannels? Soiled already. This time I'm sending your mother the bill.

FRANCIS: Do you think Mrs. Scupp would like to play badminton after lunch?

(They are gone)

APRIL: What did that dummy know? You're Roy Pitt, the best actor in the business.

ROY: What am I? Chopped Liver?

DR. PEPPER: How long do you think you'll be staying?

ROY: Just as long as we have to.

DR. PEPPER: Good. I'm going to need all the time I can get with you.

ROY: We're not as bad as we seem.

APRIL: Other people don't understand. They think it's just the sex with us.

ROY: It's the sex, it's the egos, it's the sun reflector.

APRIL: It's everything.

ROY: *(To April)* I'll probably get that movie but it doesn't go for three months.

APRIL: Listen, I wasn't going to mention this, but since you brought it up: you think there's anything in it for me?

ROY: A fantastic part. They want a name but I'll mention you for it first thing.

APRIL: I'll test, but first-class, Roy. They're gonna have to fly me out there first-class.

(They are gone. There is more and more thunder. Dr. Pepper looks up at the sky. Otto goes to wheel him in for lunch)

DR. PEPPER: Lasse!

OTTO: Herr doktor nein wolle lunchen heute? *(Dr. Pepper shakes his head)* Herr doktor wolle ein martini? *(Dr. Pepper shakes his head)* Ein kleine rubdown? Ich fach ein gut rubdown.

DR. PEPPER: Herr doktor just wants everyone to be happy.

OTTO: Happy?

DR. PEPPER: Du bist happy, Otto?

OTTO: Happy? Was ist happy?

DR. PEPPER: That's a good question. Be sure to seat Mrs. Scupp next to me at lunch, Otto.

OTTO: Ja, herr doktor.

(Dr. Pepper starts to sing "Wien" again. Otto joins him)

DR. PEPPER: Sway the chair, Otto. Gently, gently! *(Otto sways the chair in time to the music)* Thank you, Otto. *(Dolly is heard off calling "Jason, Jason!")* Is Vienna very beautiful, Otto?

OTTO: Ja, herr doktor.

DR. PEPPER: I've always meant to go there. Maybe I will next summer. Or the summer after. Who knows, Otto.

(Dr. Pepper's voice trails off. A great flash of lightning. A clap of thunder. It starts to rain)

THE END

Richard Wesley

THE PAST IS THE PAST

Richard Wesley

When Richard Wesley's double bill, *The Past Is the Past* and *Goin' Thru Changes* opened at the Billie Holiday Theatre, Brooklyn, New York, in January, 1974, Mel Gussow reported in *The New York Times:* "Mr. Wesley has been steadily growing and expanding since *The Black Terror* introduced him to Off-Broadway two years ago. In these two new short plays, he reveals an even finer emotional sensitivity and awareness of the nuances of human behavior.... In *The Past Is the Past,* we immediately recognize that the characters are father and son, but they reveal this fact gradually and, in the father's case, reluctantly. The separation is a chasm that can not be leaped. The son must find his own way without help, or even compassion, from his father.... What transforms this familiar situation into a wistful and tender evening in the theatre is the artistry of the playwright, Richard Wesley."

In his coverage of the author's *The Sirens* (presented at the Manhattan Theatre Club, May, 1974) the same reviewer wrote: "As in all his plays that I have seen, the author elevates the seemingly commonplace into remarkably human drama."

Mr. Wesley was born in Newark, New Jersey, in July, 1945, and attended Howard University in Washington, D.C., where he studied under the noted black writers Owen Dodson and Ted Shine. He received a Bachelor of Fine Arts Degree in 1967. In 1965, while a sophomore at Howard, he received an "Outstanding Playwright Award" from Samuel French, Inc. for his play, *Put My Dignity on 307.* This same play was later mounted as an experimental production at Howard in 1967, and subsequently was seen on a local television show.

In September, 1969, Mr. Wesley joined the New Lafayette Theatre of Harlem as the managing editor of *Black Theatre Magazine* which the theatre published at that time. He remained with the New Lafayette in this capacity through 1973 and during this period he also was named playwright-in-residence, a position he shared with Ed Bullins and actor-playwright J. E. Gaines.

Mr. Wesley has written over a dozen plays, both short and full-length, and has seen them all produced, either in New York or in theatres and colleges throughout the country as well as in Italy and West Germany. His most noted works include *The Black Terror,* for which he won a Drama Desk "Outstanding Playwright Award." Produced by the New York Shakespeare Festival Public Theatre, it opened on November 10, 1971, and ran for 180 performances. In 1973, The New Phoenix Repertory Company performed his *Strike Heaven on the Face* as a workshop production and it was this play that first brought him to the attention of Sidney Poitier, who was then preparing *Uptown Saturday Night.* He was engaged as a screenwriter for the film that was to co-star Poitier, Harry Belafonte and Bill Cosby and which became one of 1974's most successful motion pictures.

The author is currently a guest lecturer at Manhattanville College, Purchase, New York, where he teaches a course in Black Theatre and has participated in a number of symposiums on theatre and film.

His most recent work for the theatre, *The Mighty Gents,* was presented at the Eugene O'Neill Memorial Theatre Center in Waterford, Connecticut, during the summer of 1974, and he presently is completing work on another play.

The author and his wife and young daughter reside in Newark, New Jersey.

The Past Is the Past is published for the first time in *The Best Short Plays 1975.*

Characters:

EARL DAVIS, *mid-forties, well-dressed, generally casual wear. Probably a foreman on his job.*
EDDIE GREEN, *twenty-six. College student. Grew up in an urban Black community.*

Scene:

Lights up on Earl Davis playing pool at a solitary pool table. The only other object on stage is a jukebox in the background.

Just after the lights go up a Man's Voice is heard as Earl plays.

MAN'S VOICE:
The years separate
Us
An abyss of time
Dimming our memories
Holding back our yearnings
To reach
Out
To one
Another
Time
How short a word
Yet signifying such
A long period in
Our lives
As we slowly drift
Away
From one another
To other places
Where, alone
We must wonder
If

Our lives
Will ever
Touch
Again.

> *(Sounds of Billie Holiday come up. Eddie Green enters from the darkness upstage and stands for a long time watching Earl move cat-like about the table sinking shot after shot. Eddie approaches the table)*

EARL: *(Spying Eddie)* Hey, what's happenin'?

EDDIE: You got it.

EARL: Naw, youngblood, it's all on you.

EDDIE: *(Chuckling)* Is that so?

EARL: There can be no doubt.

EDDIE: Okay, if you say so.

EARL: You new around here?

EDDIE: Yea.

EARL: Thought so. Didn't remember ever seein' you before. Though, I got to admit there sure is somethin' familiar-lookin' about you.

EDDIE: Yea?

EARL: You look a lot like someone I used to know. *(Looks at Eddie more closely)* What's your name?

EDDIE: Eddie. Eddie Green.

EARL: Green. Where you from?

EDDIE: Oh, I'm from outta state. I'm goin' to the community college here.

EARL: A college boy. Check that out. Whatchu studyin' to be?

EDDIE: Ain't made up my mind, yet. Just takin' some general courses.

EARL: Oh. Well, whatever you do, work hard at it. Our folks need as many of you college boys as we can get. Don't mess it all up like I did.

EDDIE: You went to college?

EARL: Had a chance to, but I bullshitted around an' passed it up. Besides, World War II was on an' I got drafted. Still don't know why in hell I went. Same day I went in, some white cop shot this colored soldier in New York an'

Harlem was in flames for three days. A good friend of mine got his leg blown off that day.

EDDIE: Wow, that was some tough shit!

EARL: Forget about it! The past is the past. Know what I mean? Yea, I coulda gone on to college but by the time I got out the war I had changed my mind about everything. Just didn't care no more. If you ever have to go fight in that Viet Nam war, you'll see what I mean. That is, if you a super-sensitive cat like I used to be.

EDDIE: Maybe I am.

EARL: Naw, you kids today seem much harder than I can ever remember us bein'. Y'all got more, but you just seem unhappy. Know what I mean? Hey, you wanna play me a game?

EDDIE: I can't play that good.

EARL: Then whachu doin' in here?

EDDIE: I came in to look for...I mean, I just came in to look around.

EARL: Don't you know anything about pool?

EDDIE: About the only thing I can play is "eightball."

EARL: Solid. We'll play that. Since I'm the oldest here, I'll break. Rack 'em, "house."

EDDIE: *(Smiling)* Oh, wow, check my man out for bein' arbitrary an' shit. *(Eddie sets the balls up)*

EARL: I'll go light on you since you can't play.

EDDIE: That's okay, you don't have to give me no slack. You haven't before, have you?

EARL: Whatchu say?

EDDIE: Nothin'.

EARL: You know, you a funny dude. You always talk to yourself?

EDDIE: I wasn't talkin' to myself.

EARL: Sure seemed like it.

EDDIE: Naw, I'm straightforward an' blunt. Never talk to myself. My mother says I'm just like my father.

EARL: Yea? *(The balls are set up and Earl breaks)* You father ain't around, huh?

EDDIE: Naw.

EARL: Didn't die, did he?

EDDIE: He split after I was born. Sent my mother some bucks for awhile, but even that stopped.

EARL: Yea, son, I know that story. Nine ball corner pocket. *(He shoots)*

EDDIE: "Son?"

EARL: Six ball. Yea, I call all young men "son."

EDDIE: You got any kids?

EARL: Two by my wife. Three more here and there. Three ball.

EDDIE: Wow, man, you don't miss nothin', do ya? Hey, five kids. That's quite a brood.

EARL: That's right. I'm a nomad. Most colored men are. We *got* to be that way. Got no choice.

EDDIE: I don't know about that.

EARL: It's true. When you get out here in the real world with alla these hungry wolves snapping at your heels you'll see I was tellin' you right. I'm a foreman at my plant, now. But before that I lived all over this country: Houston, New Orleans, Chicago, Philly, Detroit, Baltimore, all over. I've slopped hogs, built battleships, waited tables, poured cement, bell hopped, did just about everything I could to survive. Not to mention killin' men in the army. Now, on top of all that what you tryin' to do is find out what this life is all about an' what you gotta do to take your place in this world. I was born down South, but I left there because I knew at some point I was gonna haveta kill me a white man. Just knew it. There was no other way I was gonna take that shit. I was all of sixteen, then. I was on my own, tryin' to make it. Kep' in school to stay outta trouble, but I loved them streets, boy. My trouble was, I had no discipline. That's what messed me up in my young days. That's why a lotta Black men is nomads. They got a lot of heart, lots n' lots courage, but they not discipline, 'cause no one's taught it to them an' there's folks out there who wanna keep it that way. So, all we do is wander when we young an' when we get old we ain't no good to nobody. We alone. Know what I mean?

EDDIE: But you got you a family.

EARL: Yea, they doin' alright. I'm one of the lucky ones, I guess. Got myself together before it was too late.

EDDIE: An' your other kids?

EARL: Five ball. They doin' okay. I s'pose. Got a daughter in Detroit. She's about twenty-eight now, I guess. She had a fine-lookin' mama. Me an' her mama was goin' together off an' on for a long time. We was really tight. *Good*-lookin' woman. Light brown skin with hazel eyes. Not beautiful, just cute. You know? Teen-age cute. Just breakin' into womanhood cute. An' had the biggest behind. We thought we was in love. Then she got pregnant. We started to fight a lot after that. I wasn't ready for the responsibility an' neither was she. Plus, her mama was fillin' her head with a whole lotta shit. She went down South to have the baby, then moved on up to Detroit. *(Pause. He smiles)* Just got a letter from that woman last week.... Two ball.

EDDIE: Oh, y'all still tight?

EARL: No, just friends, now.

EDDIE: You ever see your daughter?

EARL: Coupla times, as she was growin' up. Went to her high school graduation an' to her weddin'. I think she an' her husband separated. She look just like her mama. Ain't never been a woman like her mama, though. Better believe it. Seven ball. *(Shoots and misses)* Damn!

EDDIE: Now, it's my turn to run. Ten ball ...*(Shoots)*...twelve ball...*(Shoots)*...fourteen.

EARL: Who you tryin' to be, Cicero Murphy or somebody?

EDDIE: No, just plain Eddie Green. You know, you ain't ever told me your name.

EARL: Earl Davis. *(Eddie looks at Earl as though he recognizes him)* Ring a bell?

EDDIE: Kind of. What about your other "outside" kids, man?

EARL: "Outside kids?" What's that about? My kids is my kids, man.

EDDIE: Yea, but three of your kids grew up without you.

EARL: I did what I could. You know? My other daughter in Baltimore, Alicia; I used to see her a lot. Really looked out for her 'cause her mama died in childbirth. I spoiled her, though. She got too used to gettin' everything she wanted. Little mama is somethin' else today. Grew up with her grandparents. Started livin' with them when I got restless an' started wantin' to get back out here in these streets. Alicia's up in Newark somewhere. She got herself a good job, though. Least she ain't on welfare, or nothin' like that.

EDDIE: *(Somewhat bitterly)* An' the third child never saw you!

EARL: His mother was the first woman I ever really, really loved. She was somethin' else, man. Skin as black as night with eyes that could look right into your soul. She was *all* woman. It was like she could reach out an' touch you without ever raisin' her arms from her sides. A queen, man. Boy, did we ever have a thing goin' between us. She meant a lot to me, man. That's why it's hard for me to explain why I ever left her. You got to understand, Eddie. I just wasn't ready for any of them three children. Their mothers an' I, well, we was about tryin' to put somethin' in our lives that our parents wasn't able to put there. We was growin' up in days when every livin' minute was spent tryin' to survive an' our parents was doin' the best they could with us, but they was "out there" an' we was left, man. So, we turned to each other. It was all we had. We just wasn't ready. That's why I try to be so close to my two younger kids, now. Maybe I can make things easier for them.

EDDIE: But that third kid never saw you. He might have needed you.

EARL: Yea, I s'pose he did. But in those days I had so little to give.

EDDIE: You had yourself.

EARL: For men, that just ain't enough. A man wants to give his children the world, if he can.

EDDIE: So you ran out.

EARL: You a young cat, man. You should learn to be quiet until you've learned a few things.

EDDIE: But that was a cold shot, man. A kid grows up without his father an' spends summa the time wonderin' if he'll ever see him, an' what should he do if he ever do see him.

EARL: Nothin' he can do, except try to understand.

EDDIE: I never saw my father.

EARL: You told me. I'll tell you somethin', too. I never saw mine, either. *(Eddie looks surprised)* It's true. Nigger passed through my life like a shadow. I spent my grown years tryin' to fill in the empty gaps in my life that he left. I tried to leave some of me in all my children, even if it didn't do no more than just pass on to them through they mamas.

EDDIE: I guess that's what the third woman did, huh?

EARL: Vessie? Yea, I guess so.

EDDIE: Hey man, look at me.

EARL: Yea.

EDDIE: I mean, really *look* at me!

EARL: I'm lookin'. Been lookin'. I knew who you was the minute you walked through that door. How'd you find me?

EDDIE: By accident. I was in a restaurant eatin' when I saw you come in. That picture mama got of you is twenty years old, but you ain't really changed that much.

EARL: Naw, runs in the family, I guess.

EDDIE: This sure ain't goin' down like I expected. I had imagined a whole lotta tears an' shit.

EARL: *(Laughing)* You seen too many movies, Eddie. *(Looks at Eddie)* Yea, there was no doubt when I saw you come in. You Vessie's spittin' image.

EDDIE: You know that's really funny 'cause mom's always said I look just like you. Act like you, too.

EARL: So, what's happenin'?

EDDIE: Man, you actin' so cool about all this.

EARL: *(Perplexed)* Hey, man . . . what can I say?

EDDIE: Yea . . . I guess you right.

EARL: You lookin' mighty clean, man.

EDDIE: I got a part-time gig in a men's store. Sometimes I boost shit.

EARL: No kiddin'. An' your mama, how she doin'?

EDDIE: She doin' okay. Her an' this dude might get married.

EARL: Yea? What's he like?

EDDIE: Smooth-talkin' nigger from North Carolina. They may go down there to live. He's a lot like you in some ways.

EARL: No kiddin'?

EDDIE: That may be why I don't like him.

EARL: Yea. *(Pause)* Why you come lookin' for me?

EDDIE: 'Cause I wanted to know who you was, an' I wanted you to see me.

EARL: Yea, you a fine-lookin' boy. Couldn't miss with me for a father.

EDDIE: I had another reason for wantin' to see you. Thirteen ball.

EARL: Uh-huh.

EDDIE: You gonna be a grandaddy, man. Eleven.

EARL: No kiddin'? Hey, that's really beautiful. Congratulations, Eddie. When's it due?

EDDIE: About six months.

EARL: Where's the mother at?

EDDIE: Back home.

EARL: You goin' through much hassle?

EDDIE: Some, but no more than the usual amount.

EARL: Probably be a boy.

EDDIE: I didn't want it at first. I told her to get an abortion.

EARL: Yea, that's what I told Vessie back when I found out she was carryin' you.

EDDIE: Wow, man, you sure know how to tighten somebody's jaws!

EARL: I'm sorry, son, but it was the truth. Vessie wanted to have you, though. She was determined about that. She cried an' everything, tellin' me if she had to raise you by herself she'd do it, but nobody was gonna rip her insides out. *(Looks at Eddie)* She did well raisin' you, boy.

EDDIE: Daddy....

EARL: Why you call me "Daddy?" You don't know me that well.

EDDIE: I want to.

EARL: Yea?

EDDIE: I *need* to.

EARL: The same way that kid of yours needs to. Your old lady didn't get that abortion, did she? *(Eddie shakes his head)* I didn't think so.

EDDIE: I'm here now 'cause there're some things I need to understand. I never had you there, man. When I truly needed you around. Someone to show me how to dribble a basketball, or tell me some stories, or just teach me *somethin'*. You wasn't *there*. All your other children had you, why not *me*?

EARL: I can't explain it, man. I was still a kid myself when you was born. A child leadin' a child; what kindna shit was that? I did the best I could with what I had. An' that's all you can do with your kid. Give him everything you feel you never got from me, or at least try to. That's all I can tell you.

EDDIE: But there's got to be more.

EARL: What else is there? Oh, yea, the nights lyin' awake somewhere wonderin' what your kids are growin' up to be like, wonderin' whether or not they're growin' up to hate you an' someday kill you, or the nights when you wonder why you don't care whether they do or not. That's what it is, man.

EDDIE: There were nights when I wanted to kill you, but I wanted more than anything just to be with you, my old man, the mystery cat in the picture my mother keeps hidden in her top dresser drawer. I wanted to hear you say you love me.

EARL: You're asking for the moon, son. You're from me but not of me.

EDDIE: Because you won't let me be.

EARL: Because I *can't* let you be.

EDDIE: Why not?

EARL: Because there's too much pain, that's why.

Too many years an' tears I buried long ago. That's what you represent, boy.

EDDIE: I'm more than that. I'm your son.

EARL: A son I didn't want.

EDDIE: You were too young to understand.

EARL: I understood. *(Quietly)* I ... understood.

EDDIE: I love you, Daddy. That must mean *somethin'*. Hey, man, don't just shut me out! Don't pull this shit on me.

EARL: C'mon, Eddie. I'm not that important to you. I can't be.

EDDIE: Because you're my father an' because I don't wanna be standin' like this with my son twenty years from now.

EARL: My grandson. Wow! Will you name him after me?

EDDIE: *(Somewhat surprised by the reply)* Yea.

EARL: Tell him a little about me, an' bring him around so I can see him.

EDDIE: Why don't *you* come an' see him?

EARL: I don't know. We'll have to see.

EDDIE: Damn! Why you so cold, man?! Shit!

EARL: Eddie....

EDDIE: Forget it, man! I thought if I could get somethin' together between you an' me maybe me an' my kid.... But I guess I'll just have to push on alone trippin' over shit like you did. It shouldn't have to be like that, man. It shouldn't have to!

EARL: But it is. Eddie, I've done all I can. I told you what I could. It's just too many years an' lost chances between us.

EDDIE: Then it's supposed to continue, huh? The same ol' bullshit goin' down again. You puttin' me through the same changes you went through an' now you tellin' me to do the same with my kid.

EARL: It don't have to be that way. You can stop it right here. Maybe I can't love you. Hell, I don't even love myself, quiet as it's kept. But Vessie raised you strong. Strong enough to be able to break this cycle you talkin' about. I'm an old cat who's gonna die soon, so quit tryin' to relate to me an' deal with your son. He's the future an' I'm the past.

EDDIE: No.

EARL: Can I mean that much?

EDDIE: You're my father. *(They look at each other)* Ain't nothin' more to say, huh? *(Earl does not answer)* Look, I guess I got to make it.

EARL: We didn't finish the game.

EDDIE: Let's finish it tomorrow.

EARL: I may not be here.

EDDIE: Then I'll come day after tomorrow.

EARL: May not be here then, either.

EDDIE: Then I'll keep comin' til' I catch you.

EARL: You just like Vessie: persistent as hell.

(They both laugh)

EDDIE: I'm gonna raise. Later.

EARL: Wait a minute. *(He moves to Eddie)* I'm glad I got to see you. I always been kinda scared I never would. *(The two men shake hands warmly. Eddie might want to embrace his father, but Earl kind of keeps everything distant, yet displays a warmth that shows his aloofness diminishing. Eddie turns to leave)*

EARL: *(With a slight trace of desperation in his voice)* Eddie.

EDDIE: Yea?

(Earl starts to say something, but decides against it)

EARL: I hope it's a boy. Tell your mother I said hello.

(Eddie smiles and goes out. Lights begin to dim on Earl, who fights back any emotion as he continues playing pool)

BLACKNESS

Terence Rattigan

AFTER LYDIA
(In Praise of Love)

Terence Rattigan

Originally, *After Lydia* was part of a double bill (the curtain-raiser was a comedy, *Before Dawn)* and the overall title was *In Praise of Love.* With Joan Greenwood and Donald Sinden co-starred, it opened at the Duchess Theatre, London, on September 27, 1973. After its West End engagement, the curtain-raiser was dropped and *After Lydia* inherited the title *In Praise of Love.* The play drew wide praise from the reviewers. *Variety's* London correspondent termed it "often moving, funny and compassionate," while Sheridan Morley's coverage in *Plays and Players* magazine described it as "one of the best Rattigan plays in the last twenty years. There is a kind of greatness here, if only because Rattigan is mounting a massive defense of all the things his generation expected of their contemporaries—exquisite taste and mental elegance and a refusal to tell the truth if the truth would hurt."

The play deals with the heroic efforts of Lydia Cruttwell, herself of Estonian origin, to conceal from her apparently blunt, self-centered and typically British husband the fact that she is dying of leukemia. That she is not the sole possessor of her secret illuminates the play's main theme: "The English vice," as the husband characterizes it, "is the belief that it is demeaning to show emotion."

Now with its new title, the drama (published for the first time in the United States in *The Best Short Plays 1975)* was scheduled to open on Broadway in December, 1974, with Rex Harrison and Julie Harris in the roles of Sebastian and Lydia Cruttwell.

The year 1971 was a particularly momentous one for Sir Terence Rattigan: already a Commander of the Order of the British Empire, he was raised to knighthood by Queen Elizabeth II and on the occasion of his sixtieth birthday he was widely honored by his countrymen with galas, revivals of his plays and special showings of his films. It was a singular tribute to one of the most successful and popular of England's modern playwrights.

Sir Terence was born in London on June 10, 1911.

Educated at Harrow and Trinity College, Oxford, he sprang to prominence in 1936 with his comedy *French Without Tears* which ran for over a thousand performances in the West End. Seven years later, he was to duplicate this theatrical feat with *While the Sun Shines,* a West End landmark for 1,154 performances.

Among Sir Terence's other noted plays are: *Flare Path; Love in Idleness* (retitled *O Mistress Mine* for Broadway where it was performed by Alfred Lunt and Lynn Fontanne for almost two years); *The Winslow Boy* (recipient of the Ellen Terry Award for the best play produced on the London stage during 1946, it won the 1947-48 New York Drama Critics' Circle Award as the season's best foreign play); *The Browning Version* (the Ellen Terry Award play for 1948); *Adventure Story; Who Is Sylvia?; The Deep Blue Sea; The Sleeping Prince; Man and Boy; Separate Tables; Ross;* and *A Bequest to the Nation.*

In addition to his works for the stage, he has written more than fifteen major films and a number of original television plays.

At one of the 1971 anniversary galas, Sir Terence was lauded for his "mastery of craft, high entertainment values, compassion, care for clarity, and concern for human beings as individuals." A staunch defender of craftsmanship, he has expressed his thoughts on the subject in a preface to the collected edition of his works: "The school of thought that condemns firm dramatic shape derives, I suppose, originally from Chekhov, an author who, in my impertinent view, is not usually properly understood either by his worshippers or his active imitators. I believe that his plays are as firmly shaped as Ibsen's. The stream that seems to meander its casual length along does so between strong artificial banks, most carefully and cunningly contrived by a master craftsman. To admire the stream and ignore the artifice that gave it its course seems to me a grave oversight, and may well have led over the years to the present critical misapprehension by which laziness of construction is thought a virtue and the shapelessness of a play is taken as evidence of artistic integrity."

This marks the third time that the famed dramatist has been represented in this series of annuals: *High Summer* was included in *The Best Short Plays 1973* and *All On Her Own* in *The Best Short Plays 1970.*

Characters:

LYDIA CRUTTWELL
SEBASTIAN CRUTTWELL
MARK WALTERS
JOEY CRUTTWELL

Setting: North London
Time: The present

Act One

SCENE: *A single light illuminates the face of Lydia Cruttwell. She is sitting, motionless, staring unseeingly into space. She remains so for some length of time.*

Then the lights come on and we are in the Cruttwells' flat in Islington, where Lydia is now found sitting motionless on a settee in the living room.

We see a small hall, large living room, and part of a kitchen when the sliding doors are opened. A staircase—probably put in during conversion—runs from the living room: first, up a few steps, to the kitchen (where the Cruttwells also eat), then turns sharply to lead to the room above. No window is needed, nor fireplace. The predominant feature of the room is books, for some of which there is no space but the floor, the bookcases having been stretched to their limit. There is a bookcase even in the diminutive hall, and on top of that, looking incongruous, a man's white hatbox which once plainly contained a top hat, and may still. Other prominent objects are a small table on which some ordinary black and white chessmen are set out, plainly for use and not for decoration, a table bearing a tray of drinks, a sofa, and various armchairs. The front door and hall are at the back and a door right leads to Sebastian's workroom. From this is coming the sound of a typewriter being very intermittently used, with long pauses be-

tween short bouts, usually followed by unmistakable sounds of angry erasure. It is about six o'clock of a spring evening. The time is the present.

Sebastian comes out from his workroom, a cigarette between his lips, an empty glass in his hand, and spectacles over his nose.

SEBASTIAN: Oh good, darling, you're back. The heating has gone wrong.

LYDIA: Has it? It seems all right in here. *(She gets briskly to her feet and feels an ancient radiator)* Yes, it's on.

SEBASTIAN: *(At the bookcase)* It's icy in my room. *(Lydia goes through the open door of the workroom. Sebastian, left alone, pulls down a book and begins to search for some reference. Vainly. He puts that one on a pile near him and picks another. Same process. Lydia comes out and quietly takes his glass from his hand)*

SEBASTIAN: Oh, thank you so much, darling— *(She fills up his glass, a procedure she can carry out in her sleep)*

LYDIA: You hadn't turned it on.

SEBASTIAN: What on?

LYDIA: The heat.

SEBASTIAN: *(Deep in a book)* Really? *(He says it as if it were a matter of the most breathless interest, a sure sign with him that he hasn't heard a word. Lydia comes back with his glass)* Oh, thank you, darling. What kept you out so long? Oh, of course, old Doctor Ziegfeld. What did he say?

LYDIA: Ziegmann. He's very pleased indeed.

SEBASTIAN: What did I tell you? And you got held up by the bus strike?

LYDIA: Not really. I found a new way on the Tube.

SEBASTIAN: *(Worried)* Should you have?

LYDIA: Oh, it was quite easy—

SEBASTIAN: I meant isn't it a bit like strikebreaking?

LYDIA: Your social conscience would have preferred I walked?

SEBASTIAN: It's not all that far, is it?

LYDIA: About as far as Fleet Street—to which I notice you've had a hire-car the last three days.

SEBASTIAN: A hire-car is different.

LYDIA: Why?

SEBASTIAN: I charge it to the paper, so it's on their conscience not mine. Good. I've got what I'm looking for—which is a wonder. Darling, our books have got in the most terrible mess again. *(He pulls a book out)* Norman Mailer in the poetry section. Why? *(He throws it on to a chair)* And—I can't believe it—Sapper? *(He pulls that one out violently and throws it on the ground)* That's for burning. Darling, couldn't Mrs. MacKintyre?

LYDIA: Mrs. Higgins. It hasn't been Mrs. MacKintyre for three months.

SEBASTIAN: I call her Mrs. MacKintyre.

LYDIA: She's noticed that.

(Sebastian pulls out another book, clicking his teeth. Lydia takes it)

SEBASTIAN: Well couldn't *she—?*

LYDIA: No. She isn't, oddly enough, a trained librarian. She isn't a trained anything, come to that. She comes three times a week for two hours a day, never stops eating and costs a bomb.

SEBASTIAN: Is she worth having then?

LYDIA: Yes.

SEBASTIAN: I mean if she costs a bomb—

LYDIA: *(Loudly)* She's worth having.

SEBASTIAN: A little tetchy this afternoon, are we? *(He reaches up and grabs another book)* Plain Talk About Sex—next to *Peter Pan.*

LYDIA: *(Taking it)* That's mine.

SEBASTIAN: For God's sake, why?

LYDIA: I bought it for a train, sometime.

SEBASTIAN: *(Taking off his spectacles)* That doesn't answer my question. Darling, I mean, with your early life—

LYDIA: Perhaps it needed a bit of brushing up.

(Pause)

SEBASTIAN: *(Blowing on his glasses, carefully)* A criticism?

LYDIA: No. A comment. Where shall I put these books?

SEBASTIAN: In their proper sections. Where I suggest you might have put the others. You might go through them when you have a little time.

LYDIA: When I have a little time, it will be high on my list.

SEBASTIAN: You're in a stinking mood this evening, aren't you?

LYDIA: Am I?

SEBASTIAN: Was it what I said about your early misadventures?

LYDIA: *(Smiling)* No, stupid. You of all people have the right to talk about that. I think it was what you said about "criticism." As if I would—

SEBASTIAN: But *you* said "comment."

LYDIA: There can be good comment as well as bad, can't there?

SEBASTIAN: In theory, yes. In fact, no. Remember, darling, that you're speaking to a critic. You meant something a bit harsh by "comment." Oh, yes. I know. Now, darling, you must realize—

LYDIA: You can't be expected to bash an old skeleton. I know.

SEBASTIAN: Darling, really! That wasn't very—tasteful, was it?

LYDIA: It was your taste. You said it.

SEBASTIAN: Then you shouldn't have remembered it. Not the actual *words.* *(Looking at her)* Did I say skeleton?

LYDIA: Yes, I know. I've put on four pounds in the last four weeks. That's not an invitation—just a fact.

SEBASTIAN: *(In breathless interest again)* Have you? Have you really? Put on four pounds? Well, that's splendid—absolutely splendid. I mean it's marvelous news, isn't it. Marvelous. *(He is looking at his book)*

LYDIA: You hadn't actually noticed?

SEBASTIAN: *(Looking up from his book)* Of course I'd noticed. I mean these last six months I've been watching you like a hawk. *(Returning to his book)* I'm not so ignorant as not to know that putting on weight is the best sign of all. The conclusive sign you could call it.

LYDIA: Well, here's something even more conclusive. I was told by Uncle Constantin to show you this. *(She takes a paper from her bag)*

SEBASTIAN: Uncle—?

LYDIA: *(Giving him the paper)* Doctor Ziegmann, I've told you a hundred times he was an old family friend from Tallinn—

SEBASTIAN: *(Holding the paper without looking at it)* But not an uncle—

LYDIA: No. I just *call* him that. He's no connection. Just a fellow Estonian.

SEBASTIAN: Yes. He sounds it. I've never heard a thicker accent on the telephone. How long has he been over here?

LYDIA: As long as me. Twenty-eight years.

SEBASTIAN: As long as I, darling. *(Looking at paper)* Of course *your* English is fantastically good, but you had a start on him, I suppose. I don't understand this at all. What is it?

LYDIA: It's a blood test—my last one.

SEBASTIAN: *(Reading)* Normal, normal, near-normal, normal, normal. Sounds like a very dull party—

LYDIA: *(Turning the page over)* And there—under General Remarks.

SEBASTIAN: Dramatic progress fully maintained. Further weekly blood counts may be discontinued. Oh, darling, isn't that marvelous! *(He kisses the top of her head)* Isn't old Ziegfeld pleased?

LYDIA: I've told you—delighted. From now on I can lead an ordinary normal life. No dieting, no wagon, late nights—anything I like. Wants me to have a holiday, though.

SEBASTIAN: Oh yes, of course. Where are we now?—

April. Well, in three months time I'll take you somewhere we've never been before. Greece, if the Colonels have gone— *(Back to his book)* I've lost my place now. Here it is. All right, darling. I'll be about half an hour—*(He turns to his door)*

LYDIA: You won't.

SEBASTIAN: Won't what?

LYDIA: Be about half an hour. Mark's due here five minutes ago.

SEBASTIAN: Mark? Mark Walters? *(Lydia nods)* He's in Hong Kong... No, that's right. He's back. I spoke to him yesterday—

LYDIA: And asked him to dinner.

SEBASTIAN: On a *Thursday?* My copy day. I couldn't have—

LYDIA: You did. What's more you asked him to be sure and come an hour early.

SEBASTIAN: *(Explosively)* Damn and blast! Why didn't you stop me? I remember now. I remember perfectly. You just sat there, with your vapid smile on, and did noth-ing—*nothing*—there's loyalty—

LYDIA: I thought you must have an easy one this week.

SEBASTIAN: Easy? *Easy?* Two sodding Professors on Shakespeare's imagery taking opposing points of view. Where *is* Mark? *(He goes to the telephone)* In that hideous palace of his in Eaton Square—?

LYDIA: No. The workmen are there, adding some-thing. He's at the Savoy. *(Taking the receiver from him)* It's far too late, darling. With the bus strike and the traffic he must have started an hour ago.

SEBASTIAN: Oh, bugger!

LYDIA: *(Soothingly)* Leave it to me. When he arrives I'll tell him you've got to meet a deadline. He's a writer, too.

SEBASTIAN: *Too?* A writer is merely a euphemism, but "too" is an insult.

LYDIA: Why? I wouldn't mind your selling a million copies before your publication date, and the film rights for half a million, sight unseen—

SEBASTIAN: I see. I see. So that's going to be thrown in my face. My novels sell five thousand and make me about seven hundred pounds in all—

LYDIA: Oh, shut up! You don't write novels. I wish you did, but you don't—*(Sebastian opens his mouth to speak)* Twenty-five years ago you wrote a masterpiece, and followed it up four years later with another—

SEBASTIAN: No. The second was a mess—

LYDIA: It was as good as the first.

SEBASTIAN: It was a mess.

LYDIA: It was only that they all turned on you for not writing *Out of the Night* all over again. And so you gave up and joined the enemy. If you can't beat them, join them, I know, but you did give up a bit soon.

SEBASTIAN: Thank you very much.

LYDIA: My God, if Mark Walters took *his* notices as seriously as you did—

SEBASTIAN: His research staff and his stenographers and the man who writes the descriptive passages between bashes would all be out of a job. And Mark would still be a multi-millionaire. Oh God, the injustice of it all! *(He holds out his glass for her to refill. She takes it)* Just take some power-mad tycoon with a permanent hard-on—

LYDIA: They're not all tycoons. His last one was about a Presidential candidate—

SEBASTIAN: With a permanent hard-on?

LYDIA: Semi-permanent. His son has the permanent one—he whams it up everything in sight.

SEBASTIAN: A wham a chapter as usual?

LYDIA: Sometimes more, but it averages out. Now the son meets a lion-tamer—

SEBASTIAN: Don't go on. Being fairly familiar with the author's "oeuvre" I can catch the drift. *(He looks toward his workroom)* I'll have to work late, that's all—and you know what that does to my bladder.

LYDIA: You finish now. Mark won't mind. I can delay dinner—*(Sebastian nods gloomily and goes toward his door)* Oh—talking of novels—

SEBASTIAN: We weren't.

LYDIA: I mean *your* novels. Darling, are those notes for a new novel I came on in there the other day?

(Pause)

SEBASTIAN: "Came on" is good. "Came on" is very good. I noticed that they'd been disturbed. *(Roaring)* Is there *nothing* I can keep concealed in this house?

LYDIA: Oh—so you *concealed* them, did you? Why?

SEBASTIAN: Because I knew that once you got your X-ray eyes on them you'd be bouncing up and down, clapping your little hands and shouting: "Oh goody, goody, he's writing a novel!"

LYDIA: Well goody-goody he is.

SEBASTIAN: No. Not necessarily at all. He may well decide to give it up, because it stinks, or decided that he hasn't got time for it anyway.

LYDIA: Oh, time isn't important. You can make that—

SEBASTIAN: What utter balls you do talk sometimes—*(There is a ring at the front door)* Oh God!

LYDIA: You go in. I'll explain.

SEBASTIAN: No. I'd better say hullo.

(Lydia opens the front door to Mark. He is in the early forties, and physically the exact opposite one would imagine, of any of his power-mad, randy heroes. He has a pleasantly mild expression and a weedy physique. He pants at the mildest physical exertion and is panting now. He carries two parcels under his arm)

LYDIA: Mark, darling—this is wonderful—*(She throws her arms around his neck)*

MARK: Wonderful for me too. Let me get my breath back. Don't they have elevators in Islington?

SEBASTIAN: No.

MARK: Hell, lifts. As a resident I should remember. Hullo, Sebastian. *(They embrace briefly)* Still murdering literary reputations?

SEBASTIAN: Yours is safe.

MARK: These days no one gives me notices. Even

my friends on the *Cleveland Plain Dealer* who used to find me "compulsive" now just says "another Walters!"

SEBASTIAN: *(Snatching a parcel)* Are these presents?

MARK: You've got Lydia's. This is yours.

LYDIA: Oh, Mark, you shouldn't.

SEBASTIAN: Of course he should. It's his duty to re-distribute his wealth. Mine rattles.

MARK: *(Snatching it from him)* Then don't rattle it.

SEBASTIAN: As good as that, eh? I'll open it later, do you mind? I've got a little work to finish off. Lydia forgot it was my copy day—

LYDIA: *He* forgot.

MARK: Look if I'm a nuisance here why don't I take Lydia out for dinner and leave you to work—?

SEBASTIAN: And how do I get dinner?

MARK: Couldn't you scramble yourself some eggs?

SEBASTIAN: Are you mad?

MARK: Yes, I'm mad. For a moment I was thinking you were a normal husband.

SEBASTIAN: You look terrible.

MARK: I know. I always do.

SEBASTIAN: Why don't you look like your heroes?

MARK: If I did I'd write about heroes who looked like me, and I wouldn't sell.

SEBASTIAN: *(Having laughed)* I often think if you'd had any education you might actually write.

MARK: If I'd had any education I'd know I couldn't.

SEBASTIAN: *(Kissing his cheek)* I love you a little, do you know that? *(To Lydia)* Darling, fill this up, would you, and then get Mark a drink.

(Lydia takes his glass again)

MARK: How's Joey?

LYDIA: *(Eagerly)* Oh, he's doing wonderfully well, Mark.

SEBASTIAN: Wonderfully well? He has an unpaid job at the headquarters of a crypto-fascist political organization called the Liberal Party.

LYDIA: He's only unpaid now. After the bye-election they're going to pay him.

SEBASTIAN: Thirty pieces of silver, I should think. *(To Mark, tragically)* Helping to split the left and let the Tories in. My own son, Mark. My own son!

LYDIA: *(Paying no attention)* He's earned three hundred pounds, Mark, for a television play he's written. Isn't that marvelous? That's more than his father earned at twenty. *(She gives Sebastian his drink)*

SEBASTIAN: The B.B.C. 2 series for which this piece of pseudo-Kafka crap was written, Mark, happens to be limited to plays by authors under twenty-one—

LYDIA: It's still an achievement—and you ought to be proud.

SEBASTIAN: Oh, I am, very. *(He sips his drink)* A touch too much water, darling.

(Lydia angrily snatches the drink back)

MARK: When's this play being done?

LYDIA: Tomorrow at ten-thirty.

SEBASTIAN: Prime viewing time.

MARK: I'll try and get to watch.

SEBASTIAN: *(In a murmur)* Don't.

LYDIA: You wouldn't come and watch it here with us, would you? *(She brings the drink back to Sebastian, having added whisky)*

SEBASTIAN: Darling, what a thing to ask the poor man!

LYDIA: It's only he could see Joey, too. He's coming up from his bye-election especially to watch it with us. Don't you think that's rather sweet of him, when he could have seen it with his friends?

SEBASTIAN: I think it's wise. He knows we've got to like it.

LYDIA: Damn you, damn you! *(She begins to switch lights on)*

SEBASTIAN: Forgive her, Mark. She's been a bit hysterical lately.

LYDIA: Go and work!

SEBASTIAN: *(Soothingly)* Yes, darling, I'm just going. *(Sebastian goes to his door)*

LYDIA: Would you, Mark? I know it's an awful thing to ask but Joey would be thrilled out of his mind.

SEBASTIAN: Out of his what?

MARK: I'd love to.

SEBASTIAN: Good God!

(He goes out. Mark faces Lydia. There is a pause)

MARK: Tell me, please, that I've come for no reason.

LYDIA: You've come, Mark, and I'm very grateful. *(She kisses him fondly)* What do you want to drink?

MARK: *(Impatiently)* Anything.

LYDIA: I went out and bought a bottle of Bourbon—

MARK: All right Bourbon. I want to see your latest blood count—stop press.

LYDIA: *(Taking it out of her bag)* But do you know anything about blood counts?

MARK: Since I got your first letter I had one of my research team—

LYDIA: *(Fondly)* Darling Marcus Waldt. Darling, darling Mark Walters.

MARK: Hell, I'm not intelligent enough to research for myself. *(He fumbles in his pocket and pulls out a notebook)* I told this guy it was for a character in a book. I got figures here—

LYDIA: For what?

MARK: *(Reading)* Acute Lymphocytosis.

LYDIA: *(Handing him his drink)* Say leukemia. It's a prettier word.

MARK: *(Harshly)* I'm not taking self-pity from you yet.

LYDIA: Unkind, but justified. I drag you half-way across the world because I'm sorry for myself, and have to talk to someone. That's self-pity all right. I hope you had other reasons for coming?

MARK: *(Absorbed in his comparison of figures)* What? Yes—plenty of reasons. These figures don't fit.

LYDIA: No.

MARK: They don't fit with—O.K.—leukemia.

LYDIA: No. Nor do they fit with the word "normal" which dear Uncle Constantin has so sweetly typed in.

MARK: *(Studying another leaf)* No. They're all above normal—

LYDIA: Quite a bit above?

MARK: Well—yes, I guess—a bit—

LYDIA: Then why did Uncle Constantin make them normal?

MARK: He wants to reassure you.

LYDIA: "We are coming along most finely, my dear, improvink every day." Uncle Constantin doesn't know I can see the tears behind those pebble glasses, and anyway they might be tears of joy, because we Estonians are an emotional people. I'm getting myself a drink.

MARK: Allowed it?

LYDIA: Encouraged, Marcus, encouraged. *(She goes to the drink tray)* Vodka. American, but still vodka. *(Impatiently)* Oh, Marcus! Why am I being encouraged to drink and lead a normal life, why am I being told I need no more blood tests, why am I being conned into thinking that I've had a dramatic recovery, when that test is worse than last week's, and considerably worse than the week's before?

MARK: How did you get to see your tests?

LYDIA: I told you—I pinch them.

MARK: How?

LYDIA: Each week I have to spend a penny for a specimen. I tell him I can't do it with someone in the room, even behind a screen. *(After a sip)* Oh, God. It doesn't even *taste* like vodka. Still, press on. Anyway the old boy discreetly disappears and I rifle his desk. I've a good head for figures. Nowadays I don't even need to write them down.

MARK: *(Indicating the paper and his notepaper)* Why are these figures lower than mine?

LYDIA: Cortisone. Lashings of cortisone. What Uncle Constantin has told me are my little tonic pills. *(She opens her bag and takes out a bottle, shaking two into her hand)* Which reminds me. *(She takes them, swallowing them with vodka)* Two six times a day now. It was two four times a day until last week.

> *(Mark snatches the bottle from her hand)*
> MARK: Where does it say they're cortisone?
> LYDIA: Nowhere.
> MARK: How do you know then?
> LYDIA: Analysis at an ordinary chemist. "Oh Miss—

could you help me. I've found these in an old bottle and I'm not too sure what they are...Oh, how kind...Cortisone? Fancy. That's a powerful drug isn't it? I'll throw them away—" *(A sudden slight access of tears. She embraces him)* Oh, Marcus, I'm so happy to see you. I'm such a stranger in this land. Even after twenty-eight years I haven't anyone— anyone whom I could call a friend.

> MARK: That's hard to imagine.
> LYDIA: Well, I could have had lovers—but after—after

what Sebastian's just called my early misadventures—aren't English euphemisms wonderful? I didn't want them. But a real friend, no. Among the other refugees I suppose I could have made some, but that would have meant swapping concentration camp stories, probably in front of Sebastian, who dreads them. But so do all the English. Do the Americans?

> MARK: Some, I'd say—the ones who ape the English.

Easterners. But, hell, you *are* speaking to Marcus Waldt, Lydia. Grandfather Lithuanian Jewish. Most of us Americans *are* refugees. Not necessarily from concentration camps—but from something like them. Not as bad—but still bad. No, mainly we sympathize.

> LYDIA: In this country I learnt my lesson early. At

first, when I had an even stronger accent than now, people would politely ask me where I was from, and I'd say Estonia. Then I could see them thinking: "Now where the hell is that? Oh, yes. Baltic States. Germans *and* Russians. Jesus, we'd better not ask her *her* experiences." But some did, and I'd be silly enough to tell them, and I'd see the glassy stare of utter boredom in their eyes. And something worse—I was guilty of bad form—especially if, as I sometimes did, I cried a bit when telling. Oh, damn the English! Sometimes I think that their bad form doesn't just lie in revealing their emotions, it's in having any emotions at all. Do you like the English?

MARK: I don't quite dig them. But I like their country. So I live in it rather than mine.

LYDIA: Yes, I like their country too, and sometimes say so—and that's bad form, too. No, Mark, in England I'm very alone. Of course I have Joey—but even he gets embarrassed if I even hint at what I feel for him. As for— *(She jerks her thumb despairingly at Sebastian's room)* No. I think I should have gone away with you when I had the chance.

MARK: I think you should, too. Among other things, it would have saved me two sets of alimonies.

LYDIA: And *you* I could have told I was dying of leukemia.

MARK: No, Lydia. If that was true, mind you—*I* would have told you. At the proper time. Not till necessary. Not till you had to know. But the doctor and I would have been in league from the start.

LYDIA: Yes. Well, perhaps there are some English husbands who'd have behaved the same way. It's difficult for me to say. I've only really known one. I'm getting another drink. What about you?

MARK: *(Shaking his head)* Sebastian might have behaved the same way, if you'd given him the chance.

LYDIA: *(Laughing)*He'd have tried to, poor lamb. For a week or two he'd have remembered his upbringing at Winchester and Balliol. Manners Makyth Man. And for a week or two he'd have been quite solicitous—"Do lie down, old girl. Mustn't tire yourself, you know. I'll get you your tea—" *(She laughs)* Just to hear that I sometimes almost wish I *had* told him. But after a time, can you imagine the boredom he'd have gone through? Don't fool ourselves, Mark, a long, slow terminal illness is the worst visitation we can inflict on anyone, let alone our nearest and dearest. And Sebastian isn't the best person in the world at being bored. The glassy stare, very soon, and then going on for months and months. Then, when I came to die I wouldn't have enjoyed looking up into Sebastian's face—and seeing relief. This is morbid. Let's talk of something else. Hong Kong—

MARK: Not yet. There's still leukemia. There's no certain proof until—

LYDIA: *(Interrupting)* I've had the lumbar puncture.

MARK: *(Looking at his notebook)* Now would that be the sternum test?

LYDIA: Yes, I had it yesterday. It was positive.

MARK: The result wouldn't be through.

LYDIA: No, it isn't, officially. But Uncle Constantin's nurse is Scandinavian. Accent very like mine. I called the hospital, got the specialist's secretary, said Doctor Ziegmann needed a verbal report and couldn't speak himself as the patient was in his consulting room at that moment. She swallowed it. Said she'd look it up—

MARK: Where were you?

LYDIA: In a call-box, scared to death it would sound off before she found the report. It didn't. "Mrs. Lydia Cruttwell—Positive." Very brisk voice. No, "I'm sorry," Just "positive." Now you'll have another drink?

MARK: Yes. *(Lydia takes his glass. Mark jumps up)* No, you sit down. I'll—

(Lydia laughs)

LYDIA: Don't be silly. Cortisone makes me feel eighteen again. It's a wonderful drug. They dope racehorses with it. Honestly, I've never felt better.

MARK: There's a man in Denver, Colorado, who guarantees a seventy percent cure.

LYDIA: *(Laughing)* Denver, Colorado!

MARK: There's no money problem.

LYDIA: I know. There's no Marcus problem. There's just a Sebastian problem. And that, darling Marcus, is insoluble.

MARK: He's got to be told sometime.

LYDIA: When the ambulance comes. Perhaps not even then. Certainly not before.

MARK: If this test really *is* positive, your doctor will tell him.

LYDIA: Oh, no, he won't. Uncle Constantin promised me most sacredly—a long time ago.

MARK: I could tell him.

(Pause)

LYDIA: *(Quietly)* And guarantee my never speaking
to you again—ever, in this life.

MARK: Christ, Lydia—he's your husband.

LYDIA: No. Oh, yes, I have my marriage lines written in Russian with a British Occupation Authority stamp on
it, but Sebastian didn't take me for better, for worse, in sick-
ness and in health, to love and to cherish. He took me to give
me a passport—

MARK: For other reasons than that, for Christ sake.

LYDIA: Two, if you like. I made him enjoy going to
bed with me, because I'd learnt how. And sometimes, in
those early days, my funny English made him laugh. And a
third. I fell in love with him at once, and never really fell
out—not even now. So he felt under an obligation. Still when
we got to England we were supposed to divorce. But gradually I made myself too useful to him to be got rid of. Deliberately, Mark. Deliberately. Then we had ourselves a son—
(She stops suddenly and bites her lip) Oh, God—Joey—

(Mark is beside her, holding her tight)

MARK: Lydia, darling, you must let me help you.
You mustn't give up—you mustn't—please—

(Sebastian puts his head round the door)

SEBASTIAN: Darling, my special reading light
doesn't go on. *(Neither Mark nor Lydia show any embarrassment at their intimate attitude)* Darling, I said my special
reading light—

LYDIA: I heard you. What's the matter with it?

SEBASTIAN: *(Simply and reasonably)* It doesn't go on.

LYDIA: Probably the bulb. *(She goes past him into the
room)*

SEBASTIAN: Do forgive me, Mark. Just two more
sentences. You haven't been too bored, I hope.

MARK: Not at all. What are you writing on this week?

SEBASTIAN: That complacent old burgher of Stratford-on-Avon. God, he's so maddening. With his worship of the Establishment he makes nonsense of everything we write, don't you think?

MARK: *We?*

SEBASTIAN: *(Appalled)* Are you a *Republican?*

MARK: *(Hastily)* Gee, no. I'm a radical—

SEBASTIAN: Well, Shakespeare *must* infuriate people like us who passionately believe that no man can write well whose heart isn't in the right place.

MARK: Meaning the left place?

SEBASTIAN: *(Feeling his heart)* Which is where the heart is. Thank you, Mark. I might use that as my pay-off. *(Lydia appears)* Well?

LYDIA: It wasn't plugged in.

SEBASTIAN: Who unplugged it. Mrs. MacKintyre?

LYDIA: *(Gravely)* Probably Mrs. MacKintyre.

SEBASTIAN: You must speak to her, darling. Set up the chessmen, Mark.

(He goes into his room. There is a pause)

MARK: Now who on earth is going to look after that, if—

LYDIA: Say "when," Mark. Get used to it, please.

MARK: *(Stubbornly)* I'm not saying "when," Lydia. I'm sorry. Someone's got to keep a little hope going around here. You seemed to have resigned yourself to black despair—

LYDIA: Black despair? Me! Marcus, have you forgotten, who you're talking to? Black despair! Me. Between the ages of sixteen and twenty-two I had to face, every day and every night, the almost certain prospect of death in a hundred really horrible ways. Thirty years later I face a very gentle kind of death—*(She knocks on wood)* well, let's hope. But my books aren't frightening about it at all, and they give me about eighteen months. Eighteen months? That's a long time. And then—"To cease upon the midnight with no pain"? God, how many millions of us over there during those six years longed for just that—and didn't get it. Black despair! Me! Marcus, really!

MARK: I'm sorry. Only I'd sooner not talk about it too much, if you don't mind. *(He pulls one of his parcels out and begins to open it)*

LYDIA: Well, we've got to talk about it a little or you're not going to be much of a help, are you?

MARK: O.K., but not now. Do you mind?

LYDIA: Just one thing more. You asked a question and I've got to answer it. *(Mark is taking out a set of very beautiful, carved, Chinese chessmen, in red and white, and is methodically replacing the black and white pieces with them on the table in the corner. Lydia, obsessed with her problem, has not yet noticed what he is unobtrusively doing)* Who's going to look after *that,* (She thumbs at Sebastian's door) when *I* can't any more. Well, I've an idea—

MARK: I suppose he couldn't just look after himself?

LYDIA: Are you mad?

MARK: Hasn't he ever *had* to? Surely in the war—

LYDIA: Commission in Army Intelligence at once, and a batman. Knowing him, probably two. What are you doing over there?

MARK: Don't look yet. How does he reconcile all that with his Marxism?

LYDIA: Surprisingly easily. No, I've got an idea. There's a girl called Prunella Larkin—a journalist, who's mad about him, and I gather rather his form too, mentally *and* physically. Anyway he's been seeing an awful lot of her recently. In fact I think for the last three months they've been having a thing—

MARK: So? He doesn't seem to have things much—

LYDIA: Unlike you sex-maniac.

MARK: Don't confuse *me* with my heroes.

LYDIA: You do all right.

MARK: What makes you think it's a thing?

LYDIA: Well, he's not a master of subterfuge. He takes this Larkin out to dinner—a little business chat, you know, darling—and later gets caught in the rain when there isn't any, and stays the night with his editor who sends him a postcard the next day from Tangier. You know the form.

MARK: Who better? Only mine don't go to that much trouble. They just sleep out and when I ask where, it's mental cruelty.

LYDIA: Now the doctor says I must have a holiday. Will you take me away for ten days?

MARK: Sure. Where?

LYDIA: Ilfracombe's nice—

MARK: So's Monte Carlo. What's this to do with Miss Larkin?

LYDIA: Mrs. Larkin, divorced. Well, he'll say "who's going to look after me?" And I'll say "what about that nice girl Prunella"—and he'll jump at it. Then if the ten days are a success—well, later on, I can make plans accordingly. *(Mark is silent)* Don't you think it's a clever idea?

MARK: I can only repeat what Sebastian so often says to you: you are an extraordinary woman. All right. Now you can look. *(He carries the completed table over to the centre of the room. Lydia looks in wonder)*

LYDIA: *(Picking up a piece)* Oh, but these are exquisite.

MARK: Chinese. Nothing very grand. Modern.

LYDIA: But they're beautiful. He'll adore them. My God, if his is as good as that, I'm going to open mine. *(She snatches up the remaining parcel and begins furiously to unwrap it)*

MARK: Listen—if that doesn't suit—

(Lydia has managed to open the parcel which is a box and peers inside, past tissue paper. Then she closes the box)

LYDIA: No. Take it back.

MARK: Lydia.

LYDIA: Take it back this instant. *(But she holds on to it firmly. There is a pause. Then gathering strength, she whisks out a silver mink wrap. She gazes at it lovingly)* I said—take it back.

MARK: I heard you.

(He takes the wrap from her and holds it out for her to slip into. She does so.)

LYDIA: I didn't mean a word of what I said just now. I think you're an absolute horror.

MARK: Yes.

LYDIA: Flaunting your wealth, showing girls what they've missed by not divorcing their husbands and marrying you.

(She looks at herself from every angle in the mirror. Then she gives him a passionate embrace. Finally she takes his empty glass)

MARK: Well, maybe I sensed this was special.

LYDIA: Special it was. Thank you, dear Marcus.

(She embraces him again. Sebastian comes in)

SEBASTIAN: Have you two nothing better to do? You're not even giving the poor man a chance to smoke.

LYDIA: I haven't seen him for six months.

SEBASTIAN: Nor have I. Nor has anyone. Darling, that lovely patent folding table of yours doesn't fold—

LYDIA: *(Looking in the room)* Well, of course, it doesn't if you leave the typewriter on it.

(She flaunts her wrap in front of his eyes, to no effect whatever. Crossly she goes into the workroom)

SEBASTIAN: *(Very half-heartedly after her.)* Oh, darling—do let me—

(He takes half a step to the workroom, and three or four full and determined steps over to the drink tray)

MARK: Finished?

SEBASTIAN: More or less. I've fixed both the Professors, and the Swan is sunk in his own Avon without a trace.

MARK: Never to rise again?

SEBASTIAN: Ay. There's the rub. One has to admit that the bloody old honors-hunting bourgeois could write. William Shakespeare, Gent. Hard to forgive him for that. It should have stamped him a forgettable nonentity for the rest of creation. Instead of which—

MARK: Didn't you get something?

SEBASTIAN: An C.B.E. *(With rage)* Lydia forced me into that. She staged a sit-down strike.

MARK: Isn't an C.B.E. what's called an honor?

SEBASTIAN: I would rather not speak of it, if you please. *(He slips into the chair opposite Mark, facing him across the chessmen. He picks up a white pawn in one hand, and a red one in the other)* Now, are you prepared for your usual thrashing? *(Mark taps his left hand. Sebastian opens it, revealing a red pawn)* Good. There is no question at all that I am better playing red than—Red? *(He picks up his pawn again, feels it lovingly and then stares at the whole board. Then without a word he gets up, crosses to Mark and gives him a full, fervent kiss on the mouth)* I passionately adore you, and am prepared to live with you for the rest of my life. *(He picks up more pieces to feel them)* What is more I take everything back that I've ever written about your novels.

MARK: You've never written anything about my novels.

SEBASTIAN: Your next one will get my whole three columns—

MARK: I think I'd rather have a kiss. *(Sebastian has sat down again. Mark has moved a piece)*

SEBASTIAN: Pawn to Queen four? Ah. You've been reading your Fischer-Spassky—

MARK: You know something, I'd give a million bucks to write one novel a tenth as good as your *Out of the Night.*

SEBASTIAN: So would I. Only I haven't a million bucks. *(Picking up his King and Queen to fondle them)* These are marvelous. Of course you can't tell the King from the Queen, but when can you these days?

MARK: Are you never going to try another novel?

SEBASTIAN: That'd be telling.

MARK: Good. That means yes.

SEBASTIAN: No. You said "try." I've got to be *moved*, Mark. The war did move me and that novel was good. It wasn't Tolstoy like some idiots said, but it was good. Then the Peace didn't move me, and that novel was bad.

MARK: No.

SEBASTIAN: *(Belligerently)* Listen, who's the critic?

MARK: Sorry.

SEBASTIAN: But I'm not beyond hope about the next—if I do it. Ah *(Referring to the game)* The Queen's gambit. I thought you'd grown out of that—

MARK: I've got a new variation—

SEBASTIAN: You'll need it. My reply to the Queen's gambit makes strong men quake—*(Lydia comes in and moves ostentatiously about in front of Sebastian—showing off her wrap)* Darling, can you leave the ashtrays till later? It's a bit distracting, all that moving about. *(Lydia stands still, with a sigh)* Oh, by the way—do you see what Mark's given me?

LYDIA: I'm trying to show you what Mark's given *me*.

SEBASTIAN: *(Looking up at her)* Oh, what? *(After a pause)* Oh, that. *(Another pause. To Mark)* What fur exactly is that?

LYDIA: *(Explosively)* Don't tell him! *(Savagely)* Dyed rabbit.

SEBASTIAN: Mink? I see. *(Pause)* Very nice. *(Pause)* Isn't that light shade just a bit—forgive me, darling— on the young side—? *(Before he has finished Lydia has slipped the wrap off and has swung it at his head, disturbing several chess pieces. Outraged)* Darling, really. These are valuable—*(He and Mark pick up the pieces. Lydia goes to sit down in a sulk, hand on fist, staring at her husband with hatred)* I'd just moved pawn to King three. *(Holding a pawn)* Superb workmanship. *(He allows Mark to rearrange the board)* Where did you get them?

MARK: Hong Kong.

SEBASTIAN: Of course. *(A horrifying thought strikes him)* Oh, Mark, I may have to give them back. All that sweated labor—

MARK: Imported from Peking.

SEBASTIAN: *(With a deep sigh of relief)* Ah. Good.

MARK: It's all right if they sweat in Peking?

SEBASTIAN: They don't sweat in Peking.

MARK: Or they'd be arrested.

SEBASTIAN: Please don't make cheap jokes like that, do you mind? Now. Your move.

(They have rearranged the board. Lydia, after a questioning glance at Mark, fills up her own glass)

LYDIA: Sebastian, Mark wants to take me down to Monte Carlo for ten days or so—

SEBASTIAN: What for?

LYDIA: A holiday. A rest—like the doctor said—

SEBASTIAN: Well, can't you have a rest here?

LYDIA: Since you ask—no. Unless you go to Monte Carlo instead.

SEBASTIAN: Well, that might be an idea. I doubt if my editor would scream with joy though, seeing he's away, too.

LYDIA: In Tangier.

SEBASTIAN: Yes. How did you know? Well, can you get Mrs. MacHiggins to come in every day?

LYDIA: Not a chance.

SEBASTIAN: Just as well. It'd be very expensive.

LYDIA: But I've got a better idea. I haven't asked her, but I think I might just get Prunella to look after you.

SEBASTIAN: Prunella? Prunella Larkin?

LYDIA: Yes. Just for that little time.

(Pause)

SEBASTIAN: Are you round the bend? *(Letting himself go)* There is no such thing as a little time with Prunella Larkin. An hour is an eternity. Ten days—ten *consecutive* days with her and I'd be a gibbering lunatic.

LYDIA: *(Not displeased)* Oh. It's just that you did seem to have been seeing quite a lot of her recently—

(Pause)

SEBASTIAN: *(Carefully)* Mrs. Larkin and I do, I grant, have certain interests in common, but they are interests that can usually be shared in well under thirty minutes. If after those brief encounters I should choose not to plod back to Islington but to sleep in my editor's flat, to which I have a key, that is a matter for my conscience but not for your prurient suspicions. If you insist on skipping off on this extravagant jaunt, I shall go to the Savoy and send the bill in to Mark. If he doesn't pay I shall sell these chessmen. Now, does that settle the matter?

LYDIA: *(A shade breathlessly)* Yes. Oh, yes. Oh, yes, it does.

SEBASTIAN: Good. *(Gravely)* Your move, Mark. *(Lydia suddenly bursts into a peal of slightly drunken laughter and kisses his head)* Darling, please. This game needs concentration. Bobby Fischer won't have a camera click ten yards away—much less a hyena screeching tipsily in his ear.

LYDIA: Sorry. I was trying to kiss you.

SEBASTIAN: There is a time and a place.

LYDIA: Yes. I know both.

(Trying to be very silent, she puts down her glass, fumbles in her bag and takes out two pills from the familiar bottle. In doing so she knocks a glass over)

SEBASTIAN: Darling, go and cook dinner.

LYDIA: Yes.

(She swallows the pills with a sip of vodka. Mark sees her)

MARK: *(Sharply)* You've already had two of those—

LYDIA: Yes, but I missed two after lunch.

SEBASTIAN: What's she had two of?

LYDIA: My tonic pills.

SEBASTIAN: *(Deep in thought)* Oh, yes, those iron things. Very good for her, Mark. Put on eight pounds—

LYDIA: *(Shouting)* Two!

(Mark castles)

SEBASTIAN: The move of a coward. *(After a pause)* How did we get to know each other, Mark? It was in California when I was lecturing at U.C.L.A., but I don't remember exactly how—was it chess?

MARK: No, it was Lydia.

SEBASTIAN: Oh, yes, of course. You thought you were in love with her then, didn't you?

MARK: *(Looking at Lydia)* I think I still am.

SEBASTIAN: *(Deep in the game)* Extraordinary. *(Lydia picks up her wrap to have another go, but is warned by Mark with a gesture. Sebastian looks up)* Oh, are you still there, darling? I thought you were getting dinner.

(He makes his move. Lydia determinedly finishes her vodka, pours another and carries it to the stairs with her, which she surmounts with caution)

LYDIA: Something tells me your dinner tonight might taste a little peculu—peculiar.

MARK: *(Rising)* Can I help?

SEBASTIAN: *(Roaring)* Sit down, Mark. It's your move. *(Mark moves but keeps his hand on it. Lydia from the kitchen door gestures Mark to sit down. Sebastian looks up at her as she opens the door, her back to him. She goes inside. Sebastian looks down at the board again. There is a long pause. Sebastian leans back abstractedly. Murmuring)*

Ay, but to die and go we know not where;
to lie in cold obstruction and to rot;

(Mark who has been about to make a move stops with his hand on the piece, staring at Sebastian)

This sensible warm motion to become
a kneaded clod; and the delighted spirit—

Are you making that move?
MARK: I don't know yet. Is that Shakespeare?
SEBASTIAN:

To be imprisioned in the viewless winds,
And blown with restless violence round about
The pendant world!

Can't keep your hand on it for ever, you know—as the Bishop said to the actress—
MARK: O.K. That's my move.
SEBASTIAN: And a bloody silly one, too, if I might say so. *(He considers, and then continues softly)*

The weariest and most loathed wordly life
That age, ache, penury and imprisonment
Can lay on nature, is a paradise
To what we fear of death.

Yes, Shakespeare. One is forced to admit that he could sometimes sort out the words. Pessimistic old sod!
MARK: I thought he was a complacent old bourgeois.
SEBASTIAN: He was both—that's the trouble. *(He moves)* This move will lead to your ultimate annihilation.

,

MARK: The Cruttwell variation? It has interest, if only fleeting. *(He considers the board)* What made you choose that particular quotation?

SEBASTIAN: Hm?—Oh, it's in my article. The same man that wrote those lines also wrote:

We are such stuff as dreams are made on,
And our little life is rounded with a sleep.

The first one is Royal Court, but that one is pure Shaftesbury Avenue. Cozy, commercial and comforting. Man wasn't consistent, you see...*(Muttering)* Gent...

MARK: *(Making a move)* Check.

(A key turns in the front door and Joey comes in. His hair is long, but neat: his sweater and slacks are of sober hue. He looks what he is, a Liberal. He carries an overnight bag)

SEBASTIAN: *(Not seeing him)* I think you have fallen right into my trap.

JOEY: Hullo, Dad.

(Pause. Neither smile)

SEBASTIAN: Are we expecting you?

JOEY: No. *(With warmth)* Hullo, Mr. Walters.

MARK: *(Getting up and shaking hands)* Hullo, Joey. You look ten years older than when I last saw you.

JOEY: I feel ten years older. You don't know what canvassing in a bye-election can do to one.

(He puts down his bag. Sebastian contents himself with an abstracted Pah!)

MARK: Congratulations on getting a play done on TV, Joey. That's great.

JOEY: I'm scared to death. Anyway, ten-thirty. No one'll see it. No hope of you seeing it, is there?

MARK: Sure. I'm coming here tomorrow just for that.

JOEY: *(Awed)* Specially to see my play?

MARK: Yep.

JOEY: Jesus—

MARK: I'm sure it'll be great—

SEBASTIAN: *(Loudly)* Do you mind not yakkety-yakketing with my vote-splitting son? You are playing chess with me.

JOEY: Who's winning?

SEBASTIAN: I have him in a trap. It's only a question of how best to snap together its steel jaws.

(Joey examines the game)

JOEY: Looks the other way round to me.

SEBASTIAN: *(Snarling)* Do you mind?

JOEY: Sorry.

(Sebastian puts his hand on a piece. Joey hisses gently. Sebastian withdraws it. Then he puts his hand on another piece. Joey hisses again)

SEBASTIAN: Will you kindly cease your imitation of a cobra in heat? Faulty though it may seem to budding Empire Loyalists, I prefer my game to *be* my own.

JOEY: I just didn't want to see you lose your Knight.

SEBASTIAN: *(Who plainly hasn't seen)* My Knight?

JOEY: Two moves ahead—

SEBASTIAN: *(After a pause)* Now a Knight sacrifice might well be my plan. How do you know it isn't, eh?

(Nevertheless he withdraws his hand. After a moment he makes another move without hesitation)

JOEY: That's torn it.

SEBASTIAN: *(Explosively)* If you're so bloody good, why don't you ever play?

JOEY: I do.

SEBASTIAN: I meant with me.

(Pause)

JOEY: Two reasons, I suppose. One, you don't ask me. Two, if I did win you'd call me a fascist pig.

SEBASTIAN: Meaning I'm a bad loser?

JOEY: Meaning that anyone who stamps on your ego is always a fascist pig.

SEBASTIAN: Go away, or I'll stamp on something more painful than your ego.

JOEY: I want to watch. You don't mind, do you Mr. Walters?

MARK: Not at all.

SEBASTIAN: *(Calling)* Lydia! Lydia! *(She comes out of the kitchen)* The brood is here. Remove it before I do it violence.

LYDIA: *(With a joyous cry)* Joey! *(She begins to run down the stairs. Thinks better of it and waits half-way down for him to bound up to her. There they have a warm embrace)* Joey! Oh, how marvelous!

(She embraces him again)

SEBASTIAN: *(To Mark)* Forgive her, Mark. She hasn't seen him for five days—

LYDIA: Why didn't you let us know? Have you eaten?

JOEY: Yes. I only knew myself at the lunch break. They don't need me until Election Day—

LYDIA: Thursday? And I've got you till then?

(Joey nods. Sebastian looks up at them)

SEBASTIAN: I've got him, too.

JOEY: Don't bother, Dad. I won't be in *your* way.

SEBASTIAN: Not till Election Day? Ha! That must mean your man's given up.

JOEY: He's got it made, Dad. The latest poll gives him twelve percent over all other candidates.

SEBASTIAN: I don't believe it. *(Rising to get a drink)* The electorate, God knows, can be utterly idiotic, but it's not raving mad.

LYDIA: *(To Joey).* Could you get your mother a little sip of vodka, dear?

JOEY: I didn't know you drank vodka.

LYDIA: I've rather taken to it in the last hour.

(She sits carefully on the steps. Joey comes down into the room to get her her drink)

SEBASTIAN: It doesn't make sense. It's all Bernard Levin's fault. Centre Party! What in hell is a Centre Party?

JOEY: *(Gently, as to a child)* A party that's in the centre: That's to say, between the two extremes—of right ...*(He demonstrates)* and left. *(He demonstrates. The two are now close at the drink cupboard)*

SEBASTIAN: Don't talk to me as if I were a cretinous ape who only involved himself in politics yesterday—

JOEY: No. It was quite a long time ago, wasn't it, Dad? When Hitler was the devil, Stalin was in his heaven and all was right with the world. Times have changed, you know. You old-time Marxists are out of touch.

(He takes the vodka up the stairs to his mother. She strokes his hair)

SEBASTIAN: Out of touch, are we?

LYDIA: *(To Joey)* Careful dear. *(To Sebastian)* Did you ever have hair as beautiful as this?

SEBASTIAN: Much more beautiful. But I was in an army, fighting Fascism, and I was made to cut it short. That was for hygiene. Lice.

JOEY: Did you get many lice as an Intelligence Officer in Whitehall?

(He has sat two steps down from his mother who seems bent on stroking his hair and whom he is never averse from having do so)

SEBASTIAN: I was speaking figuratively.

JOEY: Figurative lice?

LYDIA: *(Hastily)* Don't annoy him. You know what'll happen.

SEBASTIAN: *(To Mark, with sudden venom)* Are you going to take all night?

MARK: *(Startled)* Sorry. *(He makes his move)*

JOEY: You're out of touch, Dad. It's all talk. You really don't want action any more. We do, you see—

SEBASTIAN: Flashing mirrors in the eyes of South African cricketers?

JOEY: We didn't do that. But we did get the tour stopped. And what did you do, Dad? Booked tickets for the Lord's Test.

SEBASTIAN: *(Roaring)* Don't flout the issue! A Centre Party is nothing more nor less than gross collaboration with the enemy.

LYDIA: *(Happily sipping)* Collaboration. That's very

bad. We used to get shot for that—first by the Russians, then by the Germans, then by the Russians again. It was all very confusing.

JOEY: *(Patting her hand)* Mum, that was a long time ago.

LYDIA: Yes, it was. It sometimes doesn't seem so.

JOEY: *(To Sebastian)* I suppose by "the enemy" you mean the status quo.

SEBASTIAN: *(Looking at board)* What? *(To Joey)* I mean the whole, rotten stinking mess that is Britain as it is today.

JOEY: What, mum?

(Lydia is whispering in Joey's ear)

SEBASTIAN: What's she saying?

JOEY: She says "Isn't it terrible, but she rather likes Britain as it is today."

SEBASTIAN: She's pissed!

JOEY: *(Laughing)* Are you, Mum?

LYDIA: Well, it's not a very nice way of— *(Firmly)* Yes, I am.

JOEY: Good for you.

JOEY: *(Getting up from the steps)* Dad, I'm not denying that all of us today, on both sides of the Atlantic, are living in a nightmare. But we want to *do* something—

LYDIA: *(To herself)* Nightmare— *(She titters, still happy)*

SEBASTIAN: Darling, are you going to sit there just repeating everything we say?

LYDIA: *(Defiantly)* Yes, if I want to.

SEBASTIAN: You don't think a touch of light cooking might be in order?

LYDIA: I like this discussion.

SEBASTIAN: Well, you're not making a great contribution to it.

LYDIA: How can I make a contrib—join in your discussion? I don't belong to this country.

JOEY: Mum, you do.

LYDIA: No. I'm an Englishwoman—thanks only to

the lucky accident of a British Intelligence Officer having a night out in the Russian Zone of Berlin, and stopping off at Bentinck Strasse sixteen.

SEBASTIAN: For God's sake, Lydia, Joey mightn't know we met in a whorehouse!

LYDIA: Well, he does now. *(Daintily)* And anyway I've always called it a "Maison de Rendezvous."

JOEY: *(To Sebastian)* Don't worry, Dad, I knew where you met Mum.

SEBASTIAN: Good. But it's not a thing to go roaring from all the roof tops in Islington.

LYDIA: I was not roaring it from all the roof tops in Islington. I was simply trying to remind you—all you Anglo-Saxon gentlemen—that I was born and bred in a country called Estonia, which doesn't any longer exist. *(To Sebastian)* Now England still does—by some miracle—

SEBASTIAN: *(To Mark)* Forgive the refugee bit. She doesn't do this often—

LYDIA: And England—taking it all in all—hasn't, over the last *(Trying to remember)* twenty-eight years—that's right—twenty-eight—been too bad a place for an Estonian to have lived in. I shall now go and cook.

SEBASTIAN: Yes, darling. Good idea. *(To Mark)* I don't know what's come over her, I'm so sorry, Mark.

JOEY: *(Smiling)* To *have* lived in, Mum? Why? Are you planning to leave?

SEBASTIAN: *(To Mark)* Do you really want me to take that pawn?

(Lydia suddenly clutches Joey in a fierce embrace. He is surprised. Lydia recovers quickly)

LYDIA: *(In a "matter of fact" voice)* I meant up to now, Joey, of course. *(She turns, takes a step or two quite firmly away from him, then staggers and seems likely to fall. Surprisingly, it is Sebastian and not Joey who is by her side to prevent her falling. To Sebastian)* I'm pissed, aren't I?

SEBASTIAN: As a newt, I would say. *(To Mark, who is already by his side)* Better take her up to bed…No, there's no need to carry her. I've tried it. She weighs a ton. *(To*

Lydia) Just put one foot after the other, dear—That's right. It's called walking. Well done—clever girl. Joey, your mother has plainly passed out for the night, and unless someone is prepared to do something about it, we will all be going without our dinner...

> *(Joey goes toward the kitchen. Mark, meanwhile, is helping Lydia up the stairs)*

JOEY: I'll do what I can.

SEBASTIAN: That's a good boy. *(He reaches the table. Calling)* What was your move, Mark?

MARK: *(By this time off)* Pawn to King's Rook three—

SEBASTIAN: *(At the table)* Yes...I thought it was *(He sits down)*

> *(The lights come down until only his face is visible. Then all the lights go out)*

Act Two

FIRST VOICE: *(Simultaneously)* Well, I can only repeat what I've just said...*(We now can recognize the voice as the warm and friendly one of Vic Feather's)* it's the government's responsibility to govern...*(A light comes on to illumine Joey's face as he kneels beside a TV)* but a bad law is still a bad law, whatever government's in power...

> *(Joey turns the control down to silent)*

JOEY: *(Calling)* Mum!

LYDIA: *(From the kitchen)* Yes, darling?

JOEY: What will they all be drinking?

LYDIA: *(From the kitchen)* Leave that to me.

JOEY: O.K.

> *(Lydia appears from the kitchen with a tray on which is a bottle of champagne and three glasses)*

LYDIA: This is what they'll be drinking.

JOEY: Oh, Mum. That's making too much of it.

LYDIA: You can't make too much of it. *(She has hon-*

ored the occasion with what is, perhaps, her best cocktail dress. Joey takes the tray from her) Nervous?

JOEY: Petrified. Why only three glasses?

LYDIA: Darling, if you forgive me, I think I'll stick to Vichy water. *(She sits down, exhausted)* That ought to go in a bucket. There's one in the kitchen. Put quite a lot of ice in it. It's been in the fridge—but it'll look better.

JOEY: How are you feeling now?

LYDIA: American vodka is terrible stuff. Now if it had been Estonian vodka—

JOEY: You'd probably be dead, instead of just dying.

(Lydia throws the quickest of glances at him, but is reassured by his grin)

LYDIA: Very likely. Go and get that ice.

JOEY: And another glass—

LYDIA: All right. Just a sip, in your honor.

JOEY: *(Looking at his watch)* You don't suppose Dad's forgotten, do you?

LYDIA: Of course not. He's been talking of nothing else all day. Go on.

JOEY: Where is he?

LYDIA: They wanted him at the office. An obituary or something. He'll be well on his way back by now.

JOEY: Did you call him?

LYDIA: Yes. He said he'd be back in plenty of time.

JOEY: Good.

(He runs up the stairs)

LYDIA: And Joey—*(She makes the correct sign)* Merde.

JOEY: *(Smiling)* Thanks.

(He goes into kitchen. The second he has gone Lydia is on her feet, walking quickly and silently toward the telephone. She looks up a number in a private book, then dials with speed)

LYDIA: *(Into receiver)* Mrs. Larkin?—Lydia Cruttwell. I'm sorry to be embarrassing, but this is a crisis. Is Sebastian with you?—I see. When did he leave?—That's over an hour ago. Where was he going?—Please, Mrs. Larkin, this isn't a jealous wife. I'm not jealous—I'm pleased, really. But this is important, dreadfully important.—No clue at all? Did he happen to mention that his son had a television play on tonight?—Yes. B.B.C. 2, ten-thirty—Thank you—Yes. Only twenty—thank you. Yes, that's the crisis—Something worse? What *could* be worse?—Well, he sometimes goes to his editor's flat after—talking with you. Did he say anything?—Meet some friends? Where?—Well, what's his favorite haunt up your way? After your flat, of course—*(Her face grows despairing)* But I can't ring all those. Please try and help. I've got to find out where he—*(She stops abruptly as Joey appears with the bucket and an extra glass. Laughing gaily)* Oh, that's terribly sweet of you darling—angelic of you to ask us, but I know Sebastian can't. He gets so tied up in the evenings—it's when he works you know—*(She smiles happily at Joey)* I'll get him to call you. He's due in any second. Goodbye. *(To Joey)* What a bore that woman is!

JOEY: Who?

LYDIA: No one you know. An old woman called Lady Robinson. Always trying to get us out for cocktails—

JOEY: I didn't hear the telephone ring—

LYDIA: That happens to me when *I'm* getting ice. *(The doorbell rings. Distractedly.)* That's Mark. Answer it, darling.

(Joey runs to the door. Mark is outside. He has graced the evening with a dinner jacket)

MARK: *(Shaking hands)* Well, Joey, here's wishing you everything.

JOEY: Gosh, Mr. Walters, you didn't change for me?

MARK: Of course. Always dress for a premiere. Here's a little sprig of heather for luck—*(The sprig of heather is fairly easily recognizable as a small Cartier box. Mark comes into the room and kisses Lydia)* Evening, Lydia.

LYDIA: *(Gratefully)* Marcus.

(They kiss. Joey meanwhile is opening his present. They are cufflinks)

JOEY: Are these cufflinks?

LYDIA: *(Looking at them)* No, they're earrings, and they're meant for me. *(To Mark)* What are you trying to do, Mark? Keep the whole Cruttwell family?

MARK: Well, this is a very important occasion—the début of a brilliant young dramatist.

JOEY: Dramatist—gosh—you don't get called dramatist till you're dead.

LYDIA: He let "brilliant" pass.

JOEY: No, I didn't, Mum. I just closed my ears. *(Engrossed in his cufflinks)* I don't think I've ever had a present like this. *(Belatedly)* Of course, Mum's given me some smashing things—

LYDIA: *(Arm around him)* Smashing. Nickel cigarette lighters, plastic Indian beads. Joey's going to look after Sebastian while we're away—

MARK: That's great.

JOEY: If you don't mind putting it off until after next weekend. I'm going to stay with our candidate and his family for a victory celebration.

MARK: Hadn't you better knock on wood?

JOEY: No.

LYDIA: Isn't it sweet of him to volunteer to be my replacement?

JOEY: I didn't volunteer, Mum. You had your thumbscrews squeezed really tight.

LYDIA: Joey—that's a very naughty thing to suggest—

JOEY: Anyway, we don't know what Dad's going to say.

LYDIA: *(Firmly)* Yes, we do. He said this morning that he was very impressed with how you took over last night, when your mother got a little—er—overexcited. He said the way you coped in the kitchen was excellent.

JOEY: I know how to open a tin of sardines, and where the chocolate biscuits were kept—

LYDIA: *(Firmly)* An excellent meal, he said.

MARK: And he washed up brilliantly. I would have helped but our game went on till two. That guy's like Churchill. He will never surrender.

JOEY: *(Laughing)* He did last night, though. Gosh, did he roar!

MARK: And he blamed the new chessmen, of course. They confused him. *(Pointing to the workroom)* Is he in there?

LYDIA: *(Calmly)* No. *(Looking at her watch)* He's due in any minute. *(To Joey)* Don't you think you should wear those cufflinks—for luck?

JOEY: I haven't got a shirt—I mean for links.

LYDIA: Borrow one of your father's.

JOEY: *(Slightly dismayed)* Does that mean a tie?

LYDIA: Oh, no. Don't betray your convictions. *(Joey bounds up the stairs and off. Lydia instantly becomes tense)* Mark, Sebastian's lost. It's a hundred to one he's forgotten—

MARK: Oh, God, no—

LYDIA: Go down to the porter. He lives at number seventy-five, in the basement. He's got a telephone. Call this number—*(She is hustling him toward the door)* I'll tell Joey you're reparking your car, or something—

MARK: What shall I say?

LYDIA: You don't need to say anything. I'll do the talking. Wait a moment. *(She runs to the desk, takes out an envelope and scribbles on it. Then she gives it to him)* Is that clear. My hand is so shaking with rage—

MARK: *(Reading)* "Sebastian—If after ten-thirty go away until well after eleven. And then, the first thing you say is 'Congratulations, Joey.' I'm covering for you."

LYDIA: Not even *he* can fail to follow that, can he? *(She opens the door, licks the flap of the envelope, and sticks it to the door)*

MARK: He can do some funny things.

LYDIA: You see how I'm laughing in anticipation. *(Joey comes running down the stairs, wearing a shirt much too large for him, outside his slacks. For Joey's sake)* Tell the traffic warden you're a foreigner, Mark. That always works—wait—here's the latchkey—*(She gives him a key and then closes the door quickly in his face. To Joey)* Americans always park their cars in the middle of the street.

JOEY: He won't miss anything?

(He looks at his watch. Lydia coming calmly toward him slaps his hand)

LYDIA: Plenty of time, dear. Don't fuss. You want me to fix these for you?

JOEY: Yes, please. They're complicated. *(Lydia attends to fixing the links)* Your hands are shaking, too.

LYDIA: Well, of course, I'm nervous—

(Pause)

JOEY: Are you sure Dad hasn't forgotten?

LYDIA: Positive.

JOEY: I hope he's not late. If you miss the beginning it's difficult to follow.

LYDIA: His opinion means a lot to you, doesn't it?

JOEY: Well—after all—one of the best critics in the world—Gosh! They glitter. Look.

LYDIA: Yes. You have to flash them around a bit—preferably under a light. *(She shows him how with her bracelet)* I think the shirt in, don't you? Otherwise it looks a bit like a nightdress.

JOEY: O.K. The one thing against going on living here, Mum, is—well—Dad.

LYDIA: You mean a lot to him, Joey.

(Joey laughs, not unkindly)

JOEY: Oh, Mum. No one means a lot to him, and you know it. Not even you.

LYDIA: Joey, that's a bad thing to say.

JOEY: Yes, it is, but it's the truth. And one has to tell the truth.

LYDIA: Has one?

JOEY: Honesty in this life is just about the only thing that matters.

LYDIA: Is it?

JOEY: *(Impatiently)* We both know that the only person who matters to Dad is Dad. Mum—you've admitted that to me often enough—

LYDIA: As a joke, perhaps.

JOEY: No, as the truth. Don't be dishonest, Mum, please.

LYDIA: I'm sorry. It's only—well, I still think *you* mean something to him—something special—

JOEY: Mum, he can't wait for me to get out of this house. He's said so often enough.

LYDIA: He doesn't always mean what he says—

JOEY: He means that. I agree he doesn't mean a lot of other things he talks about—like politics. He only spouts Marxist Revolution as a kind of spell to prevent it happening—like some people talk about death. You know the kind?

LYDIA: Yes. I sympathize a bit—

JOEY: *(In full spate)* I think it's dishonest to spout a theory when you personally would hate it coming true. Imagine Dad being ordered by his State-Controlled British Sunday paper to say that Evelyn Waugh was a bad writer? Or that Orwell was a lackey of the bourgeoisie? He'd be in a labor camp in a week.

LYDIA: *(Gently)* I believe these days it's a mental home.

(Pause)

JOEY: Of course, your father and brothers died in a labor camp, didn't they?

LYDIA: As far as we know.

JOEY: I'm sorry.

LYDIA: Don't be. It's all past. All you're saying, Joey, is that your father has the courage of his convictions—

JOEY: If they're about literature. About politics he just talks meaningless slogans. Sorry, Mum. Now I'm grown up I'm answering back, and he hates it. It won't work. I know it won't. Mum. I'm sorry. I can't stay on. It isn't possible. If it was just you—*(He squeezes her hand)* But it isn't.

LYDIA: You don't think the ten days—?

JOEY: If we get through them without actual bloodshed it'll be a miracle—

(The telephone rings. Lydia flies to answer it)

LYDIA: *(At telephone)* Hullo—oh hullo, darling. We were getting worried. Where are you?—You're going to watch it there—with the editor? You mean he's going to watch, too?

JOEY: Gosh! Is it color?

LYDIA: Is it color, Joey wants to know?—Very latest, of course . . . I'll give them to him for you . . . Yes. See you afterwards. *(She rings off)* He wishes you everything, Joey.

JOEY: The editor! *(He speaks as if God had announced he would be viewing)* It might get written about—

LYDIA: That must be Dad's hope, I suppose.

JOEY: Gosh! Jesus!

LYDIA: You see—he does think of you sometimes.

JOEY: Surprise, surprise! *(Suspiciously)* I bet that was your doing.

LYDIA: *(Startled)* What?

JOEY: I bet you made him get his editor watching.

LYDIA: No, it was entirely his own idea.

JOEY: Ha, ha.

LYDIA: Are you saying I'm a liar?

JOEY: Well—I bet you used pressure.

LYDIA: Now, Joey, what pressure have I ever been able to bring on your father to do something he didn't want to do?

JOEY: There you are. You're admitting it.

LYDIA: What?

JOEY: That he's a selfish old brute, and impossible to live with.

LYDIA: *(Sharply)* Joey, I won't have you talking about your father like that—do you understand!

JOEY: Yes, Mum.

LYDIA: Especially after this—very—generous thing he's doing for you tonight. Going all that way up to the city—

JOEY: *(Embracing her)* Yes, I'm sorry. I'm sorry.

LYDIA: *(Still trying to be angry)* And getting his editor—

JOEY: Yes, I know, I know. I'm sorry.

(Pause. Lydia looks down at his head, resisting the temptation to stroke it)

LYDIA: *(Bravely)* I know that during those ten days, you're going to find out a lot more about him—

JOEY: *(His voice muffled on her shoulder)* Oh, God, I hope not.

LYDIA: *(Shaking him)* Joey! I mean what he's really like.

JOEY: I know what he's really like.

LYDIA: Well—so do I, and I've lived with him happily for twenty-eight years—and will for the rest of my life.

JOEY: *(Releasing himself)* Not necessarily. You never know. Someone else might come along—

LYDIA: No one else will come along.

JOEY: Well, anyway, it's different for you. You're married to him. I'm not.

LYDIA: No. You're just his son.

JOEY: Mum—that might have been some argument in Victorian times. It's not now.

LYDIA: No, it's not. Now we know it's healthy for sons to turn against their fathers, and we encourage it. But, Joey, we also know that sons have always turned against their fathers, all through history. Sebastian turned against his—

JOEY: The Bishop? *(He laughs)* Yes. I feel sorry for the Bishop—*(He bends down to put the television on.)* Just warming it up. Oh, God! Supposing there was a fuse—

LYDIA: I'd mend it. And the Bishop revolted against his father, who was a city swindler, of enormous charm I believe. Before that there was a drunken farmer, and what father he turned against I don't know.

JOEY: *(Still at the television)* What does all this prove?

LYDIA: The enormous importance in life of pretending—

JOEY: *(Upright)* Pretending to like someone one doesn't? I'm sorry but I can't do that.

LYDIA: Have you tried?

JOEY: No, because I think it's wrong.

LYDIA: Why wrong?

JOEY: It's dishonest.

LYDIA: Take Mark. When a writer of his standing gives up a whole evening to come out to Islington to see a half-hour's first play by a twenty-year old acquaintance, and puts on a black tie and says something pleasant about the début of a brilliant young dramatist—isn't there some pretense in that? Or is honesty so damn important for you that you'd rather he'd stayed home and done what he really wanted to do tonight?

(Pause)

JOEY: *(Unhappily)* What's that?

LYDIA: I don't know. But a pleasure-loving multi-millionaire mightn't be lost for something other than driving through a traffic jam out to Islington for a sandwich and a half-hour's telly.

(Pause. She has shaken Joey)

JOEY: He's older. I can't do things like that. Besides Dad, of all people, would laugh in my face.

LYDIA: I don't think so.

JOEY: My God, I've tried—well—politeness you'd call it—

LYDIA: No, I'd call it manners. It's an old-fashioned word and I'm sorry. But there isn't a better one.

JOEY: *(Scornfully)* Manners makyth Man?

LYDIA: Yes. And it makyth other men feel better—as it's made you tonight.

JOEY: Well, I've tried it. With Dad sometimes. When he's written a good article, for instance. And what do I get always? A kick in the teeth—

LYDIA: Manners—real manners—means slipping your teeth into your pocket and pretending you're not hurt. It also means trying to feel some understanding for the man who kicked you.

JOEY: Sounds like a gooey sort of ultra-Christianity.

LYDIA: There isn't any sort of *ultra*-Christianity. There's just Christianity. And if it's gooey—well, it's gooey.

JOEY: I didn't know you were religious.

LYDIA: It's wonderful how that word today is made to sound like some curious perversion—permissible, of course, like all things, but rather unmentionable. Yes. I was brought up a Catholic—

JOEY: You don't go to *church?*

LYDIA: Oh, no. What *would* the neighbors say? I haven't been to Mass since before the war. Neither the Russians nor the Germans were exactly Jesus freaks—and—well—one gets out of things. But somehow I still—oh, no arguments, Joey—least of all on theology. Not now. Not at this moment—*(Looking at the set)* Isn't that a bit green?

JOEY: No. The faces are right. *(Violently)* Mum—if he'd only once lose an argument, say he was wrong, say he was sorry—

LYDIA: Yes, yes I know.

(Mark comes in, panting)

MARK: I know my next present to you, Lydia. Only it won't be a present to you, it'll be to me. A simple hoist is all that's needed—labeled for Mark Walters only. I'm on time anyway, aren't I?

JOEY: Yes. Two minutes.

MARK: Good. I wouldn't have missed a word.

(Joey is looking at him, puzzled, appreciative and rather sad. Mark is oblivious)

LYDIA: Sebastian called. He's going to see it on a much better set than ours.

MARK: *(Doing it well)* Oh, really? Where?

JOEY: *(Eagerly)* At his editor's.

MARK: Well now, isn't that something! I wonder if Mr. Jeremy Thorpe is watching.

JOEY: Oh, no.

MARK: Why not? One of his young hopefuls? Which is it going to be, Joey—writing or politics?

LYDIA: *(Firmly)* Both. Now you sit here, Mark.

JOEY: No, I want you to sit there, and Mr. Walters here.

LYDIA: But this is more comfortable—

JOEY: I know. It's for you.

MARK: Ah, I get it. He wants his audience attentive.

LYDIA: Well, I'm his audience.

MARK: *(Sitting in the uncomfortable seat)* You're his mother.

JOEY: *(From the set)* Sh! *(He turns the set's volume up)*

ANNOUNCER: On B.B.C. 1, in thirty seconds time, there is Match of the Week—

JOEY: Of course that's what they'll all be watching.

LYDIA: Nonsense.

ANNOUNCER: *(Through this)* Meanwhile on B.B.C. 2 there follows shortly a new thirty-minute play in the current series: Youth Theatre, entitled *The Trial of Maxwell Henry Peabody,* by Joseph Cruttwell.

(There is music)

LYDIA: *(Sharply) Joseph!* Why Joseph?

JOEY: It sounds more like a writer.

MARK: Yeah. It's a good name, Lydia. Joey's not too good. Joseph Cruttwell sounds like something—

JOEY: Thank you, Mr. Walters.

(The music stops)

FIRST VOICE: *(Loudly)* Maxwell Henry Peabody— come into court.

(There is the sound of marching feet. Lydia and Mark are both forward in that attitude of strained attention natural to people watching a TV play under the observant scrutiny of the author, who has chosen a vantage point where he can see both screen and audience.

The lights fade very quickly. There is a blackout for only a second before they come on again. Lydia, Mark and Joey are in exactly the same strained attitudes as before. One might think no one has moved even a finger to scratch his or her nose)

FIRST VOICE: Have you anything to say why sentence should not be passed against you?

SECOND VOICE: But this is ridiculous. I have done nothing, I tell you—nothing, nothing, nothing—

FIRST VOICE: I agree. You have done nothing. Nothing to help your fellow human beings, nothing to save the world from the abyss into which it must soon finally fall, nothing save for your own material advantage—

SECOND VOICE: And my wife's. She's a director of several of my companies.

FIRST VOICE: And what did you do to save your son?
(There is mocking laughter, followed by a blare of music, evidently signaling the end. Credits must follow because Joey kneels by the set, his nose practically touching it, to see his name go by. Lydia crouches with him)

LYDIA: There! Look how big his name is, Mark. Yes, Joseph is better. *(She embraces him)* Darling, I'm so proud.

JOEY: *(Impatiently)* But did you *like* it?

LYDIA: I loved it, Joey—

JOEY: *(Staring at her, puzzled)* Did it make you cry?

LYDIA: A little. Wasn't it meant to?

JOEY: *(Doubtfully)* Well, it's really supposed to make one angry.

LYDIA: *(Reassuringly)* Oh, it did that, too.

MARK: *(Choosing his words)* Congratulations, young man, on a fine achievement—

(The front door is unlocked. Sebastian appears, looking angry, holding in his hand Lydia's message which he has torn from the door)

SEBASTIAN: What in hell's this? If after ten-thirty don't come in. I'm covering up—*(He stops at sight of the television set in its prominent position, of Lydia in her smart dress, of Mark in a dinner jacket and of Joey in one of his own shirts, all staring at him with varying expressions)* Oh, Christ—

(Joey looks away from him first)

JOEY: Good night, Mum. Thanks for watching.

LYDIA: But the champagne—

JOEY: No, thanks. Good night, Mr. Walters. Thanks for coming and for these *(He indicates the cufflinks)* and for what you said.

MARK: It was good—real good, Joey. I mean it.

JOEY: Thanks.

(In silence, he walks up the stairs, hoping evidently to achieve dignity. But coming to the end he hurries his steps in a revealing way. Lydia looks after him)

SEBASTIAN: Oh, Lord—

(Lydia suddenly swings one fist at him, and then the other. They are hard blows, with real fury behind them,

and both connect. Sebastian, off balance, and slightly unsteady anyhow, is knocked off his feet and falls, upsetting a table)

LYDIA: *(With deep hatred)* You bastard!

(She turns and runs up the stairs after her son. Sebastian stays where he is, for a moment, putting his hand to his cheek, and shaking his head. Mark helps him to his feet)

SEBASTIAN: *(Indicating television)* Was it terrible?

MARK: Pretty terrible.

SEBASTIAN: *(In a chair)* Get me a drink.

MARK: What is it? Scotch?

SEBASTIAN: *(Angrily)* Of course Scotch! *(With a deep sigh)* Oh, my God! I had it written down, I'd tied knots in everything, I'd remembered it at lunch—*(He takes the drink from Mark)* And then after lunch something happened—*(Pause. He stares into his glass)* A perfect excuse, I suppose, if I could use it. Perfect. But I can't.

MARK: What was it?

SEBASTIAN: I can't tell you either. Except—*(He stares into his glass again)* I have to anyway—but not as an excuse. *(Loudly)* I have no excuses. I am as God made me, which is an uncaring shit. Oh damn! Poor little bugger. She'd covered up for me?

MARK: You were watching it with your editor.

SEBASTIAN: He's in Tangier.

MARK: The kid wouldn't have known that.

SEBASTIAN: Damn silly cover. I suppose it might have worked though. She'd have made it work. How has she been tonight—I mean apart from turning into Muhammed Ali?

MARK: Oh, fine, I thought.

SEBASTIAN: Fine, you thought. Did you look at all?

MARK: Sure. She didn't look too well, but I don't suppose she is, after her pass-out last night. Hungover, I'd say.

SEBASTIAN: Yes. Well, you'd better brace yourself, I suppose. Have you got a drink? *(Mark holds his up)* You're rather fond of this girl, aren't you?

MARK: I love her.

SEBASTIAN: And I suppose you're what might laughingly be called one of my best friends? *(Finishing his drink)* Fill it up for me, would you?

MARK: Sure.

SEBASTIAN: Are you?

MARK: I think you are what you just said, God made you, Sebastian—but maybe I'm not all that choosey about my best friends.

SEBASTIAN: Well, I'm not either, or I wouldn't choose an ignorant, illiterate porn-monger—

MARK: *(Returning with the drink)* O.K. O.K. I'm braced.

SEBASTIAN: That wasn't a pass-out last night—not an ordinary one. It was a small stroke.

(Pause)

MARK: How do you know?

SEBASTIAN: She's had them before, and these last months they're getting more frequent. It's one of the things I've been told to look out for, you see—and it's one of the things you've got to look out for, too, when you take her away. I've got a list somewhere—

MARK: Surely the vodka—

SEBASTIAN: It probably helped—that and the cortisone—so don't let her wallow in the stuff as I did last night. She's been off any drink at all for over six months—so go fairly easy out there. Mind you the odd piss-up won't make much difference. Here's that list. Now I've got the doctor's address in Monte Carlo somewhere, too—*(He fumbles in his pockets again)*

MARK: *(Quietly)* Did you say cortisone?

SEBASTIAN: What? Yes. She's been on it six weeks. She doesn't know it, of course. Thinks they're iron pills, or something. Old Conny Ziegmann—he's her doctor—"Uncle Constantin" she calls him—an ex-Estonian—he's quite a wonder. He can get her to believe anything—where the hell did I put that address? Ah, here it is. Docteur Villoret. Address is on it. *(Mark takes it from him)* Conny Ziegmann called him this afternoon, so he'll be wise to the situation, as your horrible phrase goes.

MARK: Could you, perhaps, put me wise, too?

(Pause. Sebastian looks up at him)

SEBASTIAN: I suppose so. I've been trying to put it off. I can't put it off any longer, can I? *(Another pause)* She's in the terminal stages of leukemia. *(Pause. Sebastian gets up and takes Mark's glass to fill, patting his arm as he goes)* Sorry. I had to tell you, you see, because old Conny Ziegmann wouldn't have let her go otherwise, unless I was along. I'm well-briefed, you see. What's that dreadful drink you have?

MARK: Bourbon. Did you say terminal?

SEBASTIAN: Yes.

MARK: How long does that mean?

SEBASTIAN: Three or four months. Six at most. *(He hands Mark the drink)*

MARK: Are you positive?

(Sebastian laughs)

SEBASTIAN: That's just the word, I'm afraid. *(He pulls another paper from his pocket and hands it to Mark)* This came from Conny Ziegmann by hand to the office this afternoon. He'd had it early this morning from the hospital, but couldn't call me because of Lydia. It's conclusive Lymphatic Leukemia.

(Mark stares at the paper with unseeing eyes. He knows, after all, its contents. Then he hands it back. Pause)

MARK: *(At length)* So that's the something that happened to you after lunch.

SEBASTIAN: *(Distracted)* What?—Yes. That. But I'd expected it. Conny hadn't given me any hope. He hasn't, really, for the last three months.

MARK: Who else has she seen?

SEBASTIAN: The best in the country. She doesn't know it, of course, but every man who looks her over in that hospital is handpicked. Of course they're casual with her, and don't give their names. But they've all been by courtesy of my kind Sunday paper—and all top boys on leukemia.

MARK: There are cures.

SEBASTIAN: Yes. There's this man in Denver, Colorado, who boasts a seventy percent rate. But he's cagey. He won't take a case as advanced as this—

MARK: How do you know?

SEBASTIAN: I've asked him. I gave him all the facts and figures on the telephone, and got our medical correspondent to talk to him, too. No go, Mark. He won't risk that seventy percent.

MARK: There's another man in Karlsruhe—

SEBASTIAN: I know about him, too. He's just a phony. Christ, Mark, I haven't lacked for advice. If there'd been the faintest chance I'd have taken her to Timbuctoo— and told her I was covering Saharan Literature. I'd already got my story ready for Denver. I'd induced some wretched little local college to offer me a resident lectureship. Jesus, imagine that!...Now, Winnie Slobberwicz, stop groping your neighbor and listen. Balls-ache, as you are pleased to pronounce him, is the name of an important French writer and not an occupational disease—Oh, I'm sorry, Mark. My jokes are so feeble these days, it's a wonder she hasn't seen through them. And me. But she hasn't, thank God. I mean, you've seen her alone. Does she have the faintest suspicion I'm concealing something from her?

MARK: No.

SEBASTIAN: Swear?

MARK: Swear.

SEBASTIAN: I'm good about never remembering when she's been to the doctor, getting his name wrong and never noticing when she's feeling ill. Also never on any account saying: "Look, I'll do that, darling. Don't you bother." Can you imagine anything giving the show away quicker than that?

MARK: Frankly, I can't.

SEBASTIAN: Yes. Being one of nature's shits does have its advantages when one's dealing with a dying wife. *(He turns rather abruptly and goes into the hall. There he pulls down a hatbox from the top of a bookcase where it has been visible throughout the play)* Say: "Hullo, Lydia" very loudly if you see her on the stairs. *(He opens the hatbox and pulls out a lot of documents)* Copies of all her blood-counts, from six months ago. Conny sends them to me at the office every week. Can't keep them there. Too many nosey parkers. *(He puts the latest missive on top of the others)*

MARK: Can't you find a safer place than that?

SEBASTIAN: No. She goes round this flat prying into everything. Even the notes for my new novel which I carefully hid from her in my Gibbon's *Decline and Fall*—she got her nose into those yesterday. *(He closes the lid and puts the hatbox back)* Dusting, she said. As if anyone would dust Gibbon without criminal intent—

MARK: A drawer with a lock?

SEBASTIAN: If I had one, she'd pick it. She'd never look up there. *(He points to the replaced hatbox)* Clever, don't you think? I borrowed the idea from Edgar Allan Poe.

MARK: Mightn't she want to dust the hat?

SEBASTIAN: Don't be a clot. It was a topper to go to the Palace in for that O.B.E. thing and I gave it to Oxfam the next day. I keep the box there as an ornament. Anyway I've worked it out—neither she nor Mrs. MacHiggins can reach it. Clever, I think. I wasn't in Intelligence for nothing.

MARK: Sebastian, are you quite sure you shouldn't tell her?

SEBASTIAN: Quite sure. For six long years she had nothing to think of but dying. Now that she is I'm not letting her go through it again. And then if she had any inkling about it at all she'd worry herself sick over Joey—

MARK: Not over you?

SEBASTIAN: Over *me?* Why should she worry herself over me? She knows I can look after myself—

MARK: Does she?

SEBASTIAN: Well, what with Mrs. MacHiggins and maybe Prunella—

MARK: You said yesterday—

SEBASTIAN: Yes. I laid that on pretty thick for her. Prunella's all right. She's no Lydia, but she's all right. *(Pause)* No Lydia. *(He begins to cry, fumbling for a handkerchief)* You've got to put up with this a bit, I'm afraid. Self-pity, of course. You see the thing is, Mark, I didn't begin *really* to love her until I knew I was losing her.

MARK: That happens.

SEBASTIAN: Perhaps more to uncaring shits than to other people—like you, for instance. You've always loved her—

MARK: Yes.

SEBASTIAN: And I've—I've only had about six months. My fault, of course. Anybody but me would have started twenty-eight years earlier. *(He hands out his drink to be refilled. Mark takes it. Murmuring)*
No Lydia—

"She'll come no more.
Never, never, never, never, never."

Oh, damn! I'll never review that bloody man again. I won't review anyone. After all they all make you blub some-where—if they're good. *(Angrily)* No, I'll write my own blub stuff—that's what I'll do—

MARK: Good idea.

SEBASTIAN: And *I'll* sell *ten* million paperbacks in advance—

MARK: *(Handing him his drink)* Why not?

SEBASTIAN: Without one single power-mad tycoon. Just me—and her—changed, of course. The meeting in the whorehouse is far too melodramatic. But the same balance—gratitude and duty one side, taking for granted the other—the whole adding up to—something too late—and then—*(He snaps his fingers. To Mark)* I suppose *you'll* have to be in it, as the escape she refused. Not as you are, of course. No one would believe that.

MARK: And Joey?

SEBASTIAN: Yes, Liberal Joey, I suppose. The new assenting young. Oh God, the poor little sod! He worships his mother. Too much, I suppose—but you can't blame him. Yes, he's going to be quite a handful after—*(Pause)* I'll have to try. Tonight won't have helped much, will it?

MARK: You've got ten days.

SEBASTIAN: Ten days without her. I don't like to think of that much—

MARK: Then come, too.

SEBASTIAN: No. I could—but I've got to get used to—
try to get used to—oh, damn! Did I feel about her like this from
the beginning? It's possible. It's possible. And wouldn't allow
myself to? Yes, possible. *(Angrily)* Do you know what "le vice
Anglais?"—the English vice—really is? Not flagellation, not
pederasty—whatever the French believe it to be. It's our refusal
to admit to our emotions. We think they demean us, I suppose.
(He covers his face) Well, I'm being punished now, all right—for
a lifetime of vice. Very moral endings to a Victorian novel. I'm
becoming maudlin. But, oh Mark, life without Lydia will be
such endless misery.

> *(He sees Lydia coming down the stairs. Sebastian jumps
> up from his chair and turns his back, adroitly trans-
> forming emotion into huffiness. Lydia looks at his back
> a long time. When Sebastian turns to face her he is ap-
> parently dry-eyed, and holding his jaw as if in pain)*

SEBASTIAN: *(With dignity)* Husband-beater!

LYDIA: I came to say I was sorry.

SEBASTIAN: I shall so inform my solicitors. Good
night, Mark.

MARK: Oh, am I going?

SEBASTIAN: No, I am.

> *(He gives another withering glance at Lydia, rubs his
> cheek and walks toward his workroom, even contriving
> a limp as he does so)*

LYDIA: Are you going to work? Isn't it too late?

SEBASTIAN: Yes, to the first. No, to the second.

LYDIA: Wouldn't you like some of this food?

SEBASTIAN: It would turn to ashes in my mouth. *(He
goes out)*

LYDIA: Did I hurt him?

MARK: Not enough.

LYDIA: I could have hit him much harder, you
know. And kicked him, too—on the ground. Queensbury
Rules, my fanny! Is he really working or just sulking?

MARK: Sulking, I'd say. I'm going.

LYDIA: *(Looking anxiously at Sebastian's door)* Yes,

I suppose you'd better. *(She kisses him)* Thank you so very much, Marcus. He really did appreciate it.

MARK: How is Joey?

LYDIA: He's bad, of course. *(Angrily, at the door)* How could any human being do a thing like that to his son? How *could* he? What's his excuse?

MARK: He forgot.

LYDIA: I mean his excuse for forgetting?

(Pause)

MARK: About the best a man could have, I guess.

LYDIA: *(Amazed)* You take his side.

MARK: Yes, on this.

LYDIA: Well what *is* his excuse?

MARK: Good night, Lydia. *(He goes to the door, leaving Lydia looking bewildered. Turning)* Oh, Christ! Has anybody ever been in such a spot? Look—*(He points to the hatbox)* That thing up there. It needs dusting.

LYDIA: The hatbox?

MARK: Yes. You can see the dust from here.

LYDIA: But I can't reach it.

(Mark points to some library steps. Lydia, utterly bewildered, goes to get them)

MARK: No. Not now. Tomorrow—when Sebastian's out. After you've dusted it—inside as well as out—you'll just have to play it your way—both of you. And then together or separately—tell me how *I'm* to play mine.

LYDIA: I see. He's hidden something there.

MARK: Yes.

LYDIA: Something he doesn't want me to see.

MARK: You bet.

LYDIA: The wily bastard. Love letters?

MARK: Kind of.

LYDIA: *(Aghast)* You mean—serious?

MARK: Very serious, I think.

LYDIA: Larkin—I suppose—

MARK: No. Someone else.

LYDIA: Jesus—I wish I *had* kicked him. I wish I'd

killed him. *(Suddenly loyal)* And why are you giving him away? You're supposed to be his friend.

MARK: I'm supposed to be yours, too. That's what's made my life, these last two days, a little confusing. Call you tomorrow.

(He goes out. Lydia, muttering imprecations, first looks at the hatbox, then firmly decides to resist the temptation. She comes into the sitting room and sits down demurely. Then she looks at the hatbox again, and the library steps. Then she gets up cautiously and listens at Sebastian's door. She hears him typing, and so do we. She darts to the library steps, rolls them into the hall and pulls down the hatbox, opening it and groping inside. Her fingers find what they are looking for and removes a pile of documents. Hastily she replaces the lid, and puts the hatbox back, leaving the library steps where they are. Then she puts on her glasses and settles herself onto the sofa for a belligerent, if furtive read.

Three seconds later she has shot off the sofa. She riffles through the papers. They are all of identical size, and have needed no more than a few glances. They are, after all, familiar.

After a moment or two her legs give way, and she has to fall back onto the sofa. She has opened her bag to fumble for a handkerchief when Sebastian opens his door. It is the matter of a split second for an accomplished document-peeper to stuff the papers into her bag and close it. The budding tears are a different matter. She has to brush those away. And she is conscious too of the tell-tale library steps)

SEBASTIAN: *(Gloomily)* I've been trying to write him a letter you could shove under his door. But it's no good. My mandarin style gets in the way.

LYDIA: It would.

(She gets up casually to drape herself somewhere near the hall, masking the library steps)

SEBASTIAN: I suppose I'd better see the little sod.

LYDIA: What little sod?

SEBASTIAN: Are there two in the flat? Where is he?

LYDIA: If you're referring to our son—Joseph Cruttwell, dramatist—he's in bed.

SEBASTIAN: Oh, darling, do stop sniffling. You know how I hate it.

LYDIA: I wasn't sniffling.

SEBASTIAN: You were. I could hear you from in there. *(A lie)* And those things under your eyes are tears, aren't they? *(He peers from a distance)* I'm not coming in range. I think you should know I once hit a sub-editor and he was off-duty for a week. And he wasn't any smaller than you either. However, enough of that. About Joey. What's done is done, and can by dint of my overwhelming charm, be undone. I shall speak to him personally.

LYDIA: I shouldn't rely on your overwhelming charm.

SEBASTIAN: Thank you.

LYDIA: I mean why not just let him see you once as you really are.

SEBASTIAN: I have no idea what that sibylline utterance is supposed to mean. I think I know a father's duty toward his son without prompting from you, Madam.

SEBASTIAN: Why are you leaning there like Isadora Duncan?

LYDIA: I've been putting books in their right places, under your orders, sir.

SEBASTIAN: Good. That'll be a change. All right. Go and get the little bugger down.

LYDIA: No.

SEBASTIAN: No?

LYDIA: You go up.

SEBASTIAN: *(Outraged)* Go up? Knock timidly at his door and beg leave to enter that room with all those Liberal Posters on the wall—crawl across the carpet like a penitent, abase myself like Henry IV at Canossa, scourge myself—all right, I'll go up. *(He goes to the stairs, climbing reluctantly)* Why are you looking at me like that?

LYDIA: A cat may look at a King.

SEBASTIAN: Are you pissed again?

LYDIA: Oh, yes.

SEBASTIAN: Vodka.

LYDIA: Something—kind of—headier—

SEBASTIAN: Kirsch, or Slivovitz or something? My God, darling, you'll end up in an alcoholics' ward. *(He disappears. Immediately Lydia darts into the hall, climbs the steps and deposits the papers inside. She has just wheeled the steps back when Sebastian reappears)* I looked in and the little bastard was asleep. *(Relieved)* Tomorrow, don't you think? *(He scoops some food on to a plate. Plying a fork)* Hm. This is rather good. Who made it? Joey?

(Lydia, free now moves, pulls her right fist back) Oh, *you* did?

LYDIA: It's my crab mousse, and you've had it a million times.

SEBASTIAN: It just seemed better than usual.

(Joey, in a dressing gown, is coming downstairs. Both parents watch him as he walks in a dignified manner past his father, cutting him dead, and up to Lydia)

JOEY: I'm very sorry, Mum. I left you to clear up alone.

LYDIA: Oh, that's all right, darling. I can do that myself.

JOEY: I'll help you.

(He picks up two dishes and carries them up to the kitchen. Sebastian exchanges a meaning glance with Lydia)

SEBASTIAN: *(Loudly)* Darling, would you fix that draught for me in there.

LYDIA: Oh, yes, I will.

(Joey reappears, still walking with dignity)

SEBASTIAN: I think it's coming from the window.

LYDIA: Yes. I shouldn't be surprised.

(She goes into the workroom)

SEBASTIAN: Joey, put those things down. *(Joey, at first, is inclined to disobey. Sebastian takes them from him)* Anyway I'm eating from this one.

JOEY: I'm very sorry. If I'd known I wouldn't have touched it.

SEBASTIAN: You've a perfect right to be as rude to

me as you like, and to call me every name you can think of. Tonight I behaved to you as badly as any father has ever behaved to his son. If my father had done that to me when I was your age I'd have walked straight out of his house and never talked to him again.

JOEY: You did, didn't you?

SEBASTIAN: No. I was turned out. I may have told you I walked out, because it sounds better. In fact I was booted. A little trouble with one of the maids. I can only say, Joey, that tonight I behaved like a thoughtless bastard—that's the word your Mum used. To Mark I said "shit"—"an uncaring shit" and meant it. I am that, sometimes, and I behave like that sometimes. If you like you can say usually. Or even always. It may be true. But tonight was the worst thing I've ever done to anyone, anywhere. I may do some bad things to you, Joey, in the future—if we're still seeing each other—but one thing you must know—I can't ever do anything quite as bad as I did tonight. Not even *I* can break the world record of shittishness twice—

JOEY: I don't believe you forgot. I believe you did it deliberately.

SEBASTIAN: I can see you'd rather think that. So would I. It's less damaging to the ego. The plain, sordid fact is that I forgot.

JOEY: How could you, Dad?

SEBASTIAN: I did. And I have no excuse at all. Now listen. What I intend to do is this. I shall get our television man to ask to have it re-run—

JOEY: Oh, Dad—this is all talk.

SEBASTIAN: At Television Centre, for me, for him—not for my editor who's in Tangier—and for anyone else who wants to see it. You, of course, too. And our television critic will review it. I don't know what he'll say, and it'll have to be next week, but he'll mention it in his column, I promise.

JOEY: Is this on the level, or will you forget again?

SEBASTIAN: I said you could insult me, but there's no need to kick me in the crotch. Now if I do that for you will you do something for me?

JOEY: *(Suspiciously)* What?

SEBASTIAN: Sit in that chair. *(He forces him into one and then brings over the chess table)* And show me for once how you can justify all that hissing that goes on behind my chair.

JOEY: Dad, it's late.

SEBASTIAN: Only for Liberals. Not for men. Go on. You be white. Fifty pence on it?

JOEY: I'll want a two pawns' handicap.

SEBASTIAN: One.

JOEY: Done.

(Sebastian takes one of his pawns off. Joey moves. Sebastian moves. Joey moves)

SEBASTIAN: That's not in *my* "Twelve Easy Openings for Beginners."

(Sebastian moves. Joey thinks. Lydia, who has plainly had her ear glued to the keyhole slips out of the workroom. She watches them for a second. Joey moves. Sebastian moves)

JOEY: *(Rising)* Right. My game.

SEBASTIAN: What do you mean your game?

JOEY: You moved your King three squares.

SEBASTIAN: I beg your pardon, my Queen. *(Horrified)* My *King?* Oh, blast and bugger that Mark Walters! These pieces are going straight back to Hong Kong. I told him a hundred times—

(He is putting the pieces back on the board again. Joey has stood up)

JOEY: Fifty pence, please.

SEBASTIAN: Are you mad, boy?

JOEY: The rules say firmly—

LYDIA: You must play the rules, dear.

SEBASTIAN: You keep out of this! Go and do something useful somewhere. Better still, go to bed.

JOEY: Yes, Mum. We'll clear up.

SEBASTIAN: Yes, Joey will clear up.

LYDIA: Give Joey his fifty pence.

SEBASTIAN: Oh, bugger you both!

(He forks up)

LYDIA: Charming loser, isn't he?

SEBASTIAN: Loser my arse! I didn't lose. I made a tiny human error in laying out these monstrosities of chessmen—*(Joey is going. Sebastian catches his sleeve)* Oh, my boy. Oh, no. If you think you're taking that fifty pence of mine to bed, you're making a big mistake. All right. Start again. Double or quits. Same moves, but this time with the right pieces in the right places—

(They move rapidly, in silence. Lydia watches them for a moment, putting her arm lightly on Sebastian's shoulder)

LYDIA: Well, good night.

(Joey jumps up to kiss his mother)

SEBASTIAN: *(Irritated)* Don't do that. It upsets concentration. You could have kissed her sitting down, couldn't you? *(He does exactly that, slapping her playfully on the behind. She goes to the stairs. Sebastian concentrates on the board. To Joey)* I'm afraid your Jeremy Thorpe is coming under a little pressure.

JOEY: Your Mao Tse Tung doesn't look too happy either, Dad.

(Lydia turns to look back at them)

SEBASTIAN: *(To Joey)* Yes, I can see you have played before. Well, well, well. Do you know those ten days without her might be quite fun—*(He looks up casually. If we didn't know his secret we might even believe him when he says:)* Oh, sorry, darling. Didn't see you were still there.

(Lydia smiles. In fact, radiantly)

LYDIA: I know you didn't.

SEBASTIAN: Go on. Move, Joey. *(She goes on slowly up the stairs)* We haven't got all night ahead of us. *(Lydia disappears from sight)* Except, I suppose, we have.

Curtain

Lanford Wilson

THE SAND CASTLE

Lanford Wilson

Widely recognized as one of the most important new American playwrights, Lanford Wilson was born in Lebanon, Missouri, in 1937, and was educated at San Diego State College and the University of Chicago, where he started writing plays. He inaugurated his professional career at the now defunct Caffe Cino in Greenwich Village. After having had ten productions at this pioneer Off-Off-Broadway café-theatre and six at the Café La Mama, he moved to Off-Broadway in 1965 with the presentation of *Home Free!* at the Cherry Lane Theatre. In 1966, Mr. Wilson again was represented Off-Broadway, this time with a double bill, *The Madness of Lady Bright* and *Ludlow Fair,* at the uptown Theatre East. *This Is the Rill Speaking,* another of his short plays, was seen during that same season at the Martinique Theatre in a series of six works originally done at the Café La Mama.

In 1967, Mr. Wilson won a Drama Desk-Vernon Rice Award for his play, *The Rimers of Eldritch,* a haunting dramatic study of life in a small town in the Middle West. This was followed by another full-length play, *The Gingham Dog,* which opened in 1968 at the Washington Theatre Club, Washington, D.C. In the following year, it was presented on Broadway with Diana Sands and George Grizzard as stars and Alan Schneider as director. The author returned to Broadway in May, 1970, with *Lemon Sky,* a work that prompted the following comment from Clive Barnes: "Mr. Wilson can write; his characters spring alive on stage; he holds our attention, he engages our heart."

In 1971, Mr. Wilson added another rung to his growing status when he received considerable praise for his libretto for the operatic version of Tennessee Williams' *Summer and Smoke,* which had its world premiere in St. Paul, Minnesota. The opera, with music by Lee Hoiby, was given its New York premiere in 1972 by the New York City Opera at Lincoln Center. The dramatist was associated with Tennessee Williams once again with *The Migrants,* a made-for-television feature that was nationally televised in February, 1974.

Unquestionably, his greatest success to date is *The*

Hot L Baltimore (whose title signifies a formerly beautiful but now seedy hotel's sign with one letter missing). The play, written under a Guggenheim Fellowship, originally was presented by the Off-Off-Broadway Circle Repertory Theatre Company in January, 1973, then was transferred in March to Off-Broadway's Circle in the Square Downtown for a commercial engagement. *The Hot L Baltimore,* at this writing, is now well into its second year and has been festooned with honors: it won the New York Drama Critics' Circle Award for Best American Play of the 1972-73 season; the Outer Critics' Circle Award; and an "Obie" award for Best Play. It also was named one of the "ten best plays of the New York theatre season, 1972-73" by Otis L. Guernsey, Jr., editor of the theatre yearbook.

While *The Sand Castle* was seen on the Educational Television Network several years ago, the play only recently came to the attention of this editor. A vivid and affecting study of the sometimes disturbing, sometimes funny crises which lie between youth and adulthood, *The Sand Castle* is subtitled by its author "or *There Is a Tavern in the Town* or *Harry Can Dance.*" The play appears for the first time in an anthology in this collection.

Among the author's other works for the theatre are *Balm in Gilead; Wandering; So Long At the Fair; No Trespassing; Serenading Louie;* and *The Great Nebula in Orion,* which was introduced in *The Best Short Plays 1972.*

Lanford Wilson, who has been the recipient of a Rockefeller Foundation Grant and an ABC-Yale Fellowship, will be represented this coming season by his latest work, *This Is the Lake,* to be produced by the Circle Repertory Theatre Company, the same organization that brought *The Hot L Baltimore* to national renown.

In 1974, The American Academy of Arts and Letters made an award of three thousand dollars to Mr. Wilson for the "body of his work as a playwright, the focal point being the Off-Broadway production of *The Hot L Baltimore.*"

Characters:

IRENE, *a thin, quiet woman of considerable bearing, forty*
OWEN, *her son, twenty-two*
JOAN, *her daughter, twenty*
KENNY, *her son, twelve*
SASHA, *a friend of the family, twenty*
CLINT, *Irene's boyfriend*
CALVIN, *a friend of the family, twenty-six*

Scene:

The living room and front porch of a house, the last on the street, on Ocean Beach, San Diego, California.

The porch of the house is at right. On the back wall of the living room is the door to Irene's bedroom (right) and an alcove with doors to Owen's bedroom and Joan's bedroom (left). On the wall (left) is a door to the kitchen which would be at the back of the house. The room is furnished with necessities: the sofa is a kind of iron cot with bolsters, there is a large old dining table and four unmatched chairs around it near the kitchen door. Several bookcases are against the walls. They hold a symbiotic combination of old, old novels and heavy college textbooks. The bookcase, a desk, everything is covered with papers. Papers and books are stacked in several corners. There is an overstuffed chair with a floor lamp behind it near the door to Irene's bedroom.

The floor of the house is covered with a light dusting of sand. It would be impossible to keep it out.

The high, hard beach rises behind the house and obscures the ocean which is heard distantly throughout the play. The house should seem almost to be growing up from the beach rather than being half-covered by it. The front porch is covered with sand. It piles up from the yard against the steps, almost making a ramp. The yard is surrounded by a low adobe wall, there are a few scrubby plants in the sandy yard.

It is still quite light outside when the play begins, half an hour or so after sunset.
Summer.
Irene is seated, quite proper, rather tired, in the chair, reading, Owen is playing solitaire at the dining table, Sasha, also at the table, her chair a little out from the table, is looking indifferently through an old school annual, Joan is sprawled on the sofa looking through several books. Kenny comes forward. Joan hums the first few notes of a tune, Irene says softly "shhhh," without looking up, Joan looks to her brother, who hasn't noticed, so intent on his announcement of the play, and smiles tolerantly as Kenny speaks to the audience.

KENNY: *(Brightly)* I get to begin the play now, and I get to close it later on with little narrations—little scenes or speeches. And I sing in one of the songs too, later on. *(Clears his throat)* I'm Kenny, the younger son, and there's a sister named Joan—my sister—and my brother named Owen and our mother is—we call Reen, her name is Irene. Our last name, the family name, is Renolds, after our father who was killed in the war, but you don't have to worry about that because it doesn't have anything to do with the play. *(Owen says "Thank God," without looking up. Joan laughs at this, quickly covered up. Kenny continues without hearing them)* And there's a neighbor, a girl who comes over all the time, she spends all her time here and she's just like one of...
SASHA: *(Looking up from the book, quite casually to Joan)* Who'd you have in psych? Last term? Didn't you get...(Realizes Kenny is announcing the play. Shuts up quickly with a grimace, sinks into her chair shyly and goes back to the book)*
KENNY: *(After a brief tolerant pause)* Her name is Sasha. She's a friend of my sister's. *(Joan mouths "Professor Morton" behind Kenny. Sasha mouths "Who?" Joan repeats the name, Sasha, still not understanding, repeats "Who?" then*

shrugs and goes back to the book. Kenny continues without pause) She's over all the time, they're all juniors and seniors up at State. And there's another friend of the family called Calvin. He's digging around in the bedroom right now but he comes on in a minute. He's got a boat and he's married. He studies, I think, either at State or at the Scripps Institute of . . .

OWEN: *(Interrupting)* Oh, for Christ's sake, Kenny, would you shut up and get on with it?

KENNY: *(Quickly)* Okay. *(Momentarily stopped, not knowing if he should shut up or go on, questioningly half-turns)* Well, which do you . . .

OWEN: Go on with it. God!

KENNY: *(Rapidly now)* And there's a boy friend of Reen's—that's our mother, remember—his name is Clint. He drives a bus past here and stops in. You'll see them all anyway—you see them now, and they'll—the others—will be easy enough to—you know—to—you know—to figure out. *(Pulls more erect, quite unconsciously. Everyone seems to tighten, straighten, become more aware of themselves as Kenny announces rather formally)* The Sand Castle. Or There Is a Tavern in the Town. Or Harry Can Dance. *(A tight little bow of the head in spite of himself. He turns and goes into Owen's bedroom)*

JOAN: *(Immediately to Sasha)* Professor Morton.

SASHA: Oh, god! He's a creep.

(Irene simultaneously clears her throat gently)

KENNY: *(Simultaneously, as he enters Owen's bedroom)* Okay, Calvin.

OWEN: *(Beat. Playing solitaire, directing an orchestra broadly with both hands waving in the air, sings loudly to himself)* There is! A tavern in the town!

EVERYONE: *(Including Clint, Calvin and Kenny offstage. Those on stage turn directly to the audience. Singing very loudly. Not Owen)* IN THE TOWN!

OWEN: *(Surprised)* Come on, shut up for Christ's sake; can't you hear I'm trying to concentrate? I'm nearly winning. *(Everyone is still. Owen takes three cards, looks at them, plays one. Studies a moment. Singing to himself in a high sincere falsetto)* In the town.

CALVIN: *(Enters from Owen's bedroom. He has an armload of very old comic books)* Hey, look what I found. I didn't know you had all these, Owen. *(Dumps them on the floor)*

JOAN: Oh, god!

CALVIN: Lord, remember comics?

JOAN: Don't drag those things out here, Cal, they'll be here for a month.

IRENE: Owen and Kenny must have a thousand of them.

OWEN: *(Has noticed but not said anything. Quietly to the cards)* Put them back when you're finished, too.

SASHA: *(Walking over to Calvin who has sat on the floor)* What? Good Lord, Batman.

CALVIN: There must be hundreds. There's a Wonder Woman in here somewhere. God, she was almost my foster mother. *(To Irene)* This was when I was about eight, of course.

OWEN: *(Without looking up)* Shhhhhhh.

IRENE: Owen's almost winning.

OWEN: Don't tear those up, either.

KENNY: *(From the bedroom)* Hey, Joan?

OWEN: *(Pause. Singing quietly)* And there my true love sits her down.

KENNY: *(Off)* Joan? *(Pause)*

OWEN: *(Pause. Singing quietly)*...Sits her dow-wn and...

KENNY: *(Off)* Joan?

JOAN: Well, what? For Christ's sake, Kenny, I'm not deaf—

KENNY: *(Off)* I can't find my shoes in here.

JOAN: —Honestly, you'd sit in there for an hour if nobody answered you without ever saying what, just screaming *Joan* over and over. *(Back to her book)*

KENNY: *(Off)* Joan? *(Slight pause)*

JOAN: Oh, god! Well, *what?* Jesus.

KENNY: *(Off)* I can't find my shoes, I told you and I know I took them off here because I remember last night when you said why was I wearing my shoes I had them on and when I went to bed I kicked them off at the foot of the bed by that little table there.

JOAN: *(An aside, disgruntled look at the audience, then back to the door. Portentously)* Why are you telling me all this? I haven't seen them, Kenny.

KENNY: *(Off)* Owen?

OWEN: *(Without looking up)* Go to hell!

SASHA: *(To audience)* They're this typical American family, see.

KENNY: *(Off)* Have you seen them?

JOAN: *(Reading)* What do you want with them?

KENNY: *(Entering)* I want to wear them. *(To audience)* Hi, again. That was me yelling. Wouldn't that be a great entrance if you hadn't seen me before?

IRENE: Do you need them, Kenny?

KENNY: I don't especially need them, but a fella likes to know where his shoes...

OWEN: Kenny, I'm trying to concentrate.

CALVIN: *(Reading)* God, was she great.

SASHA: He's cheating anyway.

OWEN: Who's cheating?

SASHA: *(Back to a comic)* I thought you were concentrating.

OWEN: *(Singing loudly)* Fare thee well, for I must leave you, do not let the parting grieve you...

CALVIN *and* SASHA: *(To audience. Pizzicato)* And remember that the best of friends must part. *(Sasha says "Some-times part")*

CALVIN: Take it!

SASHA: *(Instant vamp. Mock-torch singer, moving from Calvin to Owen. Much hips, breasts and sex)* Fare thee well, for I must leave you, do-oo-oo not let! The parting! Grieve you!

KENNY: *(Over the above)* I'm going out. I don't need my shoes. I guess they're just gone!

OWEN: Come on, I'm losing. Be a little quiet.
(Kenny swings out the screen door, off the porch and off)
CALVIN: We can't. We must bid farewell to your fair-weather brother. *(Waving off)* Farewell, fair-weather brother. Fare thee well. Adieu.
JOAN *and* SASHA: *(Calvin has a speech at the door over this charade. Both Joan and Sasha are up. At "Adieu" they begin to perform a kind of soft—high-stepping sister act for the audience. Obviously semi-choreographed, they dance and sing as Calvin waves off to Kenny)* Adieu! Adieu, kind friends, adieu. *(Sasha: Adieu, adieu)* I can. No longer stay with you. *(Joan: Stay with you-oo)* I must hang my head from a weeping willow tree—*(Sasha: [a rapid spoken aside] "What the hell are the words?")* AND MAY. The world go well with thee! With thee!
CALVIN: *(Over the above. Narratively. Waving off)* There he goes. Sinking into the sunset. That's the way, Kenny. Rape all the women and ravage the lands. Kill a dragon or two. Tote that barge, rape those women, lift that skirt! Look at him. There he goes across the beach—all the way to New York City, U.S.A. *You'll make it, Porgy!*
OWEN: *(Who has been trying to ignore them)* SHUT UP!
CALVIN, JOAN *and* SASHA: *(They break into a full, loud song and dance, creating a general havoc. Very bawdy, all over the stage. Also a semi-choreographed dance with kicks, etc. Owen is trying to get them out of the house. He throws a comic book at Joan. They march around his table—he tries to save his card game; destroys the game himself by tossing all the cards into the air. During this they sing loudly)*

There is a tavern in the town. In the town.
And there my true love sits him down. Sits him down.
And drinks his gin, by a weeping willow tree.
And never, never thinks of me. Of me.

(During the song Sasha comes straight to the audience—kicks her legs Can-Can fashion two or three times and says in a wildly wicked flirt: "Hi there!" "Oceanside three—four seven four nine.")

and goes back to the group. As Owen continues to push them out the front door) Fare thee well for I must leave you!

OWEN: Leave already. Leave. Part!

CALVIN, JOAN *and* SASHA: Do not let the parting grieve you!

OWEN: Like hell it grieves me, go on—outside.

CALVIN, JOAN *and* SASHA: And remember that the best of friends must sometimes part. *(As Owen continues to chase them and straighten the chairs up after them, etc. Calvin opens the front screen and they all march out)* Fare thee well for I must leave thee—do not let the parting grieve thee— And remember that the best of friends must part.

(Owen throws a pillow that hits the front screen as Calvin quickly closes it behind them)

OWEN: Friends, hell. Part! If I had a front door I could really shut them out. I'd lock them out on the porch.

(Irene through the dance, began by sitting, amused. Toward the end she stands—looking just a bit worried, apprehensive. Now she is smiling again)

KENNY: *(As Calvin, Joan and Sasha burst out onto the porch, Kenny enters with Clint, who is carrying his jacket, two six-packs of beer, his change gadget from the bus and his hat)* Clint was parking his bus.

JOAN: Hi, Clint.

CLINT: *(Handing Joan the beer)* Take this. You got any ice? They can't stay cold for long.

CALVIN: Ice! Ice!

OWEN: *(Begins to pick up the cards and return them to the table)* Damn them, I'm certain I could have won that hand, too.

IRENE: I think I heard Clint's bus.

CALVIN: Ice! *(Enters living room and crosses to kitchen)* Do you have anything perishable in the icebox? I didn't think so. I want to borrow your ice. I'll bring it right back. *(Exits to kitchen)*

IRENE: Sure, you're welcome to it, I suppose.

OWEN: Now, don't start tracking through here again. Just—

SASHA: *(Reenters. Crosses to her book, picks it up and goes back out front)* I forgot my book. We're having a picnic on the grass. Joan and I are going to strip and Kenny and Cal will play the mandolin.

IRENE: *(Laughing)* What grass?

CALVIN: *(Entering from the kitchen with a small block of ice on tongs)* We're improvising grass, actually. You should do something about your lawn.

OWEN: Perhaps we could do something about our lawn if we could get everyone off it for a minute.

CALVIN: *(To Irene)* Clint brought us a half-case of beer.

CLINT: *(Out front)* It's a stupid day to drive anyway. At least it's cooled off some from what it was.

JOAN: *(Out front)* No business probably on a Saturday.

OWEN: *(To Calvin)* You're dripping.

CALVIN: *(Not moving)* That's great of him, huh?

(Sasha opens a beer out front that spews up in the air)

IRENE: Calvin, you're not going to have time to get any work done if you don't get at it before . . .

CALVIN: Just one beer and I'll get right at it. God, what a school teacher.

IRENE: You asked me to prod you; I'm prodding.

OWEN: You're dripping all over—

CALVIN: *(Leaving the living room)* Your floor's sandy.

KENNY: *(Enters and crosses to the kitchen as Calvin goes out)* Clint's here, Reen.

CLINT: *(Simultaneously—to Calvin)* Great, great. Hey, Irene?

OWEN: *(Who has followed Calvin to the door)* Well, you'd be sandy too if you lived on a beach with a hundred maniacs running through— *(The screen door slams in his face)* —the house and all over the beach and back and forth. Wouldn't you?

JOAN: *(To Calvin about the ice)* That'll do fine.

CLINT: *(Looking up to Owen)* Hi, Owen.

OWEN: Hi, Clint. God—

CLINT: *(Coming in now. To Irene)* I left the bus running out front.

OWEN: *(Turning from the door)* —damn.

CLINT: You want a beer? I'll bring you one in.

IRENE: Hi, Clint.

(He pecks her on the cheek)

CLINT: I'll get you one. Hey, Calvin? Another one, okay? Buddy? Pitch it in.

OWEN: Pitch it in, oh, god!

CLINT: *(Catches it)* It's not too cold, I'm afraid. God, a day like this, huh? *(Opens it. It spews over the table, over Owen's cards)* Damn, look at that!

OWEN: Awh, come on, Clint. Damn!

CLINT: What's wrong? Too warm, huh?

OWEN: Your can of beer spewed up when you opened it and went all over the playing cards.

CLINT: *(Lightly tosses him a towel from the back of the chair Sasha was sitting in)* Sorry. Here. *(Lays his jacket across the chair, sits the change gadget on the table)* I just got a minute. I left the bus running. How come you got that ice, your fridge not working?

IRENE: No, it went out yesterday. I mentioned it.

CLINT: You just got the icebox? Hey—Calvin. Bring that ice back in here. Stupid. You can put the beer on top of it in the box. I ask him if there's ice and he brings it out.

CALVIN: *(From out front)* Yeah? Okay.

SASHA: Don't shake them up.

OWEN: Soaking wet. They smell like brewery passes.

CLINT: So how's your day?

IRENE: Warm, but okay. How's yours?

CLINT: Ah, bad. No problems but it's a stupid day for a bus. I'm sorry I couldn't get off. They didn't need busses today. I stopped off at the Surf and talked to the guys awhile, I'm still ahead of schedule.

IRENE: Everyone's on vacation. The beach was packed.

CLINT: It's too hot for out there.

OWEN: *(To himself)* What we need around here is a scout leader.

(Calvin, Joan and Sasha come trailing across the room with ice and beer. Sasha and Calvin go into the kitchen. Joan carries nothing, stands near the kitchen door)

CLINT: *(To Irene)* Maybe tomorrow we could take a ride—us two, okay? Up into the mountains or somewhere.

IRENE: *(Very pleased)* Wonderful. That would be fine.

CLINT: Everyone's up in the mountains anyway. It's great up there.

JOAN: God, we're all so stupid; I don't know why we didn't think of bringing the beer in instead of the ice out.

KENNY: *(Comes out of the kitchen, with a peanut butter sandwich, leans against the doorway)* Yeah, you are.

CLINT: Sure, the milk'll spoil.

KENNY: *(Over the sandwich)* There isn't any.

CLINT: Well, whatever.

OWEN: There's a little piece of butter and an empty instant coffee jar.

CLINT: Wouldn't that be fun? I'd like that.

IRENE: I'd love to. I'll pack us something to eat, if you'd like.

CLINT: Good then.

IRENE: I haven't been up in the mountains for years.

CLINT: Well, we'll remedy that. Just us.

JOAN: What?

CALVIN: *(Reentering with Sasha)* All set.

SASHA: We put them right on top.

JOAN: *(To Clint)* What?

CLINT: Just never mind, nosey.

JOAN: Well, what?

OWEN: He said never mind, nosey.

CLINT: *(To Irene)* You don't have classes on Sunday, do you? When's that thing over?

CALVIN: *(Picks up several books from the desk)* I've got to get something done.

OWEN: I don't know why, you've wasted the whole day.

IRENE: Next week. Too bad, too. It's been fun.

SASHA: *(To Irene)* Sure it has.

KENNY: *(To audience)* It's always like this. Sometimes worse.

CALVIN: *(To Sasha who is collecting Owen's cards)* Do you want to help me with this?

CLINT: *(To Irene)* College kids, huh?

SASHA: *(To Calvin)* No, thanks. What'd you want me to read to you?

IRENE: Most of them, not all.

KENNY: *(Over the sandwich. To audience)* See, Reen's a teacher out at this summer conference for writers. They have lectures and like that for two weeks every summer—like a convention. And Reen's one of the main poetry speakers. She used to be a poet—a real one, and she was published in all the little magazines and in a lot of the big ones and books and so she's this big name out there. I mean it's been twenty years probably, but she's still a great teacher. And she instructs the college graduates and all that want to be writers.

IRENE: *(Quickly)* They're not all graduates, Kenny.

CLINT: *(Finishing his beer)* Look, I gotta run. I have to put the bus in the barn and then I'm through.

IRENE: Swell.

CLINT: I've been on another twelve hours; we aren't supposed to do that. Everyone's on vacation.

JOAN: I'll bet it's good money, though. *(Joan straightens Clint's coat on the back of the chair)*

CLINT: I suppose.

IRENE: Did you leave the bus running?

KENNY: Is Jill coming over today, Calvin?

CLINT: Yeah, I'll spend all the taxpayer's money. I thought I'd just be a minute. I always stay longer. Wonder why? *(He takes the jacket)*

CALVIN: *(To Kenny)* I don't imagine, why should she? No, I don't imagine.

OWEN: She can't run all over, Kenny, my god!

JOAN: *(To Owen)* Why not?

IRENE: I'm glad you do stay, Clint.

OWEN: Well, she shouldn't.

SASHA: Why don't you still write, Reen?

IRENE: *(Softly. Quickly)* I will.

CLINT: What time you want to get started in the morning?

SASHA: Of course, how could she around here?

CALVIN: *(Having trouble trying to read)* That's what I was going to say. I can't even read.

CLINT: What time you want to start in the morning, Irene?

IRENE: What? Oh, whatever you think. Early?

OWEN: What's wrong with around here?

SASHA: *(To audience)* Isn't he great? A real jewel, huh?

CLINT: I think early, yeah. You sure you have time to fix up some food for tomorrow?

IRENE: I'm sure.

JOAN: *(Pleasantly)* What about tomorrow?

OWEN: *(To Joan)* Mind your own business.

CLINT: *(To Sasha who is finishing her beer)* You drink all that beer and I'll whack you one, you hear?

SASHA: *(Provocatively)* Clint! Please, I'm an innocent girl.

CLINT: You see her dancing around when I came up?

OWEN: She has a Salome complex.

JOAN: Sometimes we just feel like dancing.

CLINT: Just don't drink all the beer up.

SASHA: Admit it, you weak, groveling male; you're under my spell.

CLINT: *(He and Irene are moving toward the front door)* Yeah. You just leave four cans of beer for us for tomorrow or you'll be under something.

SASHA: You can only go so far with me, Clint. If you know what I mean. *(Clint and Irene laugh)*

IRENE: *(Gently)* What are we going to do with her? I don't know.

CLINT: She'll find out.

SASHA: *(A parting shot)* You want me for my body!

CALVIN: Come on, I'm trying to read.

JOAN: Honestly, Sasha.

CLINT: The bus will probably be hot as a bastard.

SASHA: *(Calling)* There's a full moon tonight.

CLINT: *(As he and Irene go out onto the front porch)* I'll full-moon you. *(To Irene)* The bus'll probably be steaming hot.

JOAN: You'd say anything. God!

OWEN: As a matter of fact, there's no moon at all tonight if you're interested.

SASHA: *(Starting to lay out the cards for a game of solitaire)* Damn! Well, no wonder nothing's working for me.

JOAN: You make such an ass of yourself.

CALVIN: Come on, I'm trying to read.

IRENE: *(To Clint)* It's beginning to cool off some.

CLINT: Muggy night.

SASHA: What can I tell you, I'm a sucker for bus drivers; you should excuse the expression.

IRENE: It is.

SASHA: I like to joke with Clint. It doesn't budge him.

CALVIN: You should excuse the—

SASHA: —Just get back to your plankton and never mind.

IRENE: That'll be wonderful tomorrow; I used to love to drive up into the mountains.

CLINT: We have to get an early start though.

IRENE: Anytime you want.

CLINT: If I stayed over we could start anytime; that's not a bad idea.

IRENE: *(She sits on the porch railing)* What's not a bad idea?

CLINT: You heard me. Of course we might not get started at all.

IRENE: Yes. I don't think it's such a good idea.

CLINT: Well, then, why don't you marry me and we could go up into the mountains every weekend. Have a place up there, maybe.

IRENE: Wonderful. With a room for Owen, and a room for Joan and one for Sasha and one...

CLINT: Sasha isn't even family. You don't have to take any of them along. Hell, they can take care of themselves by now or they never will.

IRENE: You'd think.

CLINT: Or we could move up to Fresno if that's what you want. How serious are you when you talk about moving back up there?

IRENE: Owen is dead serious, I suppose. And Joan— they can't stand it down here. Kenny it doesn't matter. He doesn't know Fresno at all, he was born down here.

CLINT: You might really go back there sometime then?

IRENE: I don't know. I don't much—I don't believe I want to, but Owen, that's the only thing he knows, and Joan's...

CLINT: Well, hell, then—that's what I thought. Why don't we get married and send *them* to Fresno. I don't want to go to Fresno. What the hell's in Fresno?

IRENE: I don't know.

CLINT: So why don't you marry me?

IRENE: Oh, god, Clint. *(Smiles at him a moment)* Look at you. I must be the most ordinary woman in the world. I feel as if I were being hooked by some vast advertising campaign.

CLINT: What do you mean, you didn't answer my question.

IRENE: To be attracted to you. Look at you.

CLINT: What?

IRENE: Well, you're Marlboro Country and the Camel Man and Randolph Scott, it's just ridiculous. All the things that we're supposed to believe are masculine and red-blooded in the pulp fiction sense. Your dreadful speech and your laughable—almost self-conscious clumsiness and your honest sincerity and middle-class, proletarian sensibility and even your total lack of good looks.

CLINT: Really?

IRENE: Really what, Clint?

CLINT: You don't think I've got any looks but you're attracted to me anyway, huh?

IRENE: *(As though studying him)* Women would consider you not classically attractive but chock full of sex appeal, I think. And I find that attractive. All-American female snob that I am, and I say to myself, Irene, that's the most obvious thing you've ever done in your life.

CLINT: You really think I'm sexy, huh?

IRENE: Well, if any of the girls in my class ever came up with a character like you—accurately described, of course—I'd wash her mouth out with soap.

CLINT: So why don't you marry me? And we'll go to Fresno or wherever, I don't care. Family or none.

IRENE: You watch it, Clint. I just might.

CLINT: *(A rather neat dodge)* I'm not going to give you another chance until tomorrow. In the meantime, just to prove what you say, I think I should stay here tonight.

IRENE: *(Just the slightest pause)* What would they say about that?

CLINT: Yeah, you're just trying to get out of it. I thought you said I was sexy.

IRENE: Of course you are.

CLINT: Sure.

IRENE: All American. Bus driver, my god, bowler, baseball fan, beer drinker, you even wear a tenement T-shirt. Those are symbols of virility in this country, didn't you know that?

CLINT: What's a tenement T-shirt?

IRENE: *(Tucks a finger under the strap of his undershirt)* That.

CLINT: Those are sexy?

IRENE: Oh, Clint, you don't know! It's absolutely the knitted materialization of American masculinity in the woman's eye.

CLINT: Cheap too, I'm even practical.

IRENE: See, you're all-over coarse hair, which is basic. You're basic which is basic and you've got nearly-but-not-quite-crossed eyes. That rather resemble a dumb animal's.

CLINT: Dumb, huh?

IRENE: Forget that—it's the animal that's important. And you're big.

CLINT: Oh, hell yes!

IRENE: That seems to be the key to the whole criterion right now. The suave gentleman is definitely out just now.

CLINT: Six-foot-two, two hundred pounds nearly...

IRENE: Well, do you realize that a few hundred years ago people never even *got* that big? You're right off the assembly line. And you've got hands that could cover a dinner plate—and my own daughter came home the other day to inform me flatly that the size of a man's hands definitely predisclosed his genital endowment.

CLINT: *(Laughing)* Joan did?

IRENE: *(Also nearly laughing now)* I've been meaning to say something to her about that but I haven't thought of anything yet. I just feel she's totally outrun all knowledge a girl her age is reasonably—at least in a healthy state of mind...

CLINT: Well, maybe she's right—

IRENE: Oh, I have no doubts about it at all. I just feel I should at least inquire if this knowledge was passed on by some teen-age sexual sage or gained first-hand through endless experiment. *(Clint laughs)* I mean, when I think of the trial and error even the simplest hypothesis has to be subjected to...

CLINT: Come on—you always get off the question at hand, Irene. You're good at that.

IRENE: What? Was there a question at hand?

CLINT: Are you going to marry me?

IRENE: Ask me tomorrow night.

CLINT: Okay. Only a dozen times.

IRENE: I'll say yes one day and we'll see how fast you run.

CLINT: Not a chance, Irene, and you know it.

IRENE: We'll see.

CLINT: You just tell me and you'll see how high I can jump.

IRENE: I bet.

CLINT: You're a damn good catch yourself, Reen. I can't go on about it like you do and joke around, but you know it.

IRENE: Let's face it, we're the match of the century.

CLINT: You're a bright woman, Irene. You know what I mean.

IRENE: And you're bright. Bright like a bonfire. Bright-smart, too; in a pseudo-stupid sort of way.

CLINT: Now see? You say a dozen good things and you end up calling me stupid. I knew it. You've got to insult me before you send me home. Every night.

IRENE: It just wouldn't work, Clint; what can I tell you? What time are you coming around tomorrow morning?

CLINT: How about seven?

IRENE: *Seven?* Well, okay.

CLINT: It'll be ten before we get anywhere even at that.

IRENE: I know, I know. I said that's fine. I'll see you at seven.

CLINT: Okay? Good night, then.

IRENE: *(As he begins to back off)* Good night, Clint; I'll see you tomorrow.

JOAN: *(Looking up from her book. Calling)* Good night, Clint.

SASHA: *(Seductively)* Good night, Clint.

JOAN: Oh, god, Sasha!

CLINT: *(Calling)* Good night. *(To Irene)* Seven in the morning, okay then? I'll see you.

IRENE: *(Turning toward the door)* Good. Get some sleep.

(Joan puts down her book and goes to the door)

CLINT: Good night.

IRENE: *(Laughing. Waves him away)* Go on! *(She comes inside, turns to look off. Joan has joined her at the door)*

JOAN: Clint strikes me as the comfortable type that

sits around the living room and watches television. The stay-at-home ilk.

IRENE: You think? Probably he would be. I wouldn't mind that, though.

JOAN: Would be? I mean by himself. Can't you just see him eating out at some coffee shop or sitting down to a whole string of Westerns with a frozen TV dinner in the oven?

OWEN: I can't see him as anything.

JOAN: The one-room, kitchenette type; sleeps on the sofa.

IRENE: Probably.

SASHA: You think?

JOAN: In his socks.

SASHA: I wouldn't think he'd be happy without a garage and woodsaws and an assortment of graduated wrenches.

IRENE: You're probably very nearly right.

SASHA: They come all rolled up in a blanket affair—the littlest one no bigger than a pin.

OWEN: Ahhhh.

SASHA: What?

OWEN: *(Sweetly)* The littlest wrench.

SASHA: Shut up!

OWEN: It sounds like a story by Oscar Wilde.

SASHA: Shut up!

JOAN: *(With an edge of superiority)* No, not at all. Clint's too tranquil to be pothering around with wrenches.

IRENE: He's quiet all right.

OWEN: Nerveless.

SASHA: *(Flatly)* He's sexy.

IRENE: Exactly. The teddy bear type.

SASHA: Right.

IRENE: All very faithful and dedicated.

SASHA: Faithful and dedicated—god, I love it.

JOAN: *(With an irritated edge)* You're going up in the mountains tomorrow?

IRENE: We thought we would.

(Calvin, who has been trying to read, with difficulty, now begins to gather up his books)

OWEN: Hey, great!

IRENE: *(To Calvin)* We're distracting you, aren't we? How much more have you got?

CALVIN: Only about a chapter. Are you going to have time to read the paper on—

IRENE: Yes, yes, of course. You don't have to ask.

SASHA: What?

IRENE: I'm his personal secretary this semester.

CALVIN: Can I help it if I can't spell?

SASHA: I'll bet she writes them for you. How much do you pay her?

CALVIN: This one's on mollusk. Shellfish. *Mollusca,* as Barnes would say; snails, whelks, oysters, that lot.

SASHA: Is there a lot of that lot?

IRENE: *(Distastefully)* Oh, lord, Calvin. I loathe shellfish. Clams?

CALVIN: Yeah, and worse.

IRENE: Oh, dear; oh, well.

CALVIN: It'll be hard enough anyway because what I know about cuttlefish you could boil in a thimble, so I mostly just rambled around with a lot of double-talk. *(He takes the books and goes to Irene's bedroom)*

OWEN: *(To Irene)* You're really driving up in the mountains?

IRENE: *(As Calvin goes in)* Shut the door, Calvin; it's all right.

CALVIN: Swell.

OWEN: That's great.

SASHA: Tomorrow's the day the teddy bears have their picnic.

JOAN: It's a lot of trouble is all.

IRENE: Not so...I have to pick up something early to make for lunch.

JOAN: I just despise picnics. Really, Reen, what a proletarian idea for Sunday afternoon. You know how long it's going to take you to get there? With traffic? It was probably a wonderful idea a hundred years ago.

SASHA: Don't be silly.

JOAN: Well, it's just absurd.

IRENE: *(Good-naturedly)* I don't think so.

JOAN: *(Irritated)* Well, Clint will just despise it.

SASHA: He knows how to drive.

OWEN: She just wants to come along and gum things up.

JOAN: Oh, be quiet, Owen; you're not even funny. You're such an ass. *(She turns to look out the door again)*

OWEN: Don't call your own brother an ass; what does that make you? The sister of an ass.

SASHA: *(Stacking up the cards from her solitaire game)* Well, that's it.

IRENE: What? Did you win?

OWEN: Did you win?

SASHA: Well, of course.

OWEN: Let's see.

SASHA: Too late.

OWEN: Good god! With my cards, too. Give them back; I haven't won once in two years.

SASHA: Of course not, you cheat. *(Picks up a comic book)* What's that one?

OWEN: Superman meets Plastic Man. Remember Plastic Man?

IRENE: Sounds like a pretty uneven match.

OWEN: They aren't enemies. Plastic Man makes his body into a shield to protect Superman from a hunk of krypton.

JOAN: *(Imitating Owen)* Remember krypton.

OWEN: You aren't funny.

SASHA: I don't know. I guess I'm getting old. I used to just love Plastic Man and any more all I can think of is all the vulgar things he could do.

OWEN: You'd destroy anything.

JOAN: *(Turning from the door)* I think I'll go over and see Jill. You want to come, Sasha?

SASHA: Jill? God, no. Not right this minute.

OWEN: I will.

JOAN: No. She doesn't want to see you. *(Disgusted—which is what she was after anyway)* You'd drive her nuts.

OWEN: What do you mean, I'd drive her nuts? Who sits around moaning all day, just *thinking* of morbid things to say. I honestly believe she just sits around thinking of ghastly tales to tell her. You should hear the things she comes out with. *I'd* drive her nuts; that's ridiculous.

JOAN: I don't want to go anyway. Forget I mentioned it.

OWEN: You say the stupidest things to her! *(Instant change to a fog of love)* Oh, Jill!

JOAN: Oh, god! You make me sick; you really do.

OWEN: You don't even know what I'm talking about. I happen to be in love with Jill...

JOAN: Come on, Calvin will hear you...

IRENE: *(Quietly)* Owen.

OWEN: I happen to feel it's a very beautiful experience to be able to love someone; I'm not ashamed of it. He knows it.

SASHA: Everyone in San Diego County knows it; it's all you ever talk about. Jill and Thomas Wolfe.

OWEN: It is not. You can just clam up, too.

SASHA: Well, I can understand being mad about her after she gets married, but when she's going to have a baby, I'd think it would turn you off a little.

OWEN: *(Adrift)* Oh, no, no. You should *see* her. She's so fragile looking, so glowing—I love pregnant girls anyway.

JOAN: God!

IRENE: Owen, Calvin is trying to read. I don't imagine he can concentrate with us discussing his wife.

OWEN: You should *see* her though.

SASHA: You should have been born in the Eleventh Century.

OWEN: No, she's so lovely. Isn't she, Reen?

IRENE: She looks fat to me. Don't ask me.

OWEN: No, she isn't. Women gain extra weight for the baby when they're pregnant.

SASHA: It's called baby fat.

(Kenny comes running up the front steps. He trots into the house)

OWEN: You people don't know anything.

KENNY: About what? Hey, guess what happened?

OWEN: —She's probably home, too. Alone, of course. I don't know how he can do that. I should probably go over there.

IRENE: *(To Joan)* See what you started?

KENNY: Reen? Guess what.

SASHA: *(To Joan)* Who did you have second year psych, you remember?

JOAN: Morton. I had him all three years.

OWEN: He's a creep.

KENNY: Where's Calvin?

SASHA: He is. What a creep.

KENNY: Who? Calvin? How come?

SASHA: Professor Morton.

KENNY: Who's he?

JOAN: A professor of psychology up at State. Jesus.

IRENE: What happened, Kenny?

KENNY: *(To audience)* Is it like this all the time or just when I come in?

IRENE: Calvin's in the bedroom.

JOAN: He gave the whole class a B minus.

KENNY: What on earth for?

SASHA: He's reading.

JOAN: About cuttlefish.

KENNY: Hey, Calvin!

IRENE: He's working, Kenny.

CALVIN: *(Off)* Yeah?

IRENE: That's okay, Calvin.

CALVIN: *(Off)* No, I'm just finishing, Reen. *(Entering)* God, this is tough.

KENNY: Did he give you a B minus?

IRENE: Are you sure you're finished?

CALVIN: Near enough. What, Kenny?

SASHA: *(Very quickly now, as Kenny starts to speak up)* How's the cuttlefish?

CALVIN: That's the paper, this is water.

JOAN: Tides, that sort of thing?

KENNY: *(Lost)* Wait.

CALVIN: Density, salinity, that sort of thing.

OWEN: *(To Sasha)* Are you going home tonight?

SASHA: *(Fliply)* Home? Certainly not, I'm going out dancing.

OWEN: *(This is a game)* Oh? Where are you going?

JOAN: God, that *is* hard.

CALVIN: You're telling me.

KENNY: Wait. *(Aside to Sasha)* I had a line in there somewhere.

OWEN: I never could get that stuff.

SASHA: Well, speak up.

KENNY: Uhh...

OWEN: Where you going dancing?

SASHA: Well, to the El Morocco, of course. With Sue and Harry.

OWEN: Sue and Harry. Oh, Sue's a great dancer.

CALVIN: You'll love Sue.

SASHA: Well, Harry's no mean stepper himself.

OWEN: I didn't know Harry could dance.

KENNY: Come on...

IRENE: Speak up, Kenny. Step in.

SASHA: You didn't know?

JOAN: If you think Sue can dance.

CALVIN: Well, of course Sue can dance.

OWEN: I didn't think Harry could dance.

SASHA: *(Brushing it aside)* Yeah, well let me tell you, Harry can dance, like, I mean Harry can dance.

KENNY: *(Rushing in to pick up the lost line. They have been adlibbing)* Guess what happened!

OWEN: About time. Jesus!

JOAN: *(Simultaneously)* Thank god, good grief, Kenny.

CALVIN: *(Simultaneously)* Way to go, Kenny.
(Owen picks up a comic book, opens it)
KENNY: Guess what happened?
OWEN: Well, *what?* God!
KENNY: I'll bet it's the most important thing that's
ever...
JOAN: Kenny, just tell it or forget it.
KENNY: *(Fading off)* In my life...
IRENE: What's that, Kenny?
KENNY: You know Sunset Cliffs?
JOAN: *(After a beat. Everyone is looking at Kenny)*
Yes, we know Sunset Cliffs. You're impossible.
KENNY: Well, they caved in.
IRENE: *(Not calm, not excited)* Really, when?
KENNY: Well—I don't know. *(He had expected a dif-
ferent reaction)* This afternoon sometime.
JOAN: How much?
CALVIN: That's wild, how much?
KENNY: *(Defensively)* How do you mean?
CALVIN: How much land?
KENNY: Oh, about—I don't know. Maybe a third of
the way to the road nearly.
CALVIN: *(Flatly)* I'll be damned.
IRENE: The last time, when was it—
KENNY: What?
IRENE: The cliffs do that every year or two; they're
weak.
CALVIN: They're just sandstone.
KENNY: Really? What does that mean?
OWEN: Well, it means they're weak for one thing.
SASHA: Every couple of years they do that. Another
chunk falls off.
KENNY: I didn't know that. It's spooky, isn't it?
They've got—
IRENE: I hope you didn't get too close.
KENNY: You can't—let me tell you—they've got pa-
trol cars along the road and they have those board fences

across the way, and no one is allowed out onto the area there because they think it might do it again.

IRENE: Was anyone hurt?

KENNY: I don't think so.

SASHA: The last time—the middle of the night, there were about four cars parked up there. I think it killed all but one.

KENNY: Really? They just went over? Car and all?

JOAN: Well, of course car and all; what do you think, it's going to take the people and leave the car?

KENNY: Golly.

CALVIN: Something like that I always remember—wasn't it Edgar Cayce who proph—

OWEN: Yeah, if you want something spooky, Kenny. That's something for you.

KENNY: What?

CALVIN: I think he's the one—he predicted the beginning and end of some war and whatever the name of the volcano in Japan that erupted and killed so many people...

KENNY: Really?

CALVIN: And the island that blew up a few years back, he predicted that. And one of the prophecies of his was that during a violent earthquake the whole state of California would slide off into the Pacific Ocean. The whole state—part of Oregon.

(Kenny holds his breath)

SASHA: What? Are you sure?

CALVIN: Sure. Sometime around now. Within ten years, it's supposed to be.

IRENE: Closer than that, I think. It makes you wonder.

JOAN: I didn't know that. *(All rather overlapping and chatty here)*

CALVIN: It's true, that's one of his predictions.

IRENE: I'm not sure it was Cayce, but someone just as accredited as Cayce.

SASHA: The whole state? Good god. I don't think I'm glad you told me. Did you know that?

JOAN: No, I didn't know that. *(To audience)* Did you know that?

OWEN: I wouldn't worry much.

SASHA: Well, I *believe* in that sort of thing.

IRENE: That's what he said—

KENNY: *(We should see it coming a mile off)* *WOW!* That is incredible! When?

JOAN: Well, don't be so happy about it.

KENNY: The whole state?

JOAN: Don't be so damned ecstatic, Kenny-baby, you live in California, don't forget.

KENNY: Well, I can swim.

JOAN: All the way to Arizona?

KENNY: Well, why not?

CALVIN: I don't think so.

KENNY: Well, that just makes Sunset Cliffs just look like nothing.

IRENE: How did it go with the reading?

CALVIN: God knows. Salinity—shmalinity, I can't see how fish can live in it. Do you want to look at the paper?

IRENE: *(Picking up the paper)* I can't correct the information, but I'm sure it's right.

CALVIN: Well, it's close.

KENNY: Is there a book about him?

CALVIN: Who, Cayce?

KENNY: Yeah.

CALVIN: Sure.

KENNY: *(To Irene)* Do we have it?

IRENE: No. *(To Calvin)* Good lord, it's enormous.

KENNY: I want to get it.

CALVIN: *(To Irene)* That's good. I'm hoping he'll grade it by the pound.

SASHA: Who would have thought you had to work that hard on Oceanography? I thought it was mostly just sailing around.

IRENE: You have to work that hard for a Master's in anything.

SASHA: I suppose. It's a damn shame, isn't it?

(Joan stays close to the front door during this scene)

IRENE: I'll take it into the room; it won't be long, I don't imagine.

CALVIN: Have you ever seen Reen read? It's disheartening; I worked three months once writing a term paper that she read in under five minutes.

SASHA: I have, I know.

OWEN: She went through *Ulysses* in about three hours. It's just her way of showing off. Are you through with these? *(Referring to the comics)*

CALVIN: Huh? Sure.

OWEN: *(Not aggressively irritated)* You could at least have put them back like I told you.

KENNY: *(To Calvin)* Did we tell you about the fireworks?

CALVIN: Why, do you have some fireworks?

KENNY: We didn't even tell you?

IRENE: He's still trying to compete with your story about Edgar Cayce.

KENNY: No, we really do. Tell him. We really do. I'll bet you can see them from across the bay. *(To audience)* Calvin and Jill live across the bay.

OWEN: *(Picking up comics)* It's weird.

KENNY: *(Back to audience)* On Point Loma.

SASHA: *(To audience)* It's very nice.

KENNY: We didn't tell Clint, I'll bet, either.

JOAN: He's ... I thought we did.

SASHA: Did you find out who did it?

KENNY: Yes. Last night we could tell; it's this first house, up on the hill. *(To audience)* We got these rich neighbors or something up on the hill that shoot off these great skyrockets every night for no reason at all.

SASHA: People do that, though.

IRENE: They probably like them, it's very nice. *(She goes into her room, shuts the door)*

SASHA: *(To audience)* You know? They really do.

OWEN: Is that all the comics you dragged out?

KENNY: Aren't they great, Owen?

OWEN: They are. They've shot off two every night for weeks now.

KENNY: Just two. Real big ones, though.

SASHA: It's probably a short-circuit in their television.

OWEN: Don't be silly. They're great. Stay and see them.

JOAN: They probably have a lot of rich kids to entertain.

CALVIN: Sure. Like they won't go to bed without their fireworks. *(Opens the door to Irene's room)* If you don't know about something, just call me.

IRENE: *(Off)* Okay, I think I'll be all right, though.

OWEN: *(To Sasha)* I should go over and visit Jill. I haven't seen her in nearly a week.

SASHA: You'd only get frustrated. I don't know why you torture yourself with seeing her. She's married. You're not going to get at her for ten years anyway.

OWEN: That's not the point.

KENNY: *(Heading for the door)* I'm going.

IRENE: *(Off)* Kenny?

KENNY: Yes?

IRENE: *(Off)* Where are you going?

(Calvin remains in the doorway to Irene's bedroom. Owen and Sasha are by the table. Joan is near the door. Kenny walks back to Irene's door, by Calvin)

KENNY: Just down to the beach.

(By now the exterior lighting should be quite dim)

IRENE: *(Off)* Well, don't go around Sunset Cliffs.

KENNY: *(Pause. Flatly)* Why not?

IRENE: *(Off)* Because it's dangerous. Okay?

OWEN: *(Quietly to Sasha)* It's wonderful just to be around her. Just to talk to her or listen to her.

KENNY: No, it isn't. There's policemen.

SASHA: God! You're such a masochist, Owen.

IRENE: *(Off)* Well, they're not immortal themselves, you know.

OWEN: *(To Sasha)* You don't seem to understand a thing. You don't know anything.

KENNY: Okay.

IRENE: *(Off)* Okay what?

JOAN: *(Turns to Owen)* Well, you are! Aside from everything else.

KENNY: Okay, I'll just go down to the beach and not over to the cliffs.

OWEN: *(To Joan)* You be quiet, too!

CALVIN: *(Closing Irene's door)* What?

(Kenny goes trotting off)

OWEN: Nothing.

JOAN: Sasha said Owen was a masochist and I agreed, because he wanted to—

OWEN: —Just never mind! You just goddamn well never mind!

CALVIN: Well, maybe he is.

OWEN: Oh, hell, yes! Maybe we all are.

CALVIN: *(Looking at the top comic on the stack)* Have you had these since they were new? Here's a 1946.

OWEN: Yes.

JOAN: He can't throw anything away.

OWEN: I assume that's supposed to have some profound meaning.

CALVIN: I'll bet they're worth something by now, you know?

OWEN: I wouldn't be at all surprised.

CALVIN: How come you haven't sold them?

OWEN: I don't want to sell them.

SASHA: Why not? I'll bet they're worth something.

OWEN: Because I don't like to throw things away.

JOAN: *(To herself)* For Christ's sake!

OWEN: What's that supposed to mean?

CALVIN: I didn't say throw them away, I said sell them.

OWEN: I'm not through with them.

JOAN: He's never through with anything.

CALVIN: I don't know where you'll put them in there. He's got more junk in— *(To Joan)* Have you seen his room?

JOAN: No. I don't look in anymore. I don't think I want to know.

CALVIN: Well, you should see it. It's something else. Did you know you can only get the door open about a foot-and-a-half in there?

OWEN: Well, that's my stuff. I know what's in there.

CALVIN: What?

OWEN: Well, a *lot* of things.

CALVIN: You're telling me. You know what you're like? Sasha, did you ever read about those brothers in New York who had the house packed floor to ceiling with newspapers? That's exactly what Owen's going to be like.

JOAN: All hermits are like that.

OWEN: Who the hell's a hermit?

CALVIN: Just incredible. There's a tunnel through the junk to Kenny's bed and about enough room on the bed for him to curl up on the side to sleep. I'm not kidding—it really is. You couldn't exaggerate it.

OWEN: Well, there's nothing wrong with that.

SASHA: *(To audience)* He just likes a lot of junk.

CALVIN: And Owen must sleep on top of all the trash. You can't find a place on his dirty old bed to even sit down. Stuff is piled up to the ceiling.

OWEN: Well, what were you doing in there anyway—digging around for comics. It's not so bad. *(To audience)* It's not so bad.

CALVIN: Not so bad? It's jammed. You can't even open the door. It's piled to the ceiling!

OWEN: Well, it's a low ceiling!

JOAN: I'll bet he hasn't cleaned his room once since we've been here.

SASHA: God, Owen!

CALVIN: How long is that?

JOAN: Since Kenny was born—twelve, thirteen years.

CALVIN: God!

JOAN: He's got a typewriter in there somewhere.

CALVIN: Really? You should look for it. My god, the way you print everything.

OWEN: It'll turn up.

JOAN: See?

CALVIN: No, really—you could use it—all of us could use it.

OWEN: Well, why should I worry about looking through all that stuff for it, anyway? It'll turn up one of these days, it's *in* there.

SASHA: Good Lord!

OWEN: Why are you all three deliberately provoking me? Or trying to.

CALVIN: We're not provoking you...

JOAN: God, paranoid...

OWEN: You are so. First I'm a masochist, now I'm paranoid. I've got to put these away. *(Picks up the stack of comics and carries them toward his door)*

SASHA: How do you know where they belong?

(Calvin picks up his book again)

OWEN: *(Entering his room with the comics)* I know where they belong—just don't worry. *(In about three tries, with the stuff piled near the door from the inside, he kicks the door shut on them)*

CALVIN: *(Looks up from his book to Sasha)* Do you know anything about this stuff?

SASHA: No. And I don't want to.

CALVIN: I've forgotten everything I learned first year.

SASHA: That's what you get for going back, they find out how stupid you are, they'll revoke your Bachelor's.

CALVIN: You know anything about this, Joan?

JOAN: *(Distractedly)* No, you're the oceanographer. *(She finally wanders out the screen door to the porch. The porch should be fairly well lighted, but the outside is quite dark by now)*

CALVIN: *(Closes the book)* Well, I don't either. *(Looks up to Sasha)* You haven't been over.

SASHA: *(Lightning fast exchange. Vampingly)* You *missed* me!

CALVIN: *(Sudden wolf—mock rape—reaching for her)* Yes, you fool!

SASHA: *(Comic, violent retreat, screaming)* Ahhhhhhhhhh!

CALVIN: *(Laughs, relaxes)* So why haven't you been over?

SASHA: Well, I didn't know you cared.

CALVIN: Jill said if I ran into you to ask you over. She never sees you up at State.

SASHA: Jill? What an excuse. You want me for my big chest. It's all over town you've got a mammary fixation.

CALVIN: Well... as a matter of fact...

JOAN: *(On the porch, moves away from the door. Toward the yard. Quietly)* Hi, Clint.

CLINT: *(Enters from the dark now)* Oh. Hello, Joan.

JOAN: I didn't know you were coming back tonight. I though you might, but I didn't know.

CLINT: I didn't either.

SASHA: *(If she and Calvin hear voices, they can't tell who Joan is talking to)* We used to have about half of our classes together until she switched to Botany.

(Calvin has opened his book again, but isn't reading)

JOAN: I heard you leaving.

CLINT: You did. When?

CALVIN: I know—you three used to be quite a team.

JOAN: The other night—when you wanted to stay overnight with Reen.

CLINT: You did. Well, your mom and I joke like that.

SASHA: I think they separated us intentionally—the three of us—We nearly blew up the campus a year ago.

CALVIN: I heard. In elementary chemistry.

SASHA: Elementary hell!

JOAN: If it was me I'd have sneaked you in the back door. I'll bet you came back for your keys.

CLINT: Did you find them? I couldn't imagine...

JOAN: ...Because you never lose things—and as a matter of fact you didn't.

SASHA: There wasn't anything elementary the way we handled it. I think we were trying to perfect the cobalt bomb.

CALVIN: And nearly succeeded, I heard.

CLINT: How did you know?

JOAN: Because I saw them in your jacket pocket and took them.

CLINT: You what? I had to walk all the way back from the barn.

JOAN: You're strong.

SASHA: It was great. Biology was best. We drove poor Smith out of his mind, though.

CLINT: I ought to take you over...

JOAN: You better not, I might like it.

CLINT: *(Flatly)* What?

CALVIN: Poor old Professor Smith.

CLINT: I'm getting all kinds of messages that I'm sure you don't mean...

JOAN: I only said if I had the opportunity I'd sneak you in the back door.

SASHA: He was a wreck.

CLINT: *(Flatly)* You would.

SASHA: We nearly drove him—I think that was only last year...

JOAN: Or maybe a walk along the beach.

CLINT: It's probably pretty chilly along the beach this evening.

JOAN: I suppose, if you're by yourself.

CALVIN: *(Hearing the voices out front now)* Hey, Joan? When were you in Biology with Smith? *(He goes toward the door)* Who are you talking... Oh, hi, Clint.

SASHA: *(Also moves toward the door)* Hi, Clint. *(To Joan)* That was last year, wasn't it? With the dog?

CLINT: *(Quickly to Joan)* You going to give me my keys?

JOAN: *(Quickly)* I probably will. *(To Sasha. She does not overreact, but is quite calm)* What?

SASHA: *(She and Calvin coming out onto the porch)* Professor Smith.

JOAN: No, that was last year.

SASHA: I thought so. That poor man.

JOAN: *(Happily)* Yes, did we ever run him ragged.

SASHA: He didn't know what to do with us. I thought you'd gone, Clint.

JOAN: *(Very naturally)* He's been down at the cliffs, apparently it's not too bad, but they've stopped cars from going by.

CALVIN: Did much go?

CLINT: *(Making it up)* No, not much.

JOAN: He said he didn't see much.

CLINT: *(Naturally now)* No, it didn't seem like so much to me—of course it's dark, down there.

CALVIN: Can you imagine Jill and Joan and Sasha in one biology class? I don't know whatever possessed them.

SASHA: It was pretty impossible. We had a ball in biology. Smith retired with an ulcer. *(She, Joan and Calvin laugh)* Everyone was working on frogs and salamanders and the three of us...*(Laughs)*

JOAN: Clint said he'd walk me down to the cliffs, I think I'll see what's happened to them.

CALVIN: It can't be much.

JOAN: I know, but when they're our only natural phenomenon closer than the Grand Canyon...

SASHA: It's too dark to see much.

CALVIN: They probably have search lights.

CLINT: *(Easily)* Oh, yeah, you can see pretty well...

JOAN: I'll give you a report...*(She and Clint walk off into the dark)*

SASHA: *(Continuing)* Anyway, everyone was working on frogs and so naturally the three of us decided to dissect a dog. *(She is laughing, remembering)*...it was absurd.

CALVIN: Yuck. You would.

SASHA: Well, there were three of us. *(Laughing)* What a mess...

CALVIN: ...Come on...

SASHA: *(Laughing)* Oh, you don't know...really—

CALVIN: You'll make me sick...

SASHA: *(Laughing)* No, come on—we started out on this very complex system and I forget what we were going to do, but we...*(Laughing through this)*...decided to follow the nerves from the testicles and see where they went—

CALVIN: You would—you three...

SASHA: *(Laughing)* But we didn't have any *idea* what we were doing...

CALVIN: *(Waits a moment as she laughs, smiling at her)* Well, what?

SASHA: *(Still laughing)* We got all hung up looking for the nerves—honestly—you—won't...*(She breaks down laughing)*

CALVIN: *(Patiently, still smiling)* Come on...

SASHA: *(Laughing, almost unable to catch her breath)* No...for three...days...we...

CALVIN: Well, did you find where it went at least?

SASHA: *(Squeaking)* It was a girl dog! *(Continues laughing)*

CALVIN: *(Sits on the porch railing while she laughs)* Come on.

SASHA: *(Laughing)* It was funny.

CALVIN: I'll bet.

SASHA: It...was...a...girl dog.

CALVIN: *(Smiling)* Yes.

SASHA: *(Calming)* Oh, God! I'll—it was so funny. I'll come over. I really will. I'd like to see Silly Jill again. I never see her at school.

CALVIN: *(Still looking at her with the same smile)* You'd better.

SASHA: I will. I've been tied up in Spanish.

CALVIN: What are you taking, anyway?

SASHA: I don't know. Everything.

CALVIN: *(Still smiling at her)* I see you running to the Education Building at three.

SASHA: *(Calmed but pleasantly merry)* Elementary education. They're too young for anything; I'm practice-teaching a pack of terrors. Eight-year-olds.

CALVIN: *(Moving in a little closer)* What are you going to be, a school teacher?

SASHA: I *hope* not!

CALVIN: *(Closer)* An old maid teacher, huh?

SASHA: I hope to hell not. Not if I can help it. *(Just a touch nervously)* How is Jill, anyway? I never see her.

CALVIN: She's all right—better than most I suppose. Tell me about your pack of eight-year-olds. The terrors.

SASHA: I make it sound worse than it is—they're only eight of them; one boy and seven girls. It's a small class but they have the strength of lions. Lionesses, as it were. I call them my pride and joy. They don't have any idea what I'm talking about.

CALVIN: *(Fingering her skirt material. Feigning great interest in her story)* My...

SASHA: *(Wickedly)* My, my, yes—what-the-hell-are-you-*doing*?

CALVIN: My, what big eyes you have, teacher.

SASHA: *(Moving away slightly)* Yes, well, the better to see you with, my dear; and you better believe it.

CALVIN: What a large mouth you have.

SASHA: Yes, well, the better to—good god!

CALVIN: I never see you with many boys, you know?

SASHA: Oh, I don't know; how many?

CALVIN: Don't back off—come on over...

SASHA: Over where? Hey! That sounds like a great war song— *(Singing)* Over where! Over where!...Calvin! *(She opens the screen door)*

CALVIN: *(Crowding against her)* What's wrong?

SASHA: Come on.

CALVIN: What's wrong?

SASHA: Come on, Calvin...*(She is trying to go inside, he is trying to make her stay out. Speaking very fast)* You're a married man—you're pregnant—er—your *wife* is married—or to— Come on, Calvin—you're—good grief.. .*(Squeezing inside the screen door)* You're going to be a *father,* for Christ's sake! Good god!

CALVIN: *(Entering the living room)* What's wrong?

SASHA: Nothing. I just don't fancy myself hitting the sack with someone's father.

CALVIN: I'm not a father yet.

SASHA: Well, you're going to be. God.

CALVIN: Come on, you know I've always been interested in you, anyway.

SASHA: Yeah, well—me too, but you got married.

CALVIN: Yeah. And?

SASHA: Well, I just don't feel like an extra-curricu-
lar activity this evening. I may act like a terrible flirt, but I
am a very *puritanical young person.*

CALVIN: Bull!

SASHA: I belong to the Protestant Youth Group, for
Christ's sake!

CALVIN: Yeah, sure.

SASHA: I assume it's for Christ's sake.

CALVIN: Well, what does your little youth group do
when they get someone worked up into a hot panting lather?
Advise a cold shower, huh?

SASHA: Don't tell me you're really irritated.

CALVIN: A little, yeah. Yes, dammit, I am a little.

SASHA: Come on, stay back.

CALVIN: You didn't answer my question, what does
your group do after they have someone panting hot down
their collar?

SASHA: Collar hell.

CALVIN: Pants then?

SASHA: Well, we're working on it!

OWEN: *(Enters from his room. Looks up at both of
them, then down)* Oh.

SASHA: We'll think of something! *(She turns to face
Owen)*

OWEN: What's up? *(Sasha looks at him blankly for a
full count before she breaks into uproarious laughter and falls
rolling on the floor)* What's so darn funny?

SASHA: *(Still laughing)* Calvin.

OWEN: *(To Calvin)* You're what?

CALVIN: Never mind. *(To Sasha)* Very, very funny.

SASHA: *(Quieting)* Well, it was.

CALVIN: It wasn't really very— I didn't think.

OWEN: What?

CALVIN: Nothing. Mind your own business.

OWEN: Well, I only asked.

CALVIN: Well, don't.

OWEN: How's Jill?

CALVIN: What do you mean, how's Jill?

OWEN: Well, how's Jill?

SASHA: We were just talking about her.

CALVIN: Pregnant.

OWEN: How is she?

CALVIN: Jill is fine, Owen. *(Acidly)* Why?

OWEN: *(Beat)* What do you mean, why? Why do I ask? Well, because she's pregnant, and very often...

CALVIN: I probably would have brought it up, Owen, if anything were seriously wrong with my wife today.

SASHA: Oh, god! *(She sits at the table)* Where did Kenny run off to, I wonder? I thought he was going to watch for the sky rockets or whatever they were.

CALVIN: *(Repeating derisively)* "How's Jill?"

OWEN: Well, you didn't say anything all day...

CALVIN: Someday you'll check the compulsion to ask after her.

OWEN: Well, why should I? Jill's been my friend since Fresno. Before school even—

CALVIN: I'd just like to see you be able to bridle it once. It's just dragged out too goddamn long, you know?

OWEN: No, I don't know. I thought you came over here to tell us how Jill was getting along. I merely asked.

CALVIN: *(Calling)* Reen? Are you nearly finished with that thing? *(Opens the door)* Are you nearly finished?

IRENE: *(Off)* Oh. Yes, nearly, I am.

CALVIN: I have to get back before long.

OWEN: Well, she never comes over anymore or anything...

CALVIN: *(Turning from the door)* Owen, get off my back, will you!

IRENE: *(Entering)* It's very good, Calvin. I haven't finished. I feel like I've spent the afternoon in a bathysphere.

SASHA: What's it on?

IRENE: A report—one of their—I guess you can't call it a field trip—ocean trips. How is fishing, anyway?

CALVIN: I haven't been much.

IRENE: I always remember you and Kenny chasing around over the beach after the grunion.

CALVIN: It's crabs now; we're collecting for some firm—it should be starfish; if someone could think of a use for starfish they'd make a fortune overnight.

IRENE: Kenny's been thinking about abalone all week. You'll have to take him out again if it isn't too dangerous.

CALVIN: It isn't too. Kenny's a good diver.

IRENE: He still talks about the—what was it?

CALVIN: I don't remember. Some kind of jellyfish probably...

IRENE: *(To Sasha)* Calvin took him out on the boat on one of his afternoons—he's still talking about it.

CALVIN: There's no money in collecting—there's no money in fishing at all, as a matter of fact. I took a couple of tourists out last week. Ten bucks each. I made fifty dollars, so we're eating this week. That's more than I made all last month trying to fish.

OWEN: Well, I'd hope.

CALVIN: What?

OWEN: Well, that you're eating well. I mean it's rather important.

CALVIN: Yeah, well, don't lose any sleep.

OWEN: I do think about it as a matter—

CALVIN: *(Sharply)* Well, *don't (To Irene, breezily)* Hey, one of the tourists—a woman—you'd have loved her. I don't think the lady's principal interest was in the ocean. At least her attention was strongly divided.

IRENE: Really?

CALVIN: I probably would have, too—

SASHA: With people there?

CALVIN: No, she went out by herself. I thought something was funny when she asked. Of course, with people there is okay, too, but it's a different thing altogether. Anyway, I would have except you can't handle my boat and her at the same time. So I may have stumbled onto a whole new money-making proposition.

IRENE: Well, if it buys the bread...

CALVIN: So, Kenny can come out with me, only where he held the nets and the traps, now he can hold the helm. He'd like that, wouldn't he?

IRENE: Oh, he'd love it. Of course, it's not like fishing.

OWEN: *(To himself)* Christ!

CALVIN: Well, not exactly—but it pays pretty well, from what I hear. I could probably afford to give him a small wage. Or maybe on special occasions—like once a week—Sundays, maybe—*I'd* take the helm and let *him* earn a few bucks. See? We'll find a new way to make money out of that wreck of a boat yet.

SASHA: I love it. *(Singing lightly)* I love it. Sailing, sailing; over the bounding waves.

OWEN: I dislike discouraging you, but there's nothing new about male prostitution. *(With defensive irritation)* You don't have to go to all the trouble of going out on the ocean in a boat.

CALVIN: But that's the beauty of it...

OWEN: You can go down to the square and stand in front of Bradley's.

CALVIN: But, Owen, the beautiful thing is I'd have this great gimmick.

OWEN: It's as old as—

SASHA: Owen, you're so impossibly Victorian.

CALVIN: *He's* Victorian?

IRENE: I think it sounds like a very sound idea, Calvin; you'll have to try it out.

OWEN: It isn't funny.

CALVIN: Sure. And Kenny could sing—Rock a bye my baby. Or maybe like a gondolier. How about that?

IRENE: I don't think Kenny has much of a singing voice—

OWEN: I don't think it's funny at all.

CALVIN: Well, I work hard on my little boat. I'm just trying to think of something easier.

IRENE: On *that* boat I'm not sure that's easier.

OWEN: That's just disgusting.

CALVIN: *(An edge coming into his voice now)* Why disgusting?

OWEN: Just because your wife happens to be pregnant you think you can joke around...

CALVIN: *(Cutting in)* Owen, that doesn't even enter into—

OWEN: Don't tell me it doesn't.

CALVIN: *(Quickly, to audience)* What do you do? You take so much and then you slug him one, right?

SASHA: *(Overlapping some)* Really, Owen, you have to look at the practical side of it.

CALVIN: Reen, haven't you told him about the birds and the bees?

OWEN: I know what you're talking about. It's your attitude about everything.

CALVIN: Owen, you don't know anything.

OWEN: I know you think your wife's pregnant and you think it's perfectly all right to go around with other women until she's available again and I think that's just disgusting...!

CALVIN: I'm not serious, for Christ's sake, Owen!

OWEN: You feel you can turn to any old whore in town—you probably spend every night down at some whorehouse on the—

CALVIN: *(Irritated now. Taking the air altogether away from him. A leap up in volume)* Look—you better read up, Owen; my wife is four-and-a-half months pregnant and though I know there is no way for you to know about those things. And you'll never know about those things. You'll just float around in an amorous fog being vaguely, idealistically romantic, I can and I intend to sleep with Jill until six weeks before the baby's born and Jill intends for me to, so we really—

OWEN: *(Shocked)* You can not! You can not...

CALVIN: *(Cutting in)* Your stupidity is embarrassing, Owen. I can't stay, I'm sorry, Reen.

OWEN: You can't do that to Jill; I'm not going to let you—

CALVIN: *(Has picked up his books and started to leave. He turns)* You must discuss it with Jill if you happen to see her again.

OWEN: *(Rushing at him as he goes through the door)* You're a disgusting, maniacal, perverted—

(Calvin has stepped off the porch, he turns as Owen reaches him. He meets Owen and pushes him just backwards—almost gently—so Owen takes a hard awkward sitdown on the top step of the porch. Sasha has sat down inside at the table, trying to look invisible. Irene has come to the door, holding the screen open. The push cuts off Owen's line. Brief pause. Calvin speaks almost offhandedly, evenly)

CALVIN: Owen, I've been meaning to tell you. You make my wife nervous coming around the house and I can't have her upset just now. Usually, because you're Reen's son I overlook a lot, but I just don't want you around our house until well after our child is born, Owen. Good night, Reen. *(Exits. Owen has sat in stunned silence. He has difficulty getting up, which makes him madder. Screaming into the darkness after Calvin, across the beach)*

OWEN: You get the hell out of here and we don't ever want to see you around here ever—with—we don't want—with your filth and dirt—we— *(Looking as if for something to throw)* You cocksucker! You bastard! You pervert! You just get the hell away from—

IRENE: *(Coming from the doorway to him)* Owen—what on earth do you. Try—

OWEN: *(Turning on her as she reaches him. She is on the top step. Owen on the bottom step. He strikes out in rage—not very effectively)* Get away! You get away from here—get away from me—you're just as bad as he is. You—

IRENE: *(Grabbing his wrists and holding him firmly,*

for all her frailty. All lines are continuous) Stop it! Now just stop it! Owen!

OWEN: Why do you have him here? Why do you allow him here?

IRENE: —You're the only person in the family who doesn't like Cal—

OWEN: He's a monster to Jill. He's killing her—

IRENE: Why are you so jealous of him?

OWEN: *(Falls down in the sand on the steps)* He said I couldn't *see* her again. He said I couldn't see her.

IRENE: Why are you jealous of Calvin, Owen? I've never seen anything like it—

OWEN: *(Overlapping)* I can't see her—I love her! I love her!

IRENE: Owen, Jill has always been our friend and now she's married to Calvin and I firmly believe there isn't a soul in the world who would be better for her than Calvin is—

OWEN: *(Cutting in. Violent, long wail)* Meeeeeeeeee! Me! Me! Me! What are you *saying*.

IRENE: I mean it!

OWEN: He's ruining her life. He's making her callous and weary—he's ruined her—

IRENE: Owen, Jill's happy with Calvin—

OWEN: She isn't! I know she isn't! Can't you *see* that? She couldn't be!

IRENE: Calvin has a boat. He works like an idiot for her. He's a top graduate student at Scripps. He's a beautiful, fine young man, Owen.

(Joan enters, followed by Kenny in a moment, during the next speech. They stand away some)

OWEN: *(Getting up)* You don't understand a goddamn thing. I know that. You don't know Jill and neither does he. He should be over with her—instead he's God knows where and she's off at school and she's working until six after school and he's off on his boat and she's cleaning the house and he's playing pool and she's cooking and he's coming in at eight or nine and she's going off to concerts at night and he lets her when she should be resting and he's dragging her all over town to show off her pregnancy and not coming home till all hours—you don't know her. He doesn't love her—he doesn't worship her or her baby or her *woman-ness* or motherness— *(Breaking down some now)* Jill's the most beautiful thing in the world and she's carrying *life* in her and she's holding in her *body* all—the—*wonder* and *mystery*— *(Turns, running through the house)* You don't know her. None of you know her at all! You don't know her at all! *(He runs through the house into the kitchen)*

JOAN: What the hell's wrong with him? He's talking about Jill?

IRENE: *(Looks at Joan for a moment. With control)* He had a run-in with Calvin.

JOAN: *(Very detached)* Why doesn't he leave Calvin alone? He can't stay off that—

IRENE: Joan, he's in love with Jill. Go on in, Kenny.

JOAN: I don't believe that anymore—

IRENE: *(Tired, almost flatly)* You may not understand it, but...

JOAN: No, I think he believes he does. She's not a love, she's a religion for him.

IRENE: Yes, well, we know that.

JOAN: So was it bad, anyway? Or is he just puffed-up?

IRENE: Calvin told him he's not to see Jill again until after the baby's born.

JOAN: *(Bored)* Oh, god!

KENNY: How come?

IRENE: Kenny, go on in, please.

KENNY: Well, how come?

IRENE: I'm sure he didn't mean it—go on in, please.

(Kenny comes up on the porch but not inside)

JOAN: Well, I'm glad.

IRENE: Joan, I don't need you now—

JOAN: No, I really am. He's just been driving poor Jill out of her ever loving mind.

(Sasha comes to the door)

IRENE: I'm sure he has been, but that's nothing new to her.

JOAN: He can't expect Calvin to stand for that.

IRENE: Well, he isn't standing for it. I don't want to talk to you, Joan.

JOAN: He takes one look at her and his eyes get so large—*(Joan's line is continuous)*

SASHA: —Come on, lay off him, poor Owen.

JOAN: I mean physically dilated, pupils and all, that you just think you're going to drown in them.

KENNY: *(At "And all")* Really?

JOAN: I honestly think he thinks it's his baby—

SASHA: Oh, come on; he knows it isn't, that—

JOAN: I mean inside *him.*

IRENE: You're being ridiculous—please go inside.

JOAN: No, now, I'm very good at snap analysis.

IRENE: I really don't need you, Joan. Kenny, go on now.

JOAN: Well, maybe not that exactly, but—

SASHA: *(Cutting in)* How was Sunset Cliffs?

JOAN: *(Briefest pause)* What?

SASHA: How was your walk?

KENNY: She wasn't down at—

IRENE: Kenny. Kenny, did you go to the cliffs?

KENNY: Uh. *(Pause)* Uh. Do you think I'd do that?

IRENE: I'll find out.

KENNY: Are you going to check the clay on my boots?

IRENE: *(Tired)* Go on inside.

KENNY: Where's Owen?

SASHA: He's inside—in the kitchen.

(Kenny enters the house and walks toward the kitchen. Sasha, Joan and Irene stay in the same position)

KENNY: *(Rather quietly)* Hey, Owen?

(Owen comes to the door of the kitchen, holding one of the cans of beer)

OWEN: What?

KENNY: What did Cal say to you?

OWEN: Nothing. *(He goes back into the kitchen. Kenny sits at the table)*

JOAN: Irene? I have—

IRENE: Joan, go on in to bed, I don't want to talk to you right now.

SASHA: I have to go anyway; I have to get my things together. *(She goes in and picks up a book, stays around the table)*

JOAN: *(Very mother-to-daughter)* No, Irene, I want to tell you something—

IRENE: Good god, Joan; you haven't called me Irene in ten years. I don't want to talk just now.

JOAN: I want to tell you—

IRENE: I don't know why you want me to know. Why is it? What compulsion is it? Anyway, you don't need to bother.

JOAN: Bother what?

IRENE: You needn't bother. I don't feel like going through it now, Joan.

JOAN: What? *(Calling)* Sasha, what did you—

SASHA: What?

IRENE: Sasha didn't say anything. My god, my window's open, you—there— *(With a weak gesture to her window)* You weren't especially quiet. It wasn't anything all that clandestine, really.

JOAN: *(Near panic, but quietly)* W-what? What? I thought—

IRENE: Don't be so damn dumb, Joan. Go in!

JOAN: I want to tell you! I know it's terrible, I know—

IRENE: TELL ME WHAT? That you finally managed to seduce my boyfriend after what? Two years of trying? I should be interested in knowing the language you'd use to tell me that but I'm not for some reason.

JOAN: I didn't want to lie—about—I've never once—

IRENE: Yes, I know; well, if you want to tell me something, you tell me now. Tell me what he said to you; tell me what did he murmur in your ear; tell me how he smells when he's worked into a sweat over my nymph daughter. Did you scream his name out, tell me, or were you transported—

JOAN: —No, don't—Irene—

IRENE: —And was he? Did you manage to contrive a climax together or did you work on it slowly; tell me about his movement. What is it like to have intercourse with the man your mother is in love with? Did you want to tell me that? You tell me now.

JOAN: I only wanted not to lie. I'm ashamed, oh, don't—I wanted to— *(Looking inside)* Sasha, did you—!

IRENE: I'm not interested; I heard as much as I—

JOAN: No, now, don't—Sasha, go home! Stay out here, mother, I thought I was in love with—I want you to know what—

IRENE: *(With control)* Go on inside and go to bed, Joan.

JOAN: I don't want Clint. I don't want him now, and for years I've—

IRENE: Go inside to bed.

SASHA: *(Inside. Softly to Owen who is in the kitchen)* Good night, Owen.

JOAN: *(Fiercely)* Sasha, don't you come out here! *(Looking at her mother. Panicky)* I'm going to leave, anyway.

IRENE: No, you're not; you know you aren't.

JOAN: I want to leave, I can go up to—

IRENE: No, you don't even want to. If you wanted to you would.

JOAN: You don't want me to stay home, and I wouldn't either. I don't want...

IRENE: *(Only tired)* I'm not asking you to leave.

JOAN: Clint won't be back. I'm sure he won't.

IRENE: I didn't imagine he would.

JOAN: *(Pause)* I'm going in to bed. *(She pushes inside the door)*

SASHA: *(With her books)* I'm going.

JOAN: What did you say to her? What did you tell her?

SASHA: Nothing.

JOAN: You did, too.

KENNY: What?

OWEN: *(From the kitchen)* Kenny, come here.

KENNY: *(Entering the kitchen)* What?

JOAN: What did you know?

SASHA: Nothing. Until I started thinking about it.

JOAN: Yes, well, that's all you ever think about, though, isn't it?

SASHA: Not necessarily.

JOAN: But think is all you can do about it, isn't it? Turn to ice when anyone touches you, don't you?

SASHA: *(Turning toward the door)* I'm leaving.

JOAN: Good.

SASHA: Good night, Owen. Kenny.

OWEN: *(Appearing in the kitchen doorway. He has a beer. He is just tipsy)* Good night, Sasha.

KENNY: Night.

SASHA: *(Leaves. As she passes Irene)* Good night, Irene.

IRENE: Good night, Sasha. We'll see you tomorrow.

SASHA: *(Casually)* No. Not for a little while—I spend too much time here—I really do—I have a hell of a lot of work piled up anyway.

IRENE: O.K. Good night.

SASHA: *(She steps up on the porch and gives Irene a quick, brief hug)* Good night, Irene. *(Exits)*

KENNY: *(Singing, not too loudly)* There is. A Tavern in the Town.

OWEN: Shut up!

KENNY: In the town!

OWEN: *(To Joan)* What's wrong with you?

JOAN: Mind your own business. What is your business just now, anyway?

OWEN: My business is getting drunk.

JOAN: Well, skoal!

KENNY: *(To audience)* That's nearly my last line until the end when I have a little speech. That's the only single time I sing anything. *(Pause)* I've got a good singing voice, too. *(There is a bright burst of fireworks in the sky off left, with a corresponding ssssss sound)* They're at it again!! *(Running out)* They're at it again! Hey, Owen? Come on!

OWEN: *(Starting to run out)* Tell them to wait!

JOAN: Reen's out there, don't go out there.

OWEN: *(As the second burst appears)* Well, so what? *(He runs out, looking up)*

JOAN: Well, just leave her alone.

OWEN: What for? *(Outside)* You see it? Look at that!

KENNY: Wow. Only two?

OWEN: Watch it. Wow!

(Joan goes into her bedroom)

KENNY: That's all they ever do—boy, some day I'm going to ask them about that. I'll bet there's some great mystery. Hi, Reen.

IRENE: Hello. Bright, wasn't it?

OWEN: You see them both? *(To Kenny)* Find out what time it is. Maybe it's the same time every night.

KENNY: Roger. *(Runs in to look and back)*

OWEN: Yeah. What are you doing out here?

IRENE: Just taking in some air. It's going to be foggy tonight. Sasha should have stayed.

OWEN: Yeah. She loves that.

KENNY: *(Returning)* Ten-thirty-five on the button.

OWEN: You can still smell it. Sulphur. God, am I drunk. I think I drank all the beer for your picnic tomorrow.

KENNY: It's getting foggy, huh? They just barely made it tonight. I'll bet some nights you can't see them if the fog comes in early. Maybe they're signaling some ship out at sea, you think?

OWEN: Lost cause tonight if they are. They won't see it out very far.

IRENE: It's cold. You come on in. Did Joan go to bed?

KENNY: Yeah. *(He goes in)* It's really cold.

OWEN: God, Jill and I used to walk in the fog, remember? It was so thick you could hardly see the rocks. Of course it was dark, too.

IRENE: *(Goes up on the porch)* Come on in.

KENNY: *(To audience)* Actually it doesn't have anything at all to do with the story and then again it does, you know?

OWEN: Well, go on in, if you want to.

KENNY: *(To audience)* I'm freezing cold, with the lights even. Just talking about cold just freezes me. *(He wraps in a blanket on the sofa-bed)*

IRENE: The ocean is heavy, too. Hear it? Your father and I used to walk—he loved it. We used to walk along the beach and we'd talk for hours and plan. When I was carrying you. I used to sit out on the rocks with the water splashing around and think about how it'd be; how wonderful everything would be. It was wonderful, with the fog coming in.

OWEN: Did you? I wonder what I was thinking?

IRENE: Probably that it was cold.

OWEN: I don't think anything in the world is as beautiful as a pregnant woman, but I can't imagine you carrying me.

IRENE: You kicked like sin.

OWEN: I wasn't even born yet. God, how young.

IRENE: We're perpetually young, you and me; but I'm afraid that makes us pretty naive and pretty vulnerable.

OWEN: God, I'm drunk.

IRENE: Come on in.

OWEN: Walk around with me for a while and I'll fall asleep in a minute.

IRENE: Come on in, Owen. You'll get a cold. Or put on a jacket.

OWEN: In a minute.

IRENE: Soon then. *(She enters the living room and goes to Joan's room. Opens the door. Quietly)* Are you awake? *(Pause)* Good night. *(To Kenny)* Joan's asleep.

KENNY: Yeah. *(He kicks the blanket off)*

IRENE: Don't go to sleep there now.

KENNY: I *won't*. My gosh.

(Owen has been wandering around the yard. As if leading a band, he waves his hands in the air and yells very

loud, singing, exactly as the popular recording, with orchestration)

OWEN: Make the world! Go away! *(Now the violins, descending the scale)* Da, da, da, da, da, da, da, da! I don't! *(Stops abruptly. Sits)*

IRENE: *(Comes to the door)* Owen, you'll wake the whole neighborhood. You're drunk.

OWEN: I won't see her again. *(Pause)* He said I wouldn't see her again. *(Pause)* Well, do you think Calvin will be back over at least?

IRENE: I don't imagine. Go to bed.

OWEN: *(Entering)* When we move up to Fresno, we should—

IRENE: Go on, come on to bed.

OWEN: I'm dizzy. And I'm sleepy. *(He sits)*

IRENE: Go on to your room now. *(She sits in the chair)*

OWEN: *(Getting up)* You know what we could do, when we go up to Fresno? We could...

IRENE: Shhhhhh. Please, Owen.

OWEN: No, really, listen. When, what we should do...

IRENE: Shhhhh.

OWEN: *(Pause. Shrugs)* Okay. Listen. What's that?

IRENE: The ocean.

OWEN: God, it's heavy. Feel how damp it is? It's not like that in Fresno. I remember that, anyway. Good night now.

IRENE: Good night.

OWEN: Is Joan asleep?

IRENE: Yes.

OWEN: What's wrong with her, anyway?

IRENE: I don't know.

OWEN: I'm going to bed. *(Exits into his bedroom)*

IRENE: *(She is seated, her back to Kenny. Pause)* Kenny? *(Pause. Without looking over to him. This is a prompt. She whispers)* Kenny? Kenny? You're supposed to— *(She looks around. Kenny is asleep on the sofa. Irene goes to him quietly, shakes him very gently)* Kenny? *(Pause. Gently)*

Kenny? *(Hesitantly, she pulls the blanket up over him to his waist, tucking it into the back of the sofa and around him. She steps back)*
 OWEN: *(Off. Making his bed, faintly singing to himself from the bedroom.)*

Fare thee well for I must leave thee
Do not let the parting grieve thee
And remember that the best of friends must sometimes part.
Fare thee well for I must leave thee do not let the parting
 grieve thee; and remember that the best of friends must part.

 IRENE: *(Comes timidly, embarrassed, to the audience)* Ah...*(Almost apologetically)* This is the end of the play. *(She almost bows to the audience, turns and walks out of the house to stand on the porch, leaning against the house, pulling a sweater around her in the cold air. There is a moment's pause)*
 CALVIN, OWEN, JOAN, SASHA *and* CLINT: *(Everyone off-stage. Beginning softly, with a slight lilt, hum the first few bars of the song, moving naturally into da, da... until they reach the last line. Singing pleasantly, liltingly)* And may. The world go well with thee! *(The lights fade out)*

 Curtain

Peter Swet

THE INTERVIEW

Peter Swet

Peter Swet makes his initial appearance in *The Best Short Plays 1975* with *The Interview,* published for the first time in this collection.

When *The Interview* orginally opened in Manhattan in 1973, it was described by Howard Thompson of *The New York Times* as "One of the most effective theatre presentations in town. It is an expressive, dramatic piece, a conversational duel between a gentle old Jewish tailor and a tough insurance investigator, that ultimately catches fire and touches the heart." Other reviewers concurred. William A. Raidy in the *Long Island Press* declared that *The Interview* was "A powerful drama...Playwright Swet knows a great deal about dramatic force and gives his play an almost super-real quality...He has more than promise as a playwright and we certainly will be hearing again from its author."

The play, directed by Ted Story and superbly performed by Joey Fitter as the tailor and Richard Creamer as the "tough, arrogant insurance man, who is trapped in the corporation web," inspired drama critic Emory Lewis to write in *The Record:* "Peter Swet is a major new talent. He has a special gift for rich characterization, and his work exudes a radiant humanism seldom found in our theatre. His creations are full-bodied, not caricatures or stereotypes tossed in as thinly disguised editorials. He reminds me of a young Clifford Odets. He has written a remarkably sensitive and mature first play."

Peter Swet was born on September 25, 1942, in Ozone Park, Queens, which he describes as "a good working class section of the city, but so far removed from Manhattan in spirit that for years all the word "theatre" managed to conjure up for me was a mental picture of a *Last Picture Show* kind of movie house that reeked of popcorn and disinfectant and played lots of Randolph Scott."

The author received his first live theatre experience in 1957 when he was given some castoff tickets to a Broadway drama. The play was a notable failure, but the experience stimulated his interest in the theatre and when he graduated at age twenty from the University of Dayton, Ohio, he returned to New York and took his own apartment—in Manhattan this time—with the determination to make his mark on the theatre.

The first draft of *The Interview* was completed in 1967. By that time, though, financial and other pressures forced his attention away from playwriting, and he stashed the play away in a trunk in favor of pursuing another, seemingly more promising career, in advertising. His wife, Mary, whom he married in 1969, also had an excellent career as fashion editor for a major national magazine and together they continued to pursue and enjoy a life of increasing affluence. This was abruptly ended, though, when they were compelled to face each other one evening in 1971 with the stunning news that they both had lost their jobs on the same day. This was a major turning point because it was then decided, at his wife's insistence, that Mr. Swet turn all his efforts toward his real ambition of writing for the theatre while she supported them both with another full time job.

The Interview received its first exposure at the Gene Frankel Theatre Workshop, where Mr. Swet was a member of the Playwright's Unit. In a professional theatre atmosphere for the first time, he was able to rework the play to the point when it was ready for an audience, and Frankel presented it as a weekend showcase at the old Mercer Arts Center. The play proved to be very popular with audiences, and near the end of its twice-extended engagement, it began to attract the attention of critics. With uniformly outstanding reviews, the decision was made to reopen the play, but this time on a commercial basis. Shortly after five o'clock on the evening that the play was to reopen, however, the Mercer Arts Center came crashing to the ground, lost forever in the tragic collapse of the Broadway Central Hotel, where it had been housed.

The only thing that seemed not to be lost was the play itself, which continues to be popular with audiences and which has since enjoyed several additional productions in New York, most notably at Town Hall, the Bouwerie Lane

Theatre, Theatre In Space, and at the Theatre De Lys Matinee Series. It is currently being translated into French for a projected Paris production.

The author maintains a close relationship with the Gene Frankel Theatre Workshop, which recently produced his second play, *Debris,* and plans to present his future works.

Peter Swet now lives on the Upper West Side of Manhattan with his wife and their newly born son, Matthew, under circumstances that are "happier, though far more humble, than ever before."

Characters:

ABRAHAM MOSCOWITZ
SHANNON

Scene:

The tailor shop of Abraham Moscowitz, New York City.

A small, rather tattered-looking shop in the Canal Street area of Manhattan. There is a cluttered work table with an old-fashioned sewing machine, the kind formerly operated by foot treadle but now fitted with an electric motor. Behind the table, a plain wooden chair facing out toward the audience. Beneath the table, a large waste paper basket filled to overflowing with garment scraps and just to the left, a large pile of additional scraps. These are all of the same dismal tones of gray and black as the cheap old secondhand suits that fill the many garment racks which crowd the room everywhere except for the sewing area and a small working area at center. The working area consists simply of a cleared space where Abie can sit on the comfortably padded straight back chair that is located there, a good place for doing any handwork that may be necessary. From the work area, a path of sorts cuts to the front of the store located at stage left. Here we see the entrance to the shop, a narrow door, glass, but covered by a ragged shade drawn throughout the proceedings. Beyond the door, there is a large window, with shades similarly drawn. At the side of the window, clearly visible to the audience, there is an old faded sign, which reads:

A. MOSCOWITZ
—FINE ALTERATIONS—

Immediately beneath this is another sign, also old and faded, and obviously hand-lettered at one point by Abie himself. This sign reads:

SECONDHAND CLOTHING
Fitted Like New

Broad pools of light from ancient shaded fixtures lo-

*cated overhead illuminate the work area, the entran-
ceway and some racks of clothing. With the lighting
concentrated as it is toward the center, we have just a
notion of the true dimensions of the room and what old,
forgotten objects and materials may be lying in its hidden, dusty corners.*

*Abie is sixty-three years old, although he actually
appears to be somewhat older. He is slightly stooped
from so many years of bending over garments and,
though he tries to keep up appearances by wearing a
shirt and tie, his pants are wrinkled and baggy and the
collar points of his rather dingy shirt are bent upwards
and frayed.*

*Abie is at work, running a garment through the sew-
ing machine. Soon, however, he takes the garment (a
pair of men's trousers) to the chair at center for some
handwork. As he sits there with needle and thread, we
hear a knock at the door. Behind the door is Shannon,
the insurance investigator, a man of average build and
height, about forty-five years old, with dark, thinning
hair. He is brusquely efficient at his job, facing it with a
kind of forced pleasantness that occasionally serves to
make his own sense of discontent that much more appar-
ent. He wears a suit, an overcoat and business hat, all
of which, although fairly neat, are not of the best quality and are several years out of fashion. He carries a
timeworn briefcase.*

NOTE: *The name "Moscowitz" is pronounced quite
differently by the two characters throughout the entire
play. Shannon uses the Americanized Moscowich, with
strongest emphasis on the first syllable, while Abie in-
sists on the correct pronunciation, Mu-SCO-veetz,
with strongest emphasis on the second syllable.*

ABIE: *(Approaching the locked door)* Who? *(We hear
a muffled reply)* Who?

(He opens the door a crack, leaving the chain lock on)
Who is it? We are closed now.

SHANNON: Mr. Moscowich?

ABIE: What is it?

SHANNON: Are you Mr. Moscowich?

ABIE: *(After a brief pause, during which he eyes Shannon up and down)* You want to buy a suit?

SHANNON: No. I'd like to talk to Abraham Moscowich.

ABIE: Mos-*co*-vitz. Abraham Mos-*co*-vitz. What is it?

SHANNON: I want to talk to you about your insurance.

ABIE: Insurance? I got plenty of insurance. I don't need no more.

(He tries to close the door but Shannon forces it back)

SHANNON: All I want is a few minutes of your time to talk to you about...

ABIE: Talk? You want to talk?

SHANNON: Yes.

ABIE: Good. Make a left and two doors down there's a florist shop with two women in it with one mouth bigger than the other. They'll talk. But me, I'm too busy now. *(He tries to close the door)*

SHANNON: Hey, I'm not a salesman, Mr. Moscowich. I'm here to talk to you about your insurance policy.

ABIE: What's this?

SHANNON: Didn't you just apply for an extension on your life insurance policy a couple of weeks ago?

ABIE: Could be. So?

SHANNON: Well, I have to talk to you before it can be approved.

ABIE: *(Annoyed, opens the lock and Shannon stands in the doorway)* What is it?

SHANNON: My name is Jim Shannon, Mr. Moscowich. *(Offers his hand, which Abie weakly accepts)* I'm an insurance investigator.

ABIE: Insurance investigator?

SHANNON: Yes.

ABIE: Mr. Shannon?

SHANNON: That's right. Do you mind if I come in for a few minutes? *(He moves further into the shop)*

ABIE: So what's an insurance investigator? I don't know nothing about investigators.

SHANNON: Well, sir, your policy is now being considered for approval, you see. And before it's approved, I have to talk to you for a few minutes. Just to check out a few things, you know, your background, your health, make sure you haven't robbed any banks lately *(Laughs, but stops at Abie's sour expression)* That sort of thing. *(He draws Abie's chair over to the sewing table and sits down at the chair that's already there, indicating that he wishes Abie to sit, too)*

ABIE: *(Drawing his chair back to its original position)* Hey, mister. I have to tell you. I'm not so sure I like this. I'm a busy man. You couldn't call first and make an appointment? That's not a common courtesy?

SHANNON: *(Removing a clipboard, pencil and questionnaire from his briefcase, prepares to take down information)* Sorry if I caught you at a bad time, but I can't work from appointments. I just have too many cases to handle.

ABIE: So, you just drop in on people. And, that way, maybe you'll catch them doing something they shouldn't be, uh?

SHANNON: Well...

ABIE: And what did you think you'd find a sixty-three year old man doing in a tailor shop at seven o'clock at night? Having a hot time? Smoking some of that LSD? Come on, mister. I don't think I like this. You better leave.

SHANNON: Mr. Moscowich, look...

ABIE: Mos-*co*-vitz.

SHANNON: You're going to have to go through this some time, so it might as well be right now.

ABIE: Mr....Shannon, is it? *(Shannon nods)* There are some things a man must do. A man must live. A man must die. A man must suffer for his sins. But a man does not have to be at the beck and call of his insurance company any time of night or day. That's where you're from, right? From the insurance company?

SHANNON: Right.

ABIE: So tell me. What is the name of my insurance company?

SHANNON: Look. All I'm going to do is ask a few questions, do a little background check on you, and if everything is all right, your policy will be approved. No problem.

ABIE: Yes. Mister. But I ask you the name of the insurance company.

SHANNON: All right. I'm not from the insurance company directly. I'm from the National Investigations Bureau. We're a company that specializes in doing insurance investigations, and that's why I'm here, Mr Moscowich, to do an investigation on you.

ABIE: Investigations?

SHANNON: Right.

ABIE: On me?

SHANNON: Yes. All we want to do is determine the risk, that's all.

ABIE: Risk? What risk? I already got one policy with this company, mister. They know me for a long time. All right, so I'm sixty-three years old, so for that I have to pay an extra bigger premium, but what risk? I pay my bills, is that what they want to know? I pay my bills! No risk!

SHANNON: Come on, Mr. Moscowich. Risk involves more than credit, you know that. Now, all I want you to do is answer a few questions and verify some information for me, all right?

ABIE: Just a minute. So maybe you are from this investigations company. Still, you must tell me the name of my insurance company!

SHANNON: Here. Let me show you my credentials. *(Removes wallet, showing Abie)* You see, don't you, where it says "James T. Shannon, Insurance Investigator"?

ABIE: Yes, yes. *(Points to his sign)* And you see, don't you, where it says "A. Moscowitz, Fine Alterations"? That sign don't make me what I am. What I have here in my hands—what I do with this suit—the things that I have buried deep in my head—*these* are the things that make me what I am. If you are who you say you are, don't show me a business card. Tell me the name of the company!

SHANNON: I work by account number. That's all that I need.

ABIE: You mean, you don't even know the name of the company? Look, I'm sorry, mister...

SHANNON: Mr. Moscowich we're a big company. We have hundreds of customers, and this is just the best way for us to do business, that's all.

ABIE: So you don't even know who you're doing this for. *(Urging Shannon out)* No. Come on.

SHANNON: Look, I don't make up the rules. These things are figured out way ahead of time by people who know a lot more about it than you or me. And people like you and me, we just have to follow it.

ABIE: This you believe?

SHANNON: Sure I do.

ABIE: This you accept?

SHANNON: What else can you do?

ABIE: Well, in my language there is a perfect word for men who believe this way.

SHANNON: What's that?

ABIE: Schmuck.

SHANNON: *What?*

ABIE: You want me to translate?

SHANNON: *(Quietly threatening)* Look here, Mr. Moscowich, there's an awful lot I have to put up with in my line of work, but if there's one thing that I will not stand for, it's abusive language!

ABIE: What's abusive? Every man is entitled to an opinion. This is my opinion about this crazy system of yours. So you just go now and leave me alone! I'm working and I'm busy and I got a deadline on this suit for tomorrow morning and you make me nervous, and you make my head like I don't know what. *(Shannon has begun to take notes)* What's this? What are you writing?

SHANNON: Never mind, Mr. Moscowich.

ABIE: What's this you are writing?

SHANNON: Just doing my job.

ABIE: So tell me what you write about me!

SHANNON: All right. You said you were nervous, didn't you?

ABIE: No! No! I am not a nervous *man*. What I mean is that *you, you* make me nervous, you and this crazy system of yours, mister! So leave! *Tell* them I am a nervous man, I don't care! If this is what the company wants to do for a little insurance, then I take my business someplace else! So go! *(Shannon packs his things)* That's it!

SHANNON: You know, of course, that I'll have to finish this report on you, anyway.

ABIE: So...go. Do it, I don't care what you do. I don't like you snoops coming around here trying to find reasons why I can't have my policy.

SHANNON: I never hand in a partial report, you see, never. When my customers order a report, they get what they pay for. So don't think I'm going to stop here. There are other ways of getting information, you know, other people to talk to.

ABIE: What are you saying?

SHANNON: Those talkative little ladies in the florist shop, for one thing.

ABIE: No. No, you don't want to talk to...

SHANNON: I don't miss a trick, Mr. Moscowich. I think you should know that. I've been very reasonable up to now. But business is business.

ABIE: I stop you. They don't tell you anything.

SHANNON: Stop me from talking to an informant? Then you have something to hide?

ABIE: Hide? Me? What have I got to hide?

SHANNON: That's exactly what I'm going to find out. You wouldn't be in such a hurry to see me leave, would you, if you thought I was the kind of man who'd automatically approve your policy.

ABIE: I don't need you. I go to another company.

SHANNON: *(At the door)* Oh, sure, go ahead. But I'll tell you something. The company you change to will probably be just another one of our customers, and in that case... I'll be back.

ABIE: No.

SHANNON: And by the time I get back, my file on Abraham Moscowich isn't going to look too good.

ABIE: *(With a start)* File?

SHANNON: *(Stops abruptly, and slowly turning around)* Yes. A file. Of course.

ABIE: I...I don't understand you with your questions and your...files. I never go through anything like this for insurance before.

SHANNON: Oh, you don't think so?

ABIE: What?

SHANNON: Your original policy. 1957. You remember that, don't you?

ABIE: Yes...yes.

SHANNON: A ten thousand dollar policy.

ABIE: Yes.

SHANNON: And it was approved.

ABIE: Yes, yes. But nobody ever came around for questions and information.

SHANNON: Oh, yes, Mr. Moscowich. We were there, all right. I have your old file right in my office. Oh, we didn't speak to *you* at the time. We spoke to your neighbors.

ABIE: My neighbors? You spoke to my neighbors?

SHANNON: Oh, no, not me! I didn't handle that case myself. That was a very simple investigation. It didn't even require a personal interview. All the investigator had to do on that case was just ask around a little bit, you know, just to make sure you were alive. I wouldn't handle a case like that. I only handle the really big cases, the ones that require the most thorough investigations, the ones that involve a lot of money. That was a much smaller policy than the one you're applying for now.

ABIE: Smaller? Why smaller? I'm applying for another ten thousand.

SHANNON: Oh, no. That's not what *I* show.

ABIE: What? How much do they say?

SHANNON: One hundred thousand dollars.

ABIE: One hundred thou...mister, that is crazy. I don't want so much...

SHANNON: What are you, changing your mind now?

ABIE: No. I want ten thousand.

SHANNON: You put in for a hundred thousand, didn't you?

ABIE: No. No. I didn't.

SHANNON: Mr. Moscowich, I happen to be the most experienced man in my entire office. They wouldn't waste my time on anything less than a hundred thousand. Why, just an hour ago I interviewed one of the most powerful businessmen in this entire country. Sat there right in his office, a room three times the size of this, Picassos on the wall and everything else. That's the kind of man I'm used to talking to, Mr. Moscowich, the men with the real power, the men who buy a million dollar insurance policy the way you buy a subway token! Now, if all you applied for was another ten thousand dollar policy, there would be a much, much smaller investigation. And they wouldn't need the services of James T. Shannon for that!

ABIE: Oh, so this is it. You are the man they send to talk to all the hot shots, uh? Well, don't you see? Your machines, your computers, or whatever you got there, they make a mistake! One too many zeros they put in! *(Taking a pencil, he marks the correction on Shannon's sheet. Shannon quickly pulls the sheet away and erases the correction)* So now, instead of saying ten thousand like it should, it says a hundred thousand. *(Conciliatory)* Oh, all this waste of time for nothing, uh? Well. You go now and tell them to send around the kind of man they should be sending out for just a little ten thousand dollar investigation. O.K.? *(Tries to usher Shannon to the door)* So come on.

SHANNON: So you think there's some kind of mistake, do you?

ABIE: Sure. It's not obvious?

SHANNON: Mr. Moscowich, I don't make mistakes.

ABIE: But...

SHANNON: All I know is that your insurance company has ordered a thorough investigation based on a one hundred thousand dollar policy. And I intend to give them what they're paying for.

ABIE: What? You mean you can't see this mistake? You can't look around this palace of mine and know that I'm not a man to take out a hundred thousand?

SHANNON: *(With a wry smile, gazing directly at Abie)* I don't like being called a schmuck, Mr. Moscowich.

ABIE: *(More to himself)* Oh. Oh, so you are a man who believes in... retribution.

SHANNON: I'm a man who believes in doing his job, that's all. I have this sneaky little feeling that you're trying to put one over on the insurance company, Mr. Moscowich, and I'm just the man to find out what it is. *(He removes his coat, throws it on the chair)* I am going to finish my investigation right now. And you are going to sit there and answer my questions. I don't think you realize just what kind of man you're dealing with here, Mr. Moscowich.

ABIE: *(Quietly)* I think I do.

SHANNON: *(Removing materials from briefcase)* All right. Now, it's important that you answer all of these questions completely and to the best of your ability, and it's only fair to advise you that any false, misleading or erroneous information can result in the immediate cancellation of your policy. Your name: Abraham Moscowich. M-o-s-c-o-w-i-t-z. Is that correct? *(No answer)* Is that correct, Mr. Moscowich?

ABIE: *(Quietly)* Yes. Mos-*co*-vitz.

SHANNON: And your address ... 3301 Ocean Parkway?

ABIE: ... 3301 ... yes.

SHANNON: In Brooklyn?

ABIE: Yes.

SHANNON: Is that a private home? *(Pause)* Mr. Moscowich, is that a private home?

ABIE: No... no... an apartment.

SHANNON: How big?

ABIE: Uh?

SHANNON: How many rooms?

ABIE: Oh...four...four-and-a-half.

SHANNON: Is that four or four-and-a-half rooms?

ABIE: I don't know...It looks like four. They call it four-and-a-half.

SHANNON: Four-and-a-half. Is that rented or cooperative?

ABIE: Rented.

SHANNON: How much rent do you pay?

ABIE: Sixty-five dollars a month.

SHANNON: You're a widower, is that correct?

ABIE: Yes...yes, that is correct.

SHANNON: You live alone, then?

ABIE: I live alone.

SHANNON: You have one son, is that right?

ABIE: Yes. A son.

SHANNON: And he's married?

ABIE: That's right.

SHANNON: Any other children...*(No answer)*...Mr. Moscowich, *do you have any other children?*

ABIE: *(Pause)* No, no...no.

SHANNON: How tall are you?

ABIE: Tall? I don't know. Five foot, six inches.

SHANNON: Five-six. You must be sure, Mr. Moscowich. Are you sure?

ABIE: Yes, yes. Five-foot-six.

SHANNON: How much do you weigh?

ABIE: Uh...one-fifty, one-sixty.

SHANNON: Is that one-*fifty* or one-*sixty?*

ABIE: Uh...around there...between there.

SHANNON: All right, one-fifty-five. Have you ever been hospitalized? *(Pause)* I *say,* have you ever been hospitalized, Mr. Moscowich?

ABIE: Huh?

SHANNON: *Have you ever been in a hospital?*

ABIE: Hospital? No...no.

SHANNON: Describe your health. Are you in good health?

ABIE: ...Yes, yes...yes.

SHANNON: *(Rapidly)* In yourself, your family or any other blood relations, has there ever been any history of heart disease, cancer, tuberculosis, diabetes, mental trouble, or any hereditary, contagious, or communicable disease?

ABIE: Uh, no...no...no.

SHANNON: All right, then. Your date of birth, 8/17/10. Could that be right?

ABIE: 1910...1910...I am sixty-three. So you think I look older? Life works harder on some people, that's all. But I am in good health, knock wood.

SHANNON: Are you superstitious?

ABIE: You make me laugh, mister. Superstition is for fools. That was an expression only. I am...I try to be...a religious man.

SHANNON: Have you had any military experience?

ABIE: Military? No...no.

SHANNON: Have you ever been rejected for the draft?

ABIE: So now you think I'm a teen-ager?

SHANNON: Mr. Moscowich, the Selective Service Act was passed in this country in 1940, which means that you could have been eligible for the draft, since you were only thirty years old at the time. Now, have you ever been rejected for the draft?

ABIE: When I was a young man, mister, I was not in this country.

SHANNON: And where were you, then? Are you from...Russia?

ABIE: Yes. I am from Russia originally. I was born there.

SHANNON: I'll bet you're wondering how I knew that. It's your name. Moscowich.

ABIE: Mos-*co*-vitz.

SHANNON: It has "Moscow" in it. Like my name's Shannon, so my family's originally from Ireland. Oh, yeah, I *notice* little things like that, Mr. Moscowich. Every little detail. Now when did you leave Moscow?

ABIE: It wasn't Moscow.

SHANNON: Oh?

ABIE: You see? You took a guess. You ask a question that's not on your form, and you are wrong. No. It was just a little town, called Afimievsk.

SHANNON: Affie...

ABIE: A-f-i-m-i-e-v-s-k.

SHANNON: When did you leave?

ABIE: I was very young, maybe six years old.

SHANNON: So that would put it at about, uh, 1916. Why did you leave?

ABIE: But this is so long ago.

SHANNON: I want to know why your family decided to leave this, uh, Affimivek.

ABIE: Afimievsk. We didn't decide, mister. The officials, the soldiers, they decided for us.

SHANNON: Oh. It was the, uh...the...

ABIE: The pogroms. Yes, of course that's what it was. They kicked us out.

SHANNON: Where did you go then?

ABIE: Well, my whole family had to split up. And me...they sent me to live with relatives, in Poland...in Warsaw.

SHANNON: And when did you come to our country?

ABIE: Your country? *(A small laugh)* 19...46. Mr. Shannon, you are a Catholic?

SHANNON: What of it?

ABIE: Do you go to confession?

SHANNON: Look, it's not part of my job to discuss religion. Now you came here...

ABIE: I am only asking, that's all. You go to confession?

SHANNON: Well, when I was a kid, maybe...listen, what is this?

ABIE: You went when you were a child. But now ...no more sins to confess?

SHANNON: Now, you said you came here in 1946...

ABIE: Just one question. I have always wanted to know. When you go to the confession, does the priest draw your sins from you?

SHANNON: Mr. Moscowich. 1946.

ABIE: Does he ask you questions and make you confess?

SHANNON: Well, sometimes, if you can't remember everything you did, he might...

ABIE: And when you leave, you know that you are forgiven? Your conscience is clear?

SHANNON: Well, that's the whole idea, isn't it? Come on, now. 1946. You came here in 1946. What did you do then?

ABIE: I had an uncle. He was able to escape from Poland, and he took my son with him. I came to join them here. Yes. 1946. After the war. After I got out of the...hospital.

SHANNON: Hospital? Hospital? You told me you were never hospitalized. I'm going to have to start getting the *truth* here, Mr. Moscowich. Now, *when* were you in the hospital? For how long?

ABIE: For...for seven months...after the war.

SHANNON: Seven months? What was your condition?

ABIE: It was...it was the war.

SHANNON: Mr. Moscowich, you just told me that you never had any military experience, right?

ABIE: Yes.

SHANNON: Then how can you say you were hospitalized because of the war? Were you recuperating from something? Were you recuperating from a...oh, no. But you have to say it.

ABIE: Yes...that's what it was.

SHANNON: *You* have to tell me.

ABIE: Yes. I'm telling you! That's what it was!

SHANNON: Say it.

ABIE: You are right! You are right!

SHANNON: Come out and say it! What was it?

ABIE: A...concentration camp!

SHANNON: Well. You should just come right out

and tell me these things. Now, how long were you there?

ABIE: Two years.

SHANNON: And what was the reason for your hospitalization?

ABIE: Mister... it was... it was... How can you ask?

SHANNON: Well, I have to know if there was anything that might affect your policy.

ABIE: Starvation, mister? Does that affect my policy? *(With sarcasm)* No, it was nothing, nothing for your files. When they released me, I was just like a new man, just like nothing ever happened. All right?

SHANNON: How long have you had this shop?

ABIE: Twenty, twenty-one years.

SHANNON: Is that twenty or twenty-*one* years, Mister Moscowich?

ABIE: 1950, about.

SHANNON: 1950! That's twenty-three years. And what were you doing from 1946, when you came here, until 1950, when you opened this shop?

ABIE: I was a tailor. I worked for my uncle. I learned the business from him, in his shop on Grand Street.

SHANNON: What address?

ABIE: Near Orchard Street. I don't remember.

SHANNON: What was the name of the shop?

ABIE: "Moses' Fine Alterations." That was my uncle... Moses Abrams.

SHANNON: Where is he now?

ABIE: Dead. He died in 1950. Then I took my own shop. Here.

SHANNON: What was the cause of his death?

ABIE: I don't know. Old age. Heart attack, I suppose.

SHANNON: You said before that there was no history of heart disease in your family. Didn't you? Well, *didn't you?*

ABIE: I did?

SHANNON: You did!

ABIE: I... don't...

SHANNON: All right, I'll ask again. In your family,

in your blood relations, any history of cancer, tuberculosis, mental disease, diabetes, heart disease, or hereditary, contagious or communicable disease?

ABIE: ...Yes. My uncle...Moses. He died from a heart attack...I think.

SHANNON: Do you work alone?

ABIE: Yes.

SHANNON: Then this is a private proprietorship?

ABIE: Yes.

SHANNON: Then it's not a corporation or a partnership?

ABIE: Correct.

SHANNON: And you do not hire help?

ABIE: No.

SHANNON: Describe the work that you do.

ABIE: Look! See what I do! Look at the sign. Look in my hands, I am a tailor of men's clothing. Can't you see that? You have eyes?

SHANNON: Come on, now, Mr. Moscowich...

ABIE: And say Mos-*co*-vitz!

SHANNON: Is there anything hazardous about your job?

ABIE: Hazard. What hazard. I sit here and I sew. And I use a sewing machine, and I make chalk marks on clothes. *What* hazard. I prick my finger with a pin sometimes. Am I dead? No. Look.

SHANNON: What is your religion?

ABIE: Religion? I look like a cardinal?

SHANNON: Just answer the question, please, Mr. Moscowich.

ABIE: Mister, I am a Jew. Can't you put together even two and two for yourself?

SHANNON: Hebrew. All right. Are you an American citizen?

ABIE: Yes. Yes, I am a citizen.

SHANNON: This question is a formality, Mr. Moscowich. Please answer "yes" or "no": Have you ever advocated the violent overthrow of our present form of government?

ABIE: Here on Canal Street, mister, a man who fixes cuffs is not a rebel.

SHANNON: "Yes" or "no," Mr. Moscowich.

ABIE: No! Of course no! What kind of questions are these?

SHANNON: Just answer them, will you please?

ABIE: But these questions tell you nothing! *(Mocking)* Do you advocate the...

SHANNON: Listen, each and every question is obviously important to the insurance company, or I wouldn't have to ask them, don't you understand? They're all figured out way ahead of time...

ABIE: Yes, yes, I know. By people who get paid to sit around and think up stupid questions, right? Well, I have a question for *you*, Mr. Shannon!

SHANNON: Look, if there's any questions to be asked around here, I'm...

ABIE: Do they laugh at you? *(Shannon is stunned into momentary silence)* I mean these big hot shot businessmen of yours, when you go in there with your briefcase and your pencils and these questions, they take you seriously?

SHANNON: *(Controlled)* At the bottom of my form, Mr. Moscowich, there's a question that says, "Do you recommend?" and *I'm* the one who says "yes" or "no." And don't think I'm afraid to say "no," no matter who it might be. I can dig up an awful lot on some of these sons of bitches out there, and they know it. They take me seriously, all right. And I suggest you do the same thing. Now...

ABIE: But these sons of bitches, these are the men with the Picassos on the wall, right?

SHANNON: Look, I don't care if they've got the whole damn Sistine Chapel! It's not my job to worry about...

ABIE: And these sons of bitches, they're the ones who have the real power, uh? They're the ones who buy a million dollars insurance the way you and me buy a subway token, right?

SHANNON: Yeah, right. So what?

ABIE: So what do *you* get out of it, Mr. Shannon?

SHANNON: *(Pause)* Me? Don't you worry about me, Mr. Moscowich, I do all right.

ABIE: Sure. That's why you have to work overtime, uh? And at the end, Mr. Shannon, after thirty or forty years of talking to your big time hot shots, what do you get then? A little handshake? A nice backslap? Good work, Mr. James T. Shannon.

SHANNON: You want to know? All right, I'll tell you. Number one, we get a pension, Mr. Moscowich, which takes care of us for life. Then we get free medical coverage for life, and life insurance too, which means that when I'm sixty-three years old, I won't have to worry about applying for a policy! And even the home office sends up a little something. Usually, it's a...it's a little, uh...well, it's a nice big basket of fruit.

ABIE: *(Pause)* That's nice.

SHANNON: All right, that might not seem like much but, well, they do show their appreciation.

ABIE: You lie to yourself, Mr. Shannon. It's all right, it's all right. I lie to myself, too. The only thing that's wrong with it is that it doesn't work. The truth about yourself has a way of, uh *(He indicates completion of the thought by using a rolling hand motion),* right?

SHANNON: I don't lie to myself, Mr. Moscowich.

ABIE: No? You are a clever man, Mr. Shannon, much smarter than this job allows you to be. Smarter, maybe, than some of these hot shots with the Picassos, uh?

SHANNON: Oh, I don't know about *that.*

ABIE: Oh, so you mean that this is all you are capable of, to be an insurance investigator?

SHANNON: I didn't say that.

ABIE: *(Ignoring Shannon's last remark; with sarcasm)* Well, then you should consider yourself very lucky, Mr. Shannon. It's not every man who realizes his full potential in life.

SHANNON: *(Quickly)* I didn't say anything like that.

ABIE: *(Same)* You are blessed!

SHANNON: *(Same)* No. Look...

ABIE: *(Same)* One in a million!

SHANNON: *(Same)* I didn't say I wasn't capable of anything else, I...There's a lot of other things I could've done, but...Now, don't get me wrong. I mean, there's nothing wrong with being an insurance investigator.

ABIE: No.

SHANNON: I mean, it's all right.

ABIE: Sure. It's a good job.

SHANNON: Oh, there was a time, maybe...but I guess those are the breaks, that's all. You should know a lot about the breaks, Mr. Moscowich.

ABIE: Yes. And now you are stuck.

SHANNON: You learn to live with what you've got.

ABIE: So you learn to live with being an insurance investigator, uh, and you don't think you are living a lie? You know, it's very strange that you should be here, Mr. Shannon. More than just a coincidence, I think.

SHANNON: All right. All right. Let's drop this now and just get on with the investigation, okay?

ABIE: Sure, by all means. Investigate. Go ahead. Continue asking these questions for a company you don't even know the name of! *(Rising, moving toward Shannon)* For a system that makes no sense to you! Continue your lie, go ahead, and if you do your job like a good boy, there is waiting for you at the end of the line a little pension and a nice, fresh basket of fruit!

SHANNON: Hey, just what do you think you're doing, anyway?

ABIE: I have met men like you before, Mr. Shannon. Oh, yes. You say, "What can I do? It's the system," and meanwhile you know better than that. That makes you a *real* schmuck, the worst kind of schmuck, because you're smart enough to know better!

SHANNON: All right, I think I've had enough of this!

ABIE: Face the truth, schmuck!
(Overlapping)

SHANNON:	ABIE:
You think you're clever, don't you?	Schmuck.

(Overlapping)

SHANNON:	ABIE:
You think you're going to throw me off track, get me on the defensive, and and maybe I'll forget what I started out to do, uh? *Stop calling me schmuck!*	Schmuck! *Schmuck!* Schmuck!

SHANNON: I said that's enough! Now you sit down. *(He shoves Abie)*

ABIE: You know it, don't you, schmuck!

SHANNON: *(Pushing Abie back into his chair)* I SAID SIT DOWN! Now. I'm warning you, I've taken all I'm going to take from you! I'm going to get to the bottom of this whole shit you're trying to pull, and you are not going to open that mouth of yours unless it's to answer my questions, is that clear?

ABIE: *(Submitting)* Yes.

SHANNON: Yes, Mr. Shannon!

ABIE: Yes...Mr....Shannon.

SHANNON: All right! *(The interview now takes on the appearance of an intense interrogation. Shannon does not record the answers)* Now! How much do you earn a year?

ABIE: Seven, eight thousand dollars.

SHANNON: *(Overlapping)* Seven or eight!

ABIE: It varies.

SHANNON: Seventy-five hundred! Any other source of income?

ABIE: No...none.

(Overlapping)

SHANNON:	ABIE:
No stocks? No bonds? No real estate? No other business interests? No investments? Nothing?	No, no...Nothing, no no... No, no, none... Nothing, only this... No... No.

SHANNON: What is the net worth of this business?

ABIE: I don't know.

SHANNON: Your gross annual sales?

ABIE: I don't know.

SHANNON: Your net worth?

ABIE: I don't know.

SHANNON: Don't you even know your *worth*, Mr. Moscowich?

ABIE: No.

SHANNON: Where is your bank?

ABIE: First National City. Mott Street.

SHANNON: How much do you have in the bank?

ABIE: Three, four...

SHANNON: Three or four!

ABIE: Three thousand, four hundred, change.

SHANNON: Do you drink?

ABIE: No.

SHANNON: Not even socially?

ABIE: No.

SHANNON: Don't you ever have a glass of wine?

ABIE: Sometimes on holidays. A little glass of wine.

SHANNON: Do you ever drink more than one glass?

ABIE: No.

SHANNON: You never have two or three or four?

ABIE: No. Never.

SHANNON: Do you smoke?

ABIE: No!

SHANNON: Do you do any sports?

ABIE: Think for yourself!

SHANNON: Answer my question! Do you do any sports?

ABIE: No.! Don't be ridiculous!

(Overlapping)

SHANNON:	ABIE:
Have you ever flown a plane by yourself? Taken aviation lessons? Flown in a private plane? Use anything other than regularly scheduled airlines?	No. No. Of course no. Think for yourself! No. Ask what's important! Stupid questions. No. No! No!

SHANNON: Do you plan to travel?

ABIE: I don't know.

SHANNON: Wouldn't you like to go to Europe?

ABIE: No.

SHANNON: To Russia?

ABIE: No.

SHANNON: Poland? To Warsaw?

ABIE: No.

SHANNON: Who are you naming as beneficiary of this policy?

ABIE: My son.

SHANNON: What does he do for a living?

ABIE: He's a lawyer.

SHANNON: And he's the sole beneficiary?

ABIE: Yes. He's the only one. My Maurie.

SHANNON: Maurie? What's that short for? Morris?

ABIE: Yes. Morris. Morris Mos-*co*-vitz. My son.

SHANNON: That's not what it says on the policy, Mr. Moscowich. It says Martin. Martin Moss. The policy reads Martin Moss, *not* Morris Moscowich. Who is Martin Moss?

ABIE: My son, my son.

SHANNON: He changed his name, didn't he?

ABIE: Yes. He changed his name.

SHANNON: Why?

ABIE: For business. He wanted a business name.

SHANNON: What's wrong with Morris Moscowich? Doesn't have that old all-American ring to it, like Martin Moss, does it?

ABIE: No. No. It's for business. Business only.

SHANNON: You didn't change *your* name for business, Mr. Moscowich.

ABIE: No. That's my name. I am a small businessman only. I don't change my traditions.

SHANNON: Why did you name your son, Morris, alias Martin, as beneficiary of your insurance policy? Your son is a lawyer. He probably makes nine or ten times the amount that you'll ever make. He has all the money he needs. Enough money to take care of you. Enough money to get you out of this dump! Why doesn't he take care of you? And why are you naming him as beneficiary of your policy? He certainly doesn't need your money!

ABIE: NO! YOU! WHAT ARE YOU SAYING! MY MORRIS IS A GOOD BOY! I WILL NOT BE A BURDEN ON HIM! WHEN I DIE, HE HAS MY MONEY! I LEAVE HIM SOMETHING! I PROVIDE! HE IS ALL I HAVE LEFT! MY MORRIS! ALL I HAVE LEFT!

SHANNON: All you have left? All you have left from what? You had other children?

ABIE: Yes.

SHANNON: *Had* other children?

ABIE: Yes.

SHANNON: How many? *(No answer) HOW MANY!*

ABIE: Two...two. A girl, a little girl...and another boy.

SHANNON: YOU TOLD ME BEFORE THAT YOU HAD ONLY ONE CHILD! MORRIS MOSCO-WICH, ALIAS MARTIN MOSS! I ASKED YOU IF YOU HAD ANY OTHER CHILDREN AND YOU SAID NO! WHAT ARE YOU TRYING TO PULL WITH ME?

ABIE: I don't think of them. I try not to think of them. They are gone. Gone. I try so hard not to think of them.

SHANNON: Gone?

ABIE: Yes.

SHANNON: You mean dead?

ABIE: Yes.

SHANNON: And your wife?

ABIE: Gone...she is gone.

SHANNON: You mean dead?

ABIE: Yes...yes.

SHANNON: You came by yourself to join your son Martin and your uncle Moses here in New York after the war in 1946, right?

ABIE: Yes.

SHANNON: The others couldn't join you?

ABIE: No.

SHANNON: Your wife, your daughter, your other son, they couldn't join you?

ABIE: No.

SHANNON: Why did you lie about your other children?

ABIE: For me...for me...it is better that they never existed.

SHANNON: Your wife? Your daughter? Your son? Well, what happened to them?

ABIE: No! No! You don't know! How I try! I try! Every year, I go to the river, you know what Yom Kippur is? I stand on the pier, and I take my handful of bread, my sins, and I throw them into the water to get buried in the sea. The tide takes my bread, yes, but I find that my sins are still there! They don't go...They never go away!

SHANNON: Tell me what happened to them, Mr. Moscowich!

ABIE: No! No!

SHANNON: I can't make guesses. You have to tell me!

ABIE: ...Gone...they are all...gone.

SHANNON: Dead?

ABIE: ...Dead.

(Overlapping)

SHANNON:	ABIE:
And what was the cause of their deaths? Was it cancer?	No, no, no,
Tuberculosis?	No.
Heart disease?	NO, NO, NO,
Mental trouble?	*NO!*
Contagious, hereditary, or	*NO, NO!*
communicable disease?	*NO!*

SHANNON: Then what was it? Mr. Moscowich, what was it? I have to know. Your wife, your son, your daughter, why aren't they here? Why did they die?

ABIE: Killed...they were killed. *(He begins to breathe with increasing difficulty, occasionally grasping at his chest)*

(Overlapping)

SHANNON:	ABIE:
Oh. Accidental death.	No!
Was it an auto accident?	No, no, no,
Plane crash?	No,
Derailment?	No,
A ship?	No, no,
Did they drown?	No!

SHANNON: Then what was it? TELL ME! *You* have to tell me!

ABIE: In the street, I saw them...Golde...little Mendel...little Shandel. Standing there, looking, looking everywhere...looking for...their papa...I had run into this doorway, you see, I thought they were right behind me...I crouch. I hide...then I slowly look out and I see them *still there*...STILL THERE in that group of people. I want to shout, "HERE! HERE IS YOUR PAPA! OVER HERE! I AM WITH YOU!" But I cannot! I dare not!...There is a guard, with a machine gun. I want to run out, to distract him...but no, I cannot move! I stay there, I hide and I watch!

SHANNON: *(Quietly)* Dear God.

ABIE: They take them across the road, where they were lined up and...*(He is unable to finish through increased sobbing)*

SHANNON: *(After a pause)* You mean that they were...

ABIE: Yes, yes, yes!

SHANNON: Please. You really have to say it.

ABIE: SHOT! Like little pigs, they are mowed down against the wall! I see them falling! I see them...die! I see them take their little bodies and my Golde...they throw them like garbage onto the truck! Later, when the uprising is all over, they take the survivors and put them into concentration camps.

SHANNON: And you were the survivor. You got away.

ABIE: No! I never get away! I live, yes, but I never get away, don't you understand that?...Ahhhhh...I cannot...breathe...Please...Golde...my heart!

SHANNON: Your heart?

ABIE: I cannot... breathe.

SHANNON: Do you have any pills? *(Abie makes a dismissing gesture, as Shannon goes to the phone and dials 911)* You knew you had a heart condition all along, didn't you?

ABIE: ...Yes...yes!

SHANNON: *(Into phone)* Yes. I've got an emergency here, a cardiac. Right. *(He turns to Abie)* That's what you've been trying to hide from me, uh?

ABIE: Yes. Yes.

SHANNON: *(Into the phone)* I need an ambulance right away. Moscowich tailor shop. M-o-s-c-o-w-i-t-z. 348 Canal Street, near Mott. Right. *(He hangs up)*

ABIE: *(While Shannon is on the phone)* No...No ....Too late...you don't need an ambulance.

SHANNON: How long have you known about your heart condition? *(Abie shakes his head)* Well, come on, was it a long time? *(Abie nods)* Five years? Ten years, longer? Did you know about it when you applied for your first policy? *(Abie nods)* Great! Here you are applying for another policy, when you're not even entitled to the first one.

ABIE: Mr....Shannon...I...have...one...son.   I must...provide! *(He falls to the floor)*

SHANNON: Oh, Jesus! *(He rushes to Abie)* God, I didn't mean to...I didn't want to...*(He loosens Abie's tie, opens his collar button, then rolls up his own coat, placing it under Abie's head)* There. Now...now, you're going to be all right, Mr. Moscowich. The ambulance will be here in just a minute.

ABIE: No, mister, you still don't understand. Listen.. .you are not here just by chance. I have been waiting for many years. Now...I am happy, you see?...I die for my children, for my Golde...I am forgiven, I have peace, understand?

SHANNON: All right...Try, try not to talk now. Just relax.

ABIE: But I must ask...you will do an old man a favor? I know that you cannot give insurance to a dead man

(A weak laugh), it's true? But on my first policy I have paid all my premiums... and you must let my Morris have it. I cannot be a burden, understand?... You tell them you came in here, you found me like this... you never had a chance for your interview, yes?

SHANNON: I, uh, I better check and see if the ambulance is coming yet. You just, uh, stay calm, I'll be right back. *(He moves toward door)*

ABIE: A dying wish, Mr. Shannon. *(Shannon stops)* You must promise me... The truth that you know, you keep here *(He points to his head),* uh? You take your forms, you throw them away... and for once in your life mark your file... incomplete.

SHANNON: Well, I... I don't know. I don't know.

ABIE: *(As we hear the ambulance approaching from the distance, its siren growing louder)* No matter. I believe you will do it for me. To show me that you are maybe not such a schmuck, after all. *(He laughs, then groans from a sudden, more severe attack)*

SHANNON: I, uh, I hear the ambulance coming now. Now, just hold on. You're going to be all right, Mr. Moscowich.

ABIE: *(With a sudden, deep breath)* Mos-co-vitz!

(As Abie falls, with a slight smile, into his final collapse, we hear the ambulance siren growing louder. Slow fade on all but Shannon, who stands motionless near the doorway until we hear the siren immediately outside and can see its red lights flashing through the door and window)

Curtain

David Trainer

MR. CURATOR'S PROPOSAL

David Trainer

David Trainer's *Mr. Curator's Proposal* might be termed a black comedy in which a wife (assisted by a darkly wily curator) manipulates the disposal of her husband and his priceless art collection. The play appears in print for the first time in *The Best Short Plays 1975*.

Mr. Trainer was born in West Hartford, Connecticut, and attended the University of Pennsylvania in Philadelphia. Now a resident of New York City, he has written a number of plays which have been produced in many areas of the country. *The Undertaking* was presented at the Playwrights Unit in New York and *Thief* at the Eugene O'Neill Memorial Theatre Center in Waterford, Connecticut. A favorite playwright at the American Place Theatre (Manhattan), his drama *The Acquisition* was successfully presented there while *The Dance Next Door* and *Cafeteria Style Lunch* were favorably received at the New Theatre for Now of the Mark Taper Forum in Los Angeles.

The author is a member of The New Dramatists, which for twenty-five years has remained at the forefront of organizations that conduct playwriting programs. Describing the essence of this highly regarded organization whose playwrights have contributed well over two hundred plays and musicals to Broadway and Off-Broadway since its inception in 1949, Mr. Trainer recently wrote: "The playwright brings the raw materials—the words—and he is provided with the essential tools with which to shape these materials: actors, a director, and space. Nothing else is required to build a play, and that is all anyone gets at The New Dramatists...When a playwright thinks he has exhausted the resources of the organization, he can take his creation to the market and sell it, or take it home and hide it. But the end result is irrelevant beside the fact that the resources of The New Dramatists, being almost entirely human, are also virtually limitless."

Mr. Trainer received an O'Neill Foundation-Wesleyan University Grant for Playwriting for 1968-69, and a collection of his plays entitled *The Undertaking, Thief* and *The Pig* was published in 1968.

Although mainly active as a playwright, Mr. Trainer admits that he also enjoys directing when the occasion permits.

Characters:

JANE
STANLEY
MR. CURATOR

Scene:

The suggestion of an opulent old living room. Two wing-back chairs, in one of which sits Stanley, looking both fierce and dour, staring straight ahead, not moving. Finally Jane enters, crosses to the empty chair, sits, looks at her husband, produces a pocket watch, checks the time, then dangles the watch mesmerically before herself.

JANE: Now, now, Stanley, it can't be all that bad.

STAN: Worse.

JANE: You always make more than necessary of the little things, you know?

STAN: Little things?

JANE: Yes.

STAN: This is no little thing, this trick you've played.

JANE: I've hardly played any tricks on you, Stanley, everything is completely open and aboveboard.

STAN: Is not.

JANE: Oh, yes, I'm afraid it is.

STAN: I'll never agree to anything, you know that don't you?

JANE: We'll see.

STAN: Never.

JANE: He certainly is taking his time, isn't he?

STAN: *Wasting* his time. I'm surprised you aren't in there hovering over his shoulder as he moves from painting to painting.

JANE: He seems a very capable fellow, dear, perfectly able to appraise a body of art works without my help. You know I've never learned the first thing about your canvases.

STAN: Tell me something.

JANE: Yes, dear?

STAN: Why did you have to do this, eh?

JANE: It seemed time.

STAN: For what?

JANE: To change the scenery, clear the air.

STAN: You're culturally deficient. I've just realized that. I should have known it all along.

JANE: I've never pretended to your knowledgeability, darling.

STAN: You'd be laughed out of the room if you tried. Well, no matter. Nothing will come of your ploys. Nothing will change. I'll never relinquish my collection of art to any museum, under any circumstances, while I'm still alive to defend myself. If you should be fortunate enough to outlive me, a doubtful prospect by the way, maybe then you'll have some say about the disposition of it all. But not until then, and never without expert help. You've never read my will, have you?

JANE: I can't say that I have, no.

STAN: You'd be surprised by what you read, I assure you.

JANE: Oh?

STAN: Yes indeed. As my wife, you probably expect to inherit not only all my wealth, but all my substance too, don't you?

JANE: I never thought about it, actually. Are you contemplating an imminent death, dear? That would be so pointless.

STAN: I'm planning to stay right here, surrounded by everything I love.

JANE: With me, you mean?

STAN: With my paintings.

JANE: Oh.

STAN: My will states very clearly: you are to receive X amount of money, some specific sum or other, I can't remember what, on an annual basis, in deference to your many years of yeoman service as my helpmate. And you are to receive one vote on a panel of twenty art experts chosen from all over the world, nineteen art experts really, plus you. I

haven't got the faintest idea how to categorize you in this instance, and this body of august and respectable people will have it as their charge to sell, donate, loan, whatever, any or all of my collected paintings. I'm trusting that their intelligence will lead them to make the kind of arrangements I myself would have made if I were still alive and didn't insist on having all my paintings hanging in one splendid room of my own house. I repeat: never, ever, will I give up a single piece so long as I live. You know you're going to look awfully foolish when I tell this... this commedian, this... mock expert, this sham in the other room that he could have saved himself a great deal of time and effort if he'd never even bothered to get out of bed this morning.

JANE: You will try to say it nicely though, won't you?

STAN: Why should I be pleasant to a bald-faced, uninvited intruder.

JANE: I invited him, and I'm asking you to be nice.

STAN: Historically, you know, a wife caught attempting to deceive her husband was laid open to any recriminations he chose to inflict.

JANE: I'm not attempting to deceive you. I can't imagine having told you any more clearly what I've decided and what I've done. If you disapprove, then we'll talk about it, but you may not go on implying I'm some shrewd sharpie trying to pick your pocket. The man in the other room is a certified, recognized appraiser of art, he represents an obscure but highly considered museum, and he's willing to discuss your collection on any terms you choose.

STAN: Why are you trying to steal my paintings?

JANE: You're exasperating, Stanley, you know that? My God, you're exasperating! I'd think you'd be looking forward to an interesting conversation with this fellow. Heaven knows *we* never have any interesting conversations.

STAN: He will bore me to tears.

JANE: Through his eyes you may see some marvelous little details in your collection that you've missed on your own.

STAN: I never miss anything.

JANE: You're so...*opinionated,* Stanley, that it's almost impossible for us to hold even a civil discussion.

STAN: I'm very put out with you.

JANE: And what about me, dear? What about your wife? We've been married for twenty years, we've always lived in this house, we have no children, we hardly ever go out, and through the years we've relinquished every friend we ever had. But then I don't mind all that too much, because I never was much of one for parties and dancing and general merrymaking. I appreciate an unencumbered existence, in which the joys of family take precedence. But you've strained my patience, Stanley. I cannot compete with fifty-five oppressive oil paintings by all the great masters of art. I cannot abide the fact that you get up every morning, slip into your smoking jacket and slippers, and without kissing me, without inquiring after my welfare, without breakfast, without a glance, or a smile, or anything, without recognizing my very existence in this house, proceed to the grand gallery, close the door behind you, and look at your paintings for three and a half hours until lunch; whereupon you emerge, bathe, dress for the afternoon, and present yourself at the dining room table to eat. But again, silence reigns. It's not that you're reading the paper, Stanley. I'd be willing to bet you have so little sense of current events you couldn't even estimate for me the year in which we're living, let alone the date. You just sit there, down at the other end of the table, expressionless, wolfing down whatever it is I've prepared before scurrying back to your damn gallery without so much as a word to me. At six sharp you emerge again, pour yourself a drink, and settle back into your chair. Then, and *only* then, and only if I'm *really* lucky, do you say anything at all. And what is it you usually say, nine times out of ten? "My, but I love my collection of fifty-five great old paintings which are the envy of the world, and which I, Stanley the Great, am keeping all to myself like a spoiled selfish son of a bitch," which is what you are, darling, I haven't a doubt in the world about it. And if those paintings don't leave this house *today,* if you aren't as nice and agree-

able and amenable as possible to this man whom I've invited here, if you don't aid and abet him in every way you can, I am prepared to take action so startling, so severe, so *final* ...that you wouldn't believe it if I told you. Do you begin to comprehend me, Stanley, dear?

STAN: You're bitter.

JANE: But I'm also getting dangerous. So watch it.

(The Curator enters, younger than the other two, dressed darkly, almost muskily)

CURATOR: There you are.

JANE: Finished browsing?

CURATOR: It's a remarkable collection, remarkable, each and every canvas delights both the mind and the eye. Seldom if ever have I spent such a stimulating afternoon in anyone's private gallery.

JANE: My husband has superb taste.

CURATOR: You're to be congratulated, sir.

STAN: I know.

JANE: We'd be happy to entertain any proposal you might have as regards the collection. I'm very glad you liked it, I want you to speak with perfect freedom, I believe my husband has a clear understanding of my intentions now, he's prepared to listen politely to yours and will hopefully respond in the affirmative.

CURATOR: Well, I really have to catch my breath first, organize my thoughts...

JANE: By all means, yes, don't let me rush you.

CURATOR   The painting, sir, of the little girl dressed in the Asian costume, sitting on the tiled floor before what seems to be some kind of stylized pagoda, holding a dog in one hand, I believe, and a riding crop in the other...

STAN: Yes?

CURATOR: You know the painting I mean?

STAN: Of course I know the painting you mean.

CURATOR: Well, where did you get it? How long have you had it?

STAN: For thirty years, a sixteenth birthday gift from my grandmother. One of my favorites.

CURATOR: Yes, yes, I couldn't take my eyes off it, you know? There's something in that painting, the dog perhaps, something in the composition...

STAN: I know.

CURATOR: Have you any idea what's so compelling in that painting?

STAN: Of course I do. Do you?

CURATOR: I believe so, yes.

STAN: Well?

CURATOR: I'm deferring to your greater knowledge of the work, sir, as you are the owner. You're a hard man to compliment, aren't you?

JANE: Stanley?

STAN: I know that painting as perfectly as it can ever be known, I appreciate its every detail, I don't need to talk about it to enjoy it.

CURATOR: The dog's teeth, you see.

JANE: What about the dog's teeth?

CURATOR: Do you know the painting we're talking about?

JANE: I hate that painting. I always have, I always will.

CURATOR: Doubtless because of that jaw. It's an extraordinary picture, really, the perfect image of some alien evil. Yet at first glance I had difficulty discerning how the painting worked. Technically, it's flawless, the subject's a bit peculiar, but what—I asked myself—what exactly is causing this acute discomfort I feel as I look at it? Then I noticed the mouth of the dog. The lips, if that's what you call the skin around the jaw of a dog, are slightly parted, revealing two perfect rows of pearly teeth sharpened to a dagger's point. The recognition of this practically took my breath away. Immediately I saw the painting in a whole new light. What at first appeared simply to be a horrible little girl enjoying some bizarre surroundings suddenly became a terrified little girl holding a murderous pup in her arms. I thought *she* was evil, but I was wrong. The painting is much more complex than that. It was the dog, with that strange glint in its eyes as it glanced toward the girl's throat, which caused my blood to freeze as I stood before the canvas.

JANE: I've always hated that girl.

STAN: All these years? Really?

JANE: She made me shudder whenever I thought of her hanging on a wall not a couple of rooms away as I moved through the house.

STAN: As I said, my dear, your perceptions are valueless. All along you've hated the girl—who by all rights deserves every ounce of sympathy you can muster—when you should have been fearing the dog, who may well have it in mind to rip *you* up when he finishes with his current victim. Mr. Curator, if you are trying to impress me with your insight, you've both failed and succeeded. You cannot impress me with what I already know, yet I admire the speed with which you clarify your deepest perceptions.

CURATOR: Thank you.

JANE: I'll be happy to have that thing out of the house.

STAN: It's not gone yet, my dear.

CURATOR: And the nude...

STAN: What about her?

CURATOR: Are you asking me, or challenging me?

JANE: I hate that one, too!

CURATOR: It's a masterpiece.

STAN: Of course it is. They all are.

CURATOR: As I stepped before that painting, involuntarily, I assure you, I blushed. Now I'm not a shy man, nor excessively puritanical, but that picture...

STAN: Embarrassed you.

CURATOR: Invited me to commit rape, I might almost say. No, not rape. That implies the imposition of my will upon the subject, who seems to be passing out carnal knowledge of herself as if that knowledge were nothing more important than an armful of wild flowers one might pick and place in a vase by the front door of one's house... or nothing *less* important than an armful of—what is the most valuable substance you can name?—for the subject obviously holds her body beyond value, too, considers herself perfection, as well she might. Ah, but imagery fails me. Wildflowers. Why do I mention wildflowers, or diamonds, or gold, which can be had anywhere, unlike this woman...who can only be had in your gallery, sir, under the approving eye of all the other masterpieces.

JANE: Ordinarily I don't interrupt my husband while he's looking at his paintings. But one day, I can't remember why exactly, awhile ago, there arose some matter so pressing that nothing would do but that I call it to his attention. Foolishly, I forgot to knock before entering the gallery. I saw my husband way down at the other end, down that long hallway of paintings. You didn't hear me, darling Stanley, you never looked up. You were on your knees before the nude, pale as a ghost, head bowed, your left hand clutching your brow, your right arm extended way above your head, toward the canvas, your fingers...just barely touching...the thigh of the woman towering high above you. I stood still for several minutes, I suppose, never once did you move, never once did she move, I looking at her, her looking at me, you...oblivious. Finally I slipped out as quickly as I had entered, I never mentioned the incident before, Stanley, because it seemed so...private. That nude woman, along with the evil dog, along with everything else, must be out of this house before dark.

CURATOR: I can see I needn't have bothered to describe the effect of that painting on myself.

STAN: No, I'm sick of description, I have complete knowledge of all I possess. If you have a proposition to make, do so. The greater your haste, the sooner you can go.

CURATOR: How much money would you demand in return for the whole collection?

STAN: Several hundred million dollars.

JANE: He's kidding.

STAN: Every time I wax hyperbolic, my dear wife feels compelled to apologize and explain for me, which is completely unnecessary. In fact, hyperbole is the farthest thing from my mind. I believe I've underestimated the price for my collection by a good deal, as it is priceless, and not for sale.

CURATOR: My museum—

STAN: I don't give a damn about your museum!

CURATOR: Have you ever seen it?

STAN: Do you think a man with a collection like mine needs to frequent museums? It would take ten lifetimes to fully appreciate what I already own.

CURATOR: Well, I understand that. And then too, not many people are privileged to visit my museum, which is not public, but private, privately endowed, filled with private collections which you could never have seen in their present setting. But let me tell you about our galleries. They are more magnificent than anything you've ever seen before, like enormous interconnected cathedrals, with high vaulted ceilings rivaling in beauty those of the Sistine Chapel. The floors are perfect white marble, as are the walls, which rise over two hundred feet to the arch of the roof. Each member's collection is hung to his specifications, in his private room, to which there is no admittance except on specific days, at the owner's approval. There is a hush in the place, a magnificent silence which is never broken, as only one member at a time is allowed to view any other particular collection. But perhaps you have to see the arrangement to fully appreciate it.

STAN: I appreciate my own arrangements, in my own house, where my privacy, and silence, and anything else you care to name, are perfectly and simply available.

CURATOR: But you have only one collection. In the museum, we have many, many more for your amusement.

STAN: Again, I am amused by only one collection, and that is mine, and that is here, and there will be no changes.

CURATOR: Your wife told me you might be hesitant to move.

STAN: Now she is taking to understatement.

JANE: Perhaps, Mr. Curator, you might tell him the rest of the arrangement. Unless my husband has remained nothing more than a total stranger to me throughout the years of our marriage, I'm sure he cannot fail to grow more interested.

CURATOR: You see, all our members have collections, if not similar to, then at least the equal of yours. Not the ordinary collection, not at all, quite the opposite, quite extraordinary, quite, well...unique. And all our members are as devoted to their collections as they are to their lives. In fact, and I'm sure you can verify this, sir, when a man spends a lifetime collecting intensely personal, evocative works of art, those works actually *become* his life. His very existence is inextricably intertwined with that of his paintings. There are very few people in the world who can appreciate this merger, very few people as great and various as what they have collected. I suspect you are among the unique, I knew it the minute I entered your gallery. Wouldn't you like to meet others as devoted to their collections as you are to your own?

STAN: No, I would find that extremely distasteful.

CURATOR: Because the museum has a very special policy. When a man joins, he may either sell or consign his works to us. He selects his gallery, his paintings are hung, and the member is free to come and go at will. So far, we sound like any other organization which proposes to display fine art to the best advantage of all concerned. However, we have a more specific program than any other museum of which I've ever heard. For a certain time each week a member must sit, or stand, pose, I guess you could say, along with his paintings while another member is allowed to browse. You see, our members know themselves, and they know their collections, but they often wonder what other kinds of people are doing the same type of thing: assembling intensely personal—

STAN: You've already described my collection quite fully, along with your assumptions about the principles under which it was brought together. You say the owner is as much on show as his works?

CURATOR: Yes, because the owner is, ultimately, a part of his own collection, and vice versa. Another member would enter your gallery, and close the door behind him. Inside he would see not only all your paintings, but you yourself, sitting absolutely still, like a statue. He would go from one to another of the canvases, always in silence, we do not allow the slightest sound to violate our galleries, looking, learning, until he came to you, sitting, thinking, posed however you like. Perhaps you'd be looking front, the visitor could see you, and you could see him, but there would be no communication, your privacy is totally secure. He would study your face, imagining your character, coming to know you in relation to what you had collected. When he was through, he would leave, and you would be free to treat your paintings however you liked until the next appointment, when the scene would be repeated, with differences if you liked, with the paintings rearranged, with yourself in another pose, with perhaps a woman visitor this time, we have some very lovely, very feminine members. However, no matter what the circumstances, the No Communication rule is strictly enforced. I hope you don't mind me saying this, madam.

JANE: I don't mind.

STAN: And then, in turn, would I be free to examine the other collections, and their respective owners? In silence, of course.

CURATOR: Absolutely.

STAN: I see.

CURATOR: Many of our members have been hesitant about the arrangement at first, but unfortunately, for reasons I'm sure you can understand, we cannot arrange a trial period. Either the system appeals to you immediately, or it doesn't. We only make the offer once, if you decline you will never hear from or about us again. You might be interested to know that many of our galleries are open for appointment seven days a week, that's how fond of being observed some of our owners have become. It's quite a privilege to be observed in these circumstances, really. Where else but in the exclusive confines of a private museum can a man be as fully appreciated as that passion to which he has given his entire life? Where else but with us can a man be sure he will be seen at his very best by only his equals? By men and women as elevated, disciplined and distinguished as himself? You have indicated you're not happy with your wife's attitude toward your collection—excuse me again, madam, but your bias is evident, however well-founded you may think it to be is beside the point. This offer provides the perfect opportunity to place yourself, and your life, and your collection, beyond her scorn.

JANE: I wouldn't have contacted you if I didn't have just that intention in mind.

STAN: Would I live in the museum?

CURATOR: If you liked. Connected to each gallery is a large and tasteful apartment, which will be decorated to your specifications. You can even take some of your paintings in there at night if you like.

STAN: That wouldn't be necessary.

CURATOR: Again, the decision is yours. I'm merely pointing out the freedom which the museum allows its members. If you wanted to live at home, that would be fine, too. You could come in every day, or on only those days when you had appointments, either to see, or be seen, whatever. A certain percentage of our members start out on a commuter basis and gradually grow to like the museum so much that ultimately they move in permanently. Their families always understand. Members become transformed by our museum, the change is obvious to all. It's really quite gratifying to see a man truly happy at last, his life and work in balance, his quality of perception valued to the fullest. Again, the museum would be more than happy to purchase your collection, if you wanted to give the money to your wife and have done with all domestic complications forever. I promise a fair price. Otherwise, if you decide to join, that is, the museum will officially borrow your paintings until you have decided on the final arrangements. In either case, full privileges of membership are granted.

JANE: Isn't it a good idea, Stanley?

STAN: I haven't made up my mind yet.

JANE: You're still not angry I invited the curator to come here, are you?

STAN: No, no I'm not.

JANE: I didn't think you were. Tell him about the final room, Mr. Curator.

CURATOR: Excuse me?

JANE: The—what do you call it—the final room.

CURATOR: Ah, yes. The final room. You see, sir, this arrangement, if you consent to it, does not end with your death. When your life is done, the museum takes full responsibility for your remains, your collection and...yourself. A member is requested to designate several of his paintings to be preserved in perpetuity in the museum. The others are sold, that's how we manage to continue operating, you see. However, the designated paintings are removed to a special room, smaller than your lifetime gallery, a room appointed precisely to your specifications. Perhaps this room might be considered a kind of crypt, for here you too are preserved, taxidermied, in the pose of your choice. We call this series of rooms the Posthumous Wing, and again, the same rules apply as do in the galleries. Any member may enter any crypt, alone of course, and in silence, and is free to spend as long as he likes admiring the favorite works of the departed person, as well as, well, the departed person himself. So far, we have thirty-two fully appointed crypts open to the membership, and a thirty-third in the final stages of completion. We have a sense of history, you see, we know that a man may die, but his work, as well as his soul, lives on. And we feel a person worthy of membership in the first place deserves the finest memorial possible. And what finer memorial could a man ask than his preserved body surrounded by his favorite paintings, eh?

STAN: It's a kind of immortality.

CURATOR: It is, an exclusive immortality.

JANE: It all makes a great deal of sense, doesn't it, dear?

STAN: I must admit it does. Rather an appealing prospect, don't you think?

CURATOR: Have you any questions? I'll try to supply the best answers I can.

STAN: Well...Can I keep on collecting? If I see something I like somewhere, can I bring it in?

CURATOR: Of course.

STAN: I wouldn't have to get your approval?

CURATOR: We trust our members' taste, utterly and completely.

STAN: I see, I see...

JANE: Stanley, dear—

STAN: Eh?

JANE: You needn't worry about me, you know. I wouldn't have invited this gentleman here today if I hadn't the highest regard in the world for his organization.

STAN: I'd like to know where you heard about it though; you've never seemed to me the kind of person who'd have an offhand knowledge of a place like this.

JANE: Well...

CURATOR: She didn't contact me, sir. I contacted her.

STAN: Oh, I see. Yes, of course...

JANE: Mr. Curator thought it best we pretend a bit, so I could sort of prepare your mind.

CURATOR: You're very highly considered in certain circles, sir, I've known about you for some time. Your reputation as a reclusive sort is legendary. I didn't want to approach you right out of the blue lest you take offense, or decline to speak to me at all. So—and we don't ordinarily do this—I enlisted your wife's support in making this presentation.

STAN: Very wise decision. Tell me, Jane: if I joined, if I moved out of here tonight, left my clothes to be sent for later, just disappeared, for good and for all, forever, if we were never to see each other again...would you miss me?

JANE: No, Stanley, I wouldn't. I'm sorry.

STAN: No, no, nothing to apologize about. I wouldn't miss you either.

JANE: That was true, what I told you before about how much I dislike our life together. If you decline this man's offer and stay here with your paintings, I swear to you, on my life, I will murder you in your bed tonight, and my conscience won't even twitch once.

STAN: Really?

JANE: Yes, Stanley. Oh, yes! The paintings must go, and since you'll never consent to part with them, you must go, too.

STAN: I never imagined there would come a day when I'd move myself and my collection out of this house. I never imagined we could find a better place. And even though I have yet to see your museum, I believe, I know it will be better by far than my home here.

CURATOR: The price you'd have to pay to remain sounds insupportably high.

STAN: You're a resolute woman, aren't you, Jane?

JANE: I have become one, yes.

CURATOR: And so, sir, if there are no more questions, I officially invite you to join the museum. We can make the detailed arrangements later. Do you accept?

(Pause)

STAN: Yes, I accept.

CURATOR: You are now a member.

STAN: It's that simple?

CURATOR: It's that simple. If you like, I'll drive you to your new home, or if you prefer, I'll call for you in the morning when some of the staff come to pick up your collection.

STAN: I'll come right now. I'm a quiet man, you know, I always keep my emotions in stern check. But really, I'm quite excited. I haven't been this excited in years. Ever, perhaps.

CURATOR: Your life is finally in order, not to mention your afterlife. You have every right to be happy. And thank you for your assistance, madam. You've made this presentation very easy, the afternoon has been as pleasant as could be.

JANE: You're welcome, and thank you, too.

CURATOR: My staff will be by in the morning. They'll cause as little inconvenience as possible. I suspect you'll never see me again, but my office will be communicating with you regarding the various financial arrangements to be made by your husband.

JANE: Very good.

STAN: I'll see you're well taken care of, my dear.

JANE: I know you will.

STAN: You always knew I'd accept, didn't you? From the first moment Mr. Curator contacted you.

JANE: Yes. I knew. Good-bye, Stanley.

STAN: Good-bye, Jane.

(They shake hands)

CURATOR: Come along, sir. You're expected for dinner at six in your new apartment.

(Mr. Curator and Stanley go out. Jane comes down toward her chair, by the side of which has been sitting a large flat object in brown paper. She sits, picks it up, unwraps it, looks at it, rises and goes to an illuminated part of the wall visible to the entire audience. She hangs the object, which is a large black and white photograph of her own face. She proceeds downstage, where she stands posed at the back of her chair. Slowly the lights fade out on her. Then slowly the lights fade out on her photograph. The room is dark)

Curtain

Israel Horovitz

SPARED

Israel Horovitz

Israel Horovitz first came to international prominence in 1968 with *The Indian Wants the Bronx,* a powerful and terrifying study of violence on a New York street. A striking Off-Broadway success, it also scored heavily in other major American cities, at the 1968 Spoleto Festival (Italy), the World Theatre Festival in England (1969) as well as in numerous other foreign countries. The play (which was published in *The Best Short Plays 1969)* won a 1968 Drama Desk-Vernon Rice Award and three "Obies," as well as a commendation from *Newsweek* magazine citing the author as one of the three most original dramatists of the year.

Mr. Horovitz was born on March 31, 1939, in Wakefield, Massachusetts. After completing his domestic studies, he journeyed to London to continue his education at the Royal Academy of Dramatic Art and in 1965 became the first American to be chosen as playwright-in-residence with Britain's celebrated Royal Shakespeare Company.

The author's first play, *The Comeback,* was written when he was seventeen; it was produced in Boston in 1960. In the decade that followed, Mr. Horovitz's plays tenanted many stages of the world. Among them: *It's Called the Sugar Plum* (paired with *The Indian Wants the Bronx* on the New York stage); *The Death of Bernard the Believer; Rats; Morning* (originally titled *Chiaroscuro,* it was first performed at the Spoleto Festival and later on a triple bill, *Morning, Noon and Night,* Henry Miller's Theatre, New York, 1968); *Trees; Acrobats* (introduced in *The Best Short Plays 1970); Line* (included in this editor's anthology, *Best Short Plays of the World Theatre: 1968-1973); Leader;* and *The Honest-to-God Schnozzola,* for which he won a 1969 Off-Broadway "Obie" award.

His newest works for the stage include: *Shooting Gallery; Dr. Hero* (presented at Amherst and various other colleges as well as Off-Broadway by The Shade Company in March, 1973); *Alfred the Great* (the first of *The Wakefield Plays,* a trilogy of three full-length plays which premiered in Pittsburgh in 1973); and *Turnstile* (presented at Dartmouth College in August, 1974).

A collection of his plays, *First Season,* was published in 1968, and his first novel, *Cappella,* was issued in 1973.

Twice the recipient of a Rockefeller Foundation Playwriting Fellowship, he also won a similar fellowship from the Creative Artists Program Service, funded by the New York State Council on the Arts, and on May 17, 1972, he received an Award in Literature from the American Academy of Arts and Letters.

The author, who lives in New York City, also has written several major screenplays, notably *The Strawberry Statement,* which won the *Prix de Jury,* Cannes Film Festival, 1970.

In *Spared,* a man's life passes in review and reflects the low and high points of his existence as he attempts to do away with himself. The play (published for the first time anywhere in this collection) was given its initial public performance at the *Centre Culturel Américain,* Paris, on April 17, 1974, under the auspices of the United States Information Service, as the latter half of a Horovitz double-bill, *Hopscotch* and *Spared,* the latter bringing forth the comment from a leading French reviewer that it is "funny and despairing...like a Theatre of the Absurd classic."

Author's Note

Voices on tape to be prerecorded by the actor, using high-pitched voice. Laughter and scream both sustained, breathy. Words to be recorded once only, spliced together and repeated without pause. Frequency as noted in text.

When actor imitates mother's words, scream and laugh, imitation must reveal taped voice as his.

Four distinct voices must be developed for performance: old man's narrative voice, harsh, deep, cynical; young man's sincere voice; boy's innocent voice; and gangsterish, rather comic voice. These voices should work as warring contraries whenever possible, within sections, even within sentences and phrases. Thus, whenever Man seems to contradict himself, correct himself, contrary voices need be chosen to personalize conflict.

Dependent on size of theatre, platform should be built of the maximum possible height to hold actor's face within sight-lines, but to create sense of maximum distance from audience-floor. Two instruments for lighting: one straight above, straight down; the second slightly above the first, focused on center of actor's face. Thus, channel of light created to allow actor to lean forward to audience during more intimate moments. Lights must be low level, soft glow, no edges, focused evenly so that no lighting changes occur with actor's forward movement.

Sense of infinite blackness and space, all around.

If house-curtain is used, lights to be preset for start of play, switched off after gunshot, faded in softly after opening monologue and left on throughout rest of play. House curtain can close to end play.

Recommend, however, that final cue be fade-out of lights to blackness, as after-image in dark useful.

Opening moments of play to be musical images, not slowed in tempo for recognition of narrative. Closing moments opposite.

General note to actor: to involve audience as listeners to bedtime story.

Characters:

MAN

Scene:

Auditorium dark. Silence.
Curtain. Lights to soft glow, revealing Man in chair. He
holds point of gun to his temple. He is at first silent. Except
for soft glow, darkness and infinite space all around.

MAN: *(Gun pressed to temple: speaks clearly)* I have
tried to destroy myself more than sixty different times. *(Pulls*
trigger. Click. No gunshot. He shrugs) Always spared. *(Gun at*
his side now. Pulls trigger. Blam! Gunshot. Man is amazed.
Blackout. Auditorium and stage in darkness. Man's voice
heard, high-pitched, manic. Speaks rapidly, almost unintelli-
gibly at first) Five, the first time. Didn't know why. Children
happy. Laughter all around. Me outside. *(Pauses)* Father
then moving. Mother all ears. Hugs abundant. Talk endless.
Food, as talk. Sister, wide-eyed, adoring. Didn't know why.
(Pauses) Knife on table, eyebrow-high. Watched it, tiptoe.
Sounds all empty. Colors mute. Smells to rancid. Tiny chest
thumping. *(Pauses)* Curled in fingers. Sounds, colors, smells,
all gone. *(Pauses)* Point pricked, no pain. Full thrust, no
blood. Eyes clenched, no scream.
(Silence. Lights to a soft glow.
Man wears white shirt, dark suit, fat clownish necktie. He
reclines, arms outstretched, dangling down into darkness.
Legs same, feet over edge of platform. Sense that chair and
Man are suspended in air, floating, is wanted.
Voice changes in age, dependent on text. Amplification
needed. Speakers surround audience, placed in six posi-
tions: one in each corner of auditorium, one above au-
dience, one in darkness above Man's head.
Interruptions marked "Voice" are taped voice of elderly
woman, always kindly, sympathetic. Unless shrill

*scream wanted: child's sustained, anguished. Accent, if
distinguishable, Boston.*

Man's face unchangingly confident, head rarely bowed)

VOICE—SPEAKER #1:   Poor child.

VOICE—SPEAKER #2:   Poor child.

VOICE—SPEAKER #3:   Poor child.

VOICE—SPEAKER #4:   Poor child.

VOICE—SPEAKER #5:   Poor child.

VOICE—SPEAKER #6:   *(Shrill scream)*

MAN: Fifteen, the second. Thanksgiving Thursday.
Aunts scrubbing, cigar smoke uncled, Fat Charlotte, the
cousin, all green and sick.

VOICE—SPEAKER #1:   Poor child.

MAN: Skeleton turkey, once dead, now eaten.
Laughter all around. *(Pauses)* Three uncles, back from fishing. Cracked the early ice. Three pickerel, easy catch. Frozen solid. In the surface. Eyes open. Still stiff. Mouths open.
Still, as well. Caught together. Near the top. Chipped free.
Grave to grave. Watched them thaw. Early evening. Never
thinking. Eye to eye. *(Pauses)* Turkey carcass, winter treasure. All still. No scream. *(Pauses)* Apple-bobbing. All cous-
ins. Heads plunged, eyes clenched, mouths plugged, stuffed,
reward. Me, outside. Ever-wondering, still, unspeaking.
(Pauses) Stood in archway, top curved, me, tall, head bowed.
All eyes on me, pull me in, push me under, no control, all
gone. *(Pauses)* No ice, no flow, easy now. Do nothing. Eyes
open, life to play? All lies, just apples bobbing by. No
breath, no sound, no voice, no scream.

VOICE—SPEAKER #1:   Poor child.

VOICE—SPEAKER #2:   Poor child.

VOICES—SPEAKER #3 *and* #6:   Poor child.

VOICES—SPEAKER #4 *and* #5:   *(Sustained shrill
scream)*

MAN: Four years slid. Women now. All in that
…what's the word? Chokes me still. All in…*(Chokes three
times. Loud sound)*…All in love. Silent then. Not a sound.
Eyes all voice. Never closed. Not a blink. Ears a team.
Never clogged. Girls all blab. Heard them come, watched

them go. Countless thrills: fifty-nine. Ruth my sixtieth. Love her even now. What's her name? Not to worry. Love her still. *What's her name?*

VOICES—SPEAKER #3 *and* #5:   Poor child.

VOICES—SPEAKER #4 *and* #6:   Poor child.

MAN: Mary! No. Not to worry. Mae it was. Mae in June. Twelfth, I think. Two o'clock. Veteran's Field. Sun still high. Number sixty. Mae was chilled. Scared to touch. Learned in time. Three o'clock. Side to side. Four o'clock. Back to front. Five o'clock. Moon and sun. Mae all sorrow, all regret. Me still dumb, staring through. Not to worry ... *What's her name?*

VOICES—SPEAKER #1, #2, #3 *and* #4:   Poor child.

MAN: Made a pact, Mae and me. Leave together— from the rocks. Climbed them, smiling. July the Fourth. Parade below. Independence. Father's friends as Indians, marching. John Kennedy, too. Senator then. All applause. Us, above it, bound to leap. Children laughing, balloons wound tight. Mother down there. Then still moving. Aunts and uncles, bellies full. *(Pauses)* From our perch, we watched them watching. Silent now, our hands ungripped. *(Pauses)* Mae edged closer, never talking. Hair was brown, her loose blouse white. *(Pauses)* A runaway balloon floated up and then beyond. I followed with my eye. When I thought of Mae again, I was alone. She was gone.

VOICE—SPEAKER #3:   Poor child.

MAN: She was broken near a 4-H float. Not a sound. No cry, no scream.

VOICES—ALL SPEAKERS: *(Shrill scream)*

MAN: No pact nor promise since. No hope, no plan, no desire, no scream.

VOICE—SPEAKER #1:   Poor child.

VOICE—SPEAKER #2:   Poor child.

VOICE—SPEAKER #3:   Poor child.

VOICE—SPEAKER #4:   Poor child.

VOICE—SPEAKER #5:   Poor child.

VOICE—SPEAKER #6:   Poor child.

MAN: When I was twenty-two, I played a game

called Houyhnhnm Roulette. *(Pauses)* All cylinders of the pistol were filled, but for one. *(Pauses)* I played the game each night for five consecutive nights. *(Pauses)* Finally, my nerves gave out. I had to stop playing. *(Pauses)* I've never been much of a good-loser. *(Pauses)* Played another game, six months later. *(Pauses)* A big talent scout passed through town and picked me for his television quiz show, in Boston. Boston's first. *(Pauses)* Heartbreak. *(Pauses)* That was the name of the show: Heartbreak. *(Pauses)* By answering twenty obvious questions in my choice category, Romantic poetry, specifically, Blake, I won more than $18,000 in valuable old two-dollar bills. *(Pauses)* All of America watched me win. *(Pauses)* Outside the studio, I was mugged four times. *(Pauses)* Twice more at the subway. *(Pauses)* In the parlor car on the Boston & Maine to Wakefield, the rear pockets were ripped from my trousers. *(Pauses)* Before leaving the train, a series of Buddliners hooked together. I was mugged seventeen different times. *(Pauses)* The most bizarre attempt was an old lady, who filled a hefty bag full with water and threw it at me. While my trousers were drying, she stole them. *(Pauses)* I was naked upon arrival in Wakefield. *(Pauses)* The remainder of the year passed without incident. *(Pauses)* Twenty-three. All repaired, Emily then. Our town. One son. Brown hair and eyes. Nose mine, enormous. *(Pauses)* No. No son. Never could.

    VOICES—SPEAKER #1 *and* #3:   *(Shrill scream)*

    MAN: She stayed with me nine years. No point going on. My fault. She was...normal. *(Pauses)* She left as she first came, but nine years older. Neither of us had grown taller. Nothing visibly good had sprung from it. I wonder why we tried?

    VOICE—SPEAKER #3:   *(Female laughing)*

    MAN: *(Voice normal)* I ran. *(Pauses)* During the final month of my thirty-second year, I ran 235.6 miles. 7.6 miles per day, on, as they say, the average. *(Pauses)* I did skip a few. In the middle. *(Pauses)* Had to kick out an extra mile or two at the end of the month. *(Pauses)* Eleven. *(Pauses)* The day before my thirty-second birthday, I sprinted recklessly for eleven consecutive miles. *(Pauses)* On March first, I weighed in at one hundred thirty-three pounds. By the thirty-first of the month, I had bloated to one hundred thirty-four. *(Pauses)* 235.6 miles in one month and I gained a pound, which is to say I lost...nothing. *(Pauses)*

VOICES—ALL SPEAKERS: *(Female laughing)*

MAN: *(Pauses; young man's voice used here)* Thirty-four, cleaning dishes for the Hazelwood Cottage on Main. One-fifty an hour. Selling out. *(Pauses)* My first earned room. Chestnut Street, top floor right. Cold in winter, warm in summer. No pets permitted, not that I would have. *(Pauses)* All the Hazlewood food a man might dare. A bit soggy, a trifle—well—*touched. (Pauses)* Food and a room. Never happier. *(Pauses)* Gus, the short-order German, said I had style. Brought a certain *je ne sais quoi* into the old rathole. Easy for Gus, nose dripping in the *soupe du jour. (Pauses)* I said little, of course. Always certain to be caught brooding. These lines in the face, even then. All that *practice!* Never saw wisdom in all that gravity—just couldn't control myself—couldn't stop squinting. Reading books again. *(Pauses)* My room was perfect to me. Amazing sun in the morning. Sunsets through the window by the stove. *(Pauses)* Why do I remember all the kitchens of my life? *(Pauses)* Nancy was the first to visit there. Beautiful thing, Nancy. Long, straight hair, dark brown. Wonderful legs: thick and tight with muscles from her walks. *(Pauses; voice changes to old age)* Wonderful leg, I should say. I never actually saw both of them together. Within one...viewing. *(Pauses)* I never actually saw her walk, either. *(Pauses; voice younger)* I'm sure she must have. How else could she have gotten into my room? *(Pauses)* She had one leg or the other bundled in a quilt most of the time. Maybe *all* of the time. Certainly, *most* of the time. *All* of the time *I* was nearby, which is, strictly speaking, *most* of the time. *(Pauses)* There was *something* going on under the quilt. *(Pauses)* I kept my distance. *(Pauses)* Warmed her belly with pots of Lapsang souchong tea I'd read in Boswell, bought in Boston. *(Pauses)* She loved me for every ounce of it. *(Pauses)* We had a gentle time at first. A lot of reading. Blake: all of *Jerusalem.* Me, in my orange bath-robe, in the easy chair, reclining. *(Pauses)* I never liked sit-ting much then. Standing either: I especially avoided standing. The recline suited me best. *(Pauses)* The less said about Nancy's body, the better. *(Pauses)* My Hazelwood days were numbered from the moment I reflected upon the stack. I counted: three hundred dishes, two hundred cups, the same in saucers, and, roughly, countless spoons. *(Pauses)* I couldn't. I didn't. *(Pauses)* "Gus," I said, "I've got the dread disease." "God bless you," he belched. *(Pauses)* I left immediately. He'd never asked me *which* disease. *(Pauses)* He trusted me, old Gus. God bless him. *(Pauses)* She stuck it out with me five months, until the money ran out. First hers, then mine. *(Pauses)* Hers actually ran out just before I'd met her. Which is to say, just before I found her in my room. *(Pauses)* That's not quite the case, either. *(Pauses)* I found the room with Nancy in it. It was a furnished place: easy chair, Murphy-bed, naturally, table, silverware and dishes, the usual, plus a plump book of verse, quilt and, of course Nancy, herself. *(Pauses)* She said she'd worked the year be-fore in the B.P.L. *(Pauses)* I believed her. *(Pauses)* A woman wouldn't lie about working in a library. *(Pauses)* We kept our little idyll, as they say, *up,* until my ignominious parting from Hazelwood and money. *(Pauses)* Her note said she'd found work in England. *(Pauses)* I must not have wanted to follow her, because I didn't. *(Pauses)* I wonder. *(Pauses)* In all that time together, we never once raised our voices in anger or regret.

VOICES—ALL SPEAKERS: *(Female laughing)*

MAN: Actually, we never much raised our voices at all. I don't really remember much talk beyond the reading. *Jerusalem. (Pauses)* I never warmed to the didactical *or* the symbolical. *(Pauses)* Thirty-six. Changed rooms. Alone again. Took a smaller one, top floor down on West Water. Cheaper. *(Pauses)* Not the only reason. *(Pauses)* Couldn't stop finding *her* in the old room. Bits and scraps: nothing solid. I mean, nothing like the original find of the quilt and, of course, Nancy herself. A bobby-pin once, dozens of em-

ery boards, a plump book of verse. *(Pauses)* The painful letter was in it. Tucked. *(Pauses)* "Dear Nancy. I copied your
name and address from your notebook cover. I hope you
don't find it too froward of me, but I found you to be so
lovely, I have to try. Would you see me? Perhaps a film together?" *(Pauses)* His address next, then his telephone, then
his name: Blake. *(Pauses)* What was the honorable thing to
do? *(Pauses)* I called him during the middle of each successive night for thirty nights. Woke him up. Gave him something to think about. *(Pauses)* I never spoke, of course. He
sounded lonely, our Mr. Blake. Jim. He sounded lonely. Always home when I called. Probably firing off his letters.
(Pauses) I wrote to him in March, asking for a meeting.
Signed a woman's name—Aphra Behn. I thought it might be
nice to have a look. Waited nearly an hour. He didn't show.
(Pauses) Burned the letter, finally. Nothing solid. Nothing to
keep, certainly not to lug around. *(Pauses)* I moved. *(Pauses)*
Forty. Went with Evelyn to Utah. Her people were there.
(Pauses) Met Evelyn at Hazelwood. Never paid much attention to her. Nancy would have been jealous. Evelyn was
quite something. Straight back. Rich girl's shoulders.
(Pauses) She worked at the copy-center, Lakeside office Park.
Came East for money. *(Pauses)* She was a bit frightened
of how her folks would take to me. Baptists. I reminded her
that I'd grown up with Baptists on all sides. *(Pauses)* She
warned me about the Grace ritual—not to take down any of
their food, without thanking God first. *(Pauses)* I hated her
for telling me that. *(Pauses)* Her old man gave me a brandy-
and-water. I blessed it. "Dear Lord, bless this brandy-and-
water and cause it to bring peace into this strange land."
Then I sang *Rock of Ages*. A half-hour later, I prayed over
her mother's clam dip and Fritos, and then an hour later, I
blessed the Puss 'n' Boots they put out for their cats. *(Pauses)*
Dinner went down without so much as a nod to God.
(Pauses) Left Utah, but stayed West. Forty-three, talking
more than ever. Not saying much, but speaking well. Easterners grow ten times more learned west of the Mississippi.
(Pauses) Found Los Angeles, and a job. Names from my

childhood, to my amazement, here and well-known. Mine, as always, an unheard-of thing, never pronounced as written, always misspelled, never listened to, thus never remembered. *(Pauses)* One face from fifth grade appeared on my television screen. The nose known as target of frequent successful pickings, Warren School, thirty-seven years before, now wrinkled, perplexed. Above serious lips, speaking of politics and honesty. Concerned words. No scream. *(Pauses; voice gangsterish)* I never wanted a *social* life, exactly, but I had hoped for a life. *(Pauses; voice again normal)* My job was counting. I worked for an inventory service, supermarkets our specialty, meat and poultry mine. *(Pauses)* I met Ethel there, in the counting. She worked spices. We met in early morning, one Monday, just before absolute totals. *(Pauses)* She was fifty, old Ethel. Amazing tits and ass. She'd been married before. Widowed young. Three sons not yet grown. I had my first with her. Happened so fast, I can't remember deciding to...*(Pauses)* Must have, though. *(Pauses)* We named him Alfred, after Ethel's father, not quite deceased, which is to say, still alive. *(Pauses)* He was in Chevrolets, Ethel's father. Near a major freeway. Can't remember the name of his place—just the brand. *(Pauses)* He was extraordinarily loyal. *(Pauses)* Owned four Chevrolets: one for the missus, one for himself, one for Ethel's retarded brother, Alfred—oh, yes, the brother was Alfred, too. Alfred III, actually. My poor Alfred was at the end of a long—as they say—line. *(Pauses)* Ethel got the coupe. *(Pauses)* Ethel's father, Alfred I, was, well, grateful. Old Alfred the grateful. He never liked me much, but he was full of...shhh... well...gratitude. Ethel wasn't what you'd call much of a bargain, what with her three imbecile children and her awful malady. *(Pauses)* Hiccups. Ethel had hiccups. Had them nearly thirty years before I met her. *(Pauses)* It was funny at first. Cute, I suppose. A large woman, wonderful tits and ass, hiccupping through every sentence. *(Pauses)* I learned to loathe every hic and belch. After five years, I thought of... well...destroying her. *(Pauses)* I tried every known method of cure. Jumping out of closets was kidstuff for me and old

Ethel. I once drove the coupe straight off Laurel Canyon Road. Mulholland, actually. Through the white fence and straight over the side. *(Pauses)* I didn't do it on purpose. I'm not crazy. I was daydreaming. Thinking of ways to end her hiccing. Thought for God knows what reason, we were at her father's Chevie showroom. I turned a left through the white fence, over the side of Mulholland and into the canyon. *(Pauses)* Ethel figured it was just another ploy to shut her up—so she wasn't scared at all. *(Pauses)* She didn't even believe my blood on my face. Or, afterwards, the scar. *(Pauses)* I did it. *(Pauses)* I did. *(Pauses)* I couldn't stand the hiccing—worse yet, I could not stand what came between: the endless babble, the endless babble of Ethel's words. *(Pauses)* I downshifted the coupe into second gear, pulled left into the fence, drove through, and then eased it into neutral. Ethel landed on my shoulders. I carried her on my shoulders, all the way down. Bizarre. It became a sort of St. Christopher act of self-destruction. *(Pauses; voice a child's)* This purple scar on my face, that's all.

> VOICES—SPEAKER #1 *and* #3:   Poor child.
> VOICES—SPEAKER #2 *and* #4:   Poor child.
> VOICES—SPEAKER #3 *and* #5:   Poor child.

MAN: We divorced immediately. I took nothing, she took the rest. *(Pauses)* Most of all, old Alfred hated me for wrecking his car. *(Pauses)* At the airport, all alone. No sound, no voice, no scream.

> VOICES—SPEAKER #1, #3 *and* #5:   *(Sharp shrill scream)*

MAN: *(Voice old again)* East, again. The Big Apple. Got a job selling life insurance. Twenty-payment-life my specialty. Made a fortune. Bought a car: a Ford. *(Pauses)* Thirty-five thousand miles the first year and never left New York for a one of them. *(Pauses)* Just as many dollars as miles that year and no end in sight. *(Pauses)* Never happier. *(Pauses)* Sold an Executive Planner Policy, Tarrytown, Tuesday, May eighth. Two hundred fifty thousand, face value. Borrow cash value, increasing term rider: very neat. *(Pauses; voice normal)* Can't remember the street. Wooded, dark. *(Pauses)* When I got back to my Ford L.T.D., there was a small Oriental man in the back seat. Saying nothing. Worse: not speaking. *(Pauses)* I asked him to leave. He wouldn't answer. *(Pauses)* I asked him his name. He wouldn't answer. *(Pauses)* He never answered me! *(Pauses)* I started to cry. *(Pauses)* Sobbing, I handed the keys to him and left the car. *(Pauses)* Not one word!—the little yellow bastard never spoke!—not one word! *(Pauses)* Good car, the Ford L.T.D. Nothing quite like it. *(Pauses; voice old again. Very confident)* Fifty-six and back in Boston. Marlborough Street, just before Kenmore. *(Pauses)* Old ground. *(Pauses)* Very confident. *(Pauses)* Sold the old policy again out of an office in Chestnut Hill over Stop and Shop. Very seedy, compared to my old Gramercy Park operation. *(Pauses)* Millionaires' Club in six months and more than forty thousand for me, after taxes. *(Pauses)* Never happier. *(Pauses)* Couldn't be. *(Pauses)* It became more than a job for me, really. Selling the twenty-payment became...well...a mission. *(Pauses)* Most of my clients actually died. That doesn't *sound* astonishing, but it was. Of the hundred and twelve Metropolitan men in my ordinary district, I was the only one who actually had a client die. *(Pauses)* My rate was three a week. *(Pauses)* No one who knew my reputation would ever buy a policy from me. *(Pauses)* I had to watch my step. I changed my name several times. Most men my age would be squeamish about changing names—that late in the game and all. Didn't bother me at all. Still doesn't. *(Pauses)* It did present some minor problems now and again. When I delivered the widow's money, I'd often have to do a bit of research to find out exactly who I was at the time of the sale. *(Pauses)* It was also difficult when I sold to family. But those who bought died and the problem came to a natural conclusion. *(Pauses)* I sold to everyone in my family, parents included. *(Pauses)* Eventually, by the age of sixty-one, I'd come into a great deal of money. Quite an embarrassment for a man of my years. *(Pauses)* Three and a half million, precisely. *(Pauses)* No friends. No time. *(Pauses)* No family, of course. *(Pauses)* No complaints from me...no time. *(Pauses)* No scream.

VOICES—SPEAKER #1 *and* #2:   Poor child.
VOICES—SPEAKER #3 *and* #4:   Poor child.
VOICES—SPEAKER #5 *and* #6:   Poor child.
VOICES—ALL SPEAKERS: *(Sharp shrill scream)*
MAN: I always thought that if I ever were to tell it, I would tell it more...elegantly—more elegantly than this. *(Pauses)* It did start well, I thought. *(Pauses; tone brightens)* When I first spoke—first learned—I was very close with people. In the beginning. *(Pauses)* I asked him, my father, why I was born: what purpose he'd had in mind for me. *(Pauses)* He slapped me. *(Pauses)* I asked my mother. She told me to ask my father. I never brought the question up again. No need. No purpose to it. No scream. *(Pauses)* If he had made me a monk, I would have been one. If he had make me a killer, that too. There was nothing I wouldn't have done for him. *(Pauses)* There was nothing he wanted. *(Pauses)* I've tried...to destroy myself...more than sixty different times. *(Pauses)* Always spared. *(Pauses; voice old again, confident)* When I was four-foot-two, I swallowed a bottle of pills. My mistake, vitamins: E and B12. *(Pauses)* I grew a foot in seven months, which is to say, I became twelve inches taller. *(Pauses)* That next year, at five-foot-two, I hurled myself into Lake Quannapowitt. The water was only four-foot-two. I was a year late. *(Pauses)* Caught an awful head cold. *(Pauses)* The next year I tried fire. *(Pauses)* Burned all the woods by the West Ward School. *(Pauses)* Nearly got the little red prison itself. *(Pauses)* The tree I'd tied myself to was the only one left intact. *(Pauses)* Horse-chestnut tree. *(Pauses)* The firemen found me. Bound to it. *(Pauses)* They wouldn't believe me when I said I'd tied myself. *(Pauses)* Neither did the police. *(Pauses)* Neither did the Wakefield Daily *Item* or the Boston *Post* or *Traveler*. *(Pauses)* Once the rock of scandal rolls out of control, logic and truth present no worthy obstacle. *(Pauses)* Tried that, too. *(Pauses)* Tied myself to an enormous boulder and tried to roll the West Ward hill. *(Pauses)* Never got the stone out of the mud. *(Pauses)* Ropes held then, too. Didn't surprise me any when all papers, local and national, passed the second story by.

(Pauses) Spent one whole night lying tied in front of a parked Sears and Roebuck trailer-truck. Driver finally came out in the morning. Backed up. *(Pauses)* He couldn't imagine who had tied up a kid in front of his truck. He would have called the papers except he didn't much care to have the world know where he'd spent the night. *(Pauses)* Me neither. *(Pauses)* No regrets now. Not really. *(Pauses)* The next year, on March thirty-first, my birthday, I tied myself to the train track, northbound side. *(Pauses)* Twenty-two hours, freezing all night, sweating all day. *(Pauses)* The Boston & Maine was on strike. Fare increase threat. Trains didn't run again for six weeks. *(Pauses)* Took me the full twenty-two hours to get my hands free. *(Pauses)* Opened the knots, finally, mid-day, April first. April Fool's Day. *(Pauses)* Never stopped trying. Simply never, well, succeeded. *(Pauses)* Hardly failed. Money, children, wives, travel, books, several foreign tongues. God *knows* I've still got my health. *(Pauses)* I'm an international ideal. *(Pauses; voice to gangster's)* Sixty-two and my reputation'd spread beyond repair. I couldn't have sold a policy to a dying man—*especially* a dying man. *(Pauses; voice to old man's)* Kiss of death. *(Pauses)* That's what they called me: kiss of death. Benjy was the first. At an awards dinner in Boston. The district agent was handing me my twenty-eighth medal for excellence. He was searching for an adjective, I suppose. From the audience, down below, Benjy's voice came booming up: "Kiss of death! That's what the ghoulish son-of-a-bitch is: kiss of death!" The audience laughed first. Then they clapped. Everybody knew me. I was a legend all over the country. *(Pauses; voice to normal)* Kiss of death. *(Pauses)* I worked another six months after that, but once a problem has a label that's easy to remember, it's instantly solved, or incurable. *(Pauses)* Mine was incurable. Everybody knew who I was—and now—*what* I was. *(Pauses)* No point in going on with it. *(Pauses)* None. *(Pauses)* I missed a few. I missed a couple I'd have liked to sold. *(Pauses)* Benjy. I'd pay his premiums myself. Over now. What's the point? *(Pauses; voice to gangster's)* When I was sixty-four, I met a twenty-three-year-old girl who said she

loved me. *(Pauses; voice to old)* Sixty-five, I moved out here. The house is small, quiet. Just me and a cairn terrier. *(Pauses)* Never knew an animal to be so faithful. Always with me. Wakes when I wake, sleeps when I sleep, eats when I eat. Walks with me. Watches me constantly. *(Pauses)* I did nothing to deserve such treatment. He certainly didn't know I was wealthy. I mean, he couldn't have been in it for the money. *(Pauses)* Gone now. Hit twice by a Chevrolet. Once wasn't enough. The old lunatic had to back up to see what he'd done. *(Pauses)* I'd like to think Murphy didn't know what hit him. He did. He knew. *(Pauses)* Took him sixty-eight days to die. *(Pauses)* One day for every year. *(Pauses)* Sixty-eight now. Me. *(Pauses)* All that time dying. Not fair.

VOICES—ALL SPEAKERS: Poor child.

(Laugh, scream)

MAN: *(Voice now old)* During my sixty-fifth year I survived eight known incurable diseases. *(Pauses)* The most bizarre was called "la maladie Charcot." *(Pauses)* The first hint came on March thirty-first, the first day of my first Medicare year. *(Pauses)* The big toe on my left foot went numb. I wouldn't have known, but for the way I tend my toenails. I've always used that very toe as my barometer. *(Pauses)* When the nail of my left-hand big toe reaches the innermost point of my left-hand shoe, I clip them all. *(Pauses)* Although the toe was dead, the nail was in every way tip-top. *(Pauses)* I was given then to Adidas sneakers, the all-white variety. Wore them twenty-four hours a day. Simultaneously, I was rarely given to cleaning my toenails, except during manicure. Which is to say *pedicure.* *(Pauses)* On Tuesday, March thirty-first, at two-thirty P.M., precisely, I kicked my alarm clock, which was set for nine in the morning, but rang five and one-half hours late, and had fallen on the floor—not me—the clock. *(Pauses)* I heard the most peculiar sound, like the sound of a toenail striking a plastic clockface. *(Pauses)* It was with my left foot, I'd kicked the face of my clock, its hands at two-thirty. My left-hand toenail had poked through my left white Adidas sneaker. I had heard the sound, but felt nothing. *(Pauses)* What faced me was the dread disease. *(Pauses)*

Thirty days later, the last in April, my left foot was dead to the knee. By the end of May, my entire leg to my chest. The whole right leg joined in one fantastic overnight freeze, in July. By the start of September, I could do no more than blink my left eyelid for *yes* and my right eyelid for *no*. *(Pauses)* Rather flirtatious messages for a man in my condition. *(Pauses)* My young doctor, Johnson, attempted euthanasia. And succeeded. Not me. The hag across the hall. *(Pauses)* He injected air into an artery—at least, that's what the paper said. He was found innocent, of course, and quickly. *(Pauses)* On September thirtieth, the last, he bent over as if to hear my breath. *(Pauses)* "Do you want a shot?" I blinked my left lid. *(Pauses)* As soon as the air hit my brain, all limbs unlocked. *(Pauses)* Without malice of forethought my elbow joint constricted, causing my fingers to clench into a fist, causing, in Dr. Johnson's groin, a hernia of almost landmark proportions. *(Pauses)* When the dust, as they say, settled, Johnson was unconscious, and every muscle in my entire body was absolutely functional, except for those controlling the lids to my left and right eyes. *(Pauses)* To this day, I don't blink. I can *force* a blink, but the normal, everyday state of my eyes is…wide open. *(Pauses)* The other diseases are hardly worth a mention. *(Pauses; voice is younger)* If I could have been a runner— *(Pauses; voice returns to normal age)* Benjy reappeared not more than a year ago. He'd aged: been awfully sick. *(Pauses)* He wanted me to sell him a policy. I don't know how the hell he found me all the way up here but he did. My reputation, probably. *(Pauses)* He should have known. *(Pauses)* He named it. *(Pauses)* I could have. But now that he *wanted* one, I couldn't. To tell you the truth, I was pleased to see his old face. Not that we ever actually drunk together, let alone talked. Still and all, there was a face there I'd seen before. And a name with it. *(Pauses)* I asked him to stay. He did. Three months. Stayed in the back bedroom. Didn't stray out from it much. Stayed in bed, I guess. *(Pauses)* That's where I found him. Buried him myself out in back. *(Pauses)* Wasn't much of a talker, Benjy. Never was. Never will be. *(Pauses)*

The thing about Benjy that intrigued me was his height. He had almost none. Couldn't have been more than three-nine, maybe three-ten. *(Pauses)* Benjy's problem in the insurance game was doorbells. *(Pauses)* Winters, too. Snowbanks. It's hard to imagine what it would feel like to sink in up to your eyes. *(Pauses)* He had a big heart, Benjy. Never saw a little woman-chaser like that before. Had a lot of style, especially with the tall ones. They used to mother him. *(Pauses)* Sixty years old and he'd ask 'em if he could sit on their laps. So he could hear better. *(Pauses)* They loved it. *(Pauses)* Shows how sick a woman is at the core. *(Pauses)* He carried a big knife, Benjy. *(Pauses)* People used to like to hurt him. Never saw anything like it. I hated to walk on the street with him. People used to come up, out of nowhere, and pinch his cheeks, or poke his arm. *(Pauses)* "How'd you get so little, fella? Didn't drink your milk?" *(Pauses)* Then he'd show them his big knife. They moved on. Nobody really liked the sight of a little man with such a big knife. *(Pauses)* Kiss of death, he called me. *(Pauses)* I did. *(Bows head)* I did it.

(Pauses; voice now young) So small. Everything born, dies. Once you see the thing itself, you can't pretend. *(Pauses)* I never had a son. How could I? *(Pauses)* Over the years, I lost track of what was real and what was imagined. The distinctions between the two became...unimportant. Style was another matter. *(Pauses)* I'd hoped to tell it well. The beginning was...well...not bad. *(Pauses)* I wish it might have continued that way. Oh, I suffered. But no more, no less, than...well...him. He was my father and, as such, naturally, got to the best and worst of it *before* I could. But no more, no less, really. *(Pauses)* It's all the same.

VOICES—ALL SPEAKERS: *(Scream)*

MAN: *(Pauses; voice now gangster's)* American women with their brassieres. *(Pauses; voice now young)* This is hardly the voice I'd planned on— *(Pauses; voice again old)* Two days ago, my things were stolen. Everything I owned, gone. *(Pauses)* Caruso. The handyman. He did it. *(Pauses)* I knew right away. He was the one to tell me about the first break-in. He was shaking. *(Pauses)* I came home. He was there, in my living room, with his wife. *(Pauses)* Bald. *(Pauses)* His wife. Erica. Stone bald. *(Pauses)* She was standing behind him, with her mannish, muscular arms folded across her enormous lungs. Quite a contradiction to consider, this union of Caruso and Erica. *(Pauses)* Caruso was shaking. He couldn't look at me. His eyes always kept darting about the room. He couldn't look at me. *(Pauses)* The window-shutters were whacking and thumping—the way they do in cheap movies. *(Pauses)* The sofa was gone. So was the chaise-longue, the desk, the desk chair, the bookcases and all books but for a plump book of verse. *(Pauses)* Caruso was sweating. "You've been robbed," he said. Then she punched his arm. They looked deeply into each other's eyes. Then they either kissed or talked intimately: I couldn't be sure in that surprisingly inferior lighting. Then she sang an awful aria in that horrid contralto voice of hers. She punched his arm again, they laughed and both left. Later, I noticed that all the lamps had left as well. *(Pauses)* The next night, all bric-a-brac; rugs and carpets, occasional tables, long tables, three end tables, new, by Drexel. Paintings by all prominent landscapists, trash-can and ash-can Americans and, by God, an early Lipshitz. *(Pauses)* Four Van Velde lithographs. Etchings by Baskin, Robbins, Wells, Rich and Green, Lestrille's famous gouaches, old lady watercolors. Copious aquatints. Frames for everything mentioned, except the Lipshitz, which was, of course, a large bulbous statue. *(Pauses)* No mirrors. Never. Not ever. No need. *(Pauses)* Ice bucket and bar utensils, all gone. Wines: St. Emilion and Medoc, California, and upstate Burgundies, five varieties of Gallo—all in red. *(Pauses)* I admit to nothing wonderful in white. *(Pauses)* A medium bottle of something called "The Love Potion." *(Pauses)* Purple. *(Pauses)* Candles and candlesticks. All gone. *(Pauses)* Insurance trophies—hundreds. Some gold, some silver, some copper, some bronze, and a slew in lucite. All gone. *(Pauses)* I needn't mention the appliances or every shred of identity—passport and driver's license, birth certificate and childhood locks of hair. All gone. *(Pauses)* Every scrap moved from its natural place. All order broken. All gone. *(Pauses)* Sixty-eight years of careful accumulation, moved in a mere twenty-one days. *(Pauses)* The rhythm boggles the brain. *(Pauses)* Caruso and Erica. *(Pauses)* They must have been obsessed. *(Pauses)* By the night of the tenth day, there was nothing left in the house, but my bed and a small revolver, .22 caliber. *(Pauses)* This morning, shortly after I woke, Caruso and Erica took my bed. They said nothing. They simply walked into my room and she took it. *(Pauses)* I gave up trying to reason with them, days ago. I don't think Caruso would steal from me if he weren't pushed into it—by her—the bald wife. *(Pauses)* I can only guess at what time the bed left. I haven't had a clock in any form for more than a week. Ten-thirty, maybe eleven. At noon or half-past twelve, Caruso came into the bathroom, where I was sitting. He still had trouble looking at me. "Somebody took your bed," he said. I spat at him. He said it again. "Somebody took your bed." *(Pauses)* He was crying when she came in. The bald one. Erica. They carried me out of my house and left me there, at the trellis. I heard them bolt the door locked, from the inside. *(Pauses)* The gun was in my pants pocket. *(Pauses)* There was no reasoning with them. *(Pauses)* I said I was sorry. God only knows what it was I did. They didn't care. There was no reasoning with them. *(Pauses)* They laughed. Man's laughter: two words. Join them together—marry them—one word: manslaughter. They laughed. *(Pauses; voice normal)* I tried again. *(Pauses)* No sense to it. Point pressed into chest. Inside thumping up to it. Finger still fighting, after all. *(Pauses)* Waited for life to pass in front of eyes. Legend faulty. Never did. *(Pauses)* Four years old. Woke all shivers. Mid-July. Nearing dawn. *(Pauses)* Before me, I stood: *(Voice to old)* Sixty-eight, spoiled, exactly as I am before you now. *(Pauses; voice normal)* We touched. *(Pauses)* He lifted me to his full height and he kissed me. He lowered me again, softly, gently, to my bed. He touched my eyelids: lowering me completely. *(Pauses)* Eyes again open. Mother there. Then still moving. I: all words. *(Pauses; voice child's)* "Kiss me, Mama. Hold me gentle." *(Pauses)* Down she smiled. "Poor child," she said.

    (Note: "Poor child" exactly as on tape. Pauses; voice young) I then screamed, so shrill and sudden, all sound

stopped, all colors bled. *(Pauses; voice normal)* Mother's pity joined my scream. Those two sounds would never leave me. Those and all other sounds would only float momentarily away. All sounds in space, floating to and from me, at will, their will, not mine. *(Pauses)* I could not continue to hear my returning ignorancies without end. Voice without end. Sound without end. No pardon. No amen. *(Pauses; screams as on tape)* No matter how I tried, I could not end it. *(Pauses; laughs as on tape)* Trying since beginning. Five, the first time. Didn't know why. Children happy. Laughter all around. Me outside. *(Pauses)* Father then moving. Mother all ears. Hugs abundant. Talk endless. Food, as talk. Sister, wide-eyed, adoring. Didn't know why. *(Pauses)* Gun in pocket, eyes open. Felt the weight of it. Pushed it in as if to stab. *(Pauses)* Sounds all empty. Colors mute. Smells to rancid. Tiny chest thumping. *(Pauses)* Lump pricked through. No pain. Full thrust, no blood. Eyes clenched, no scream. *(Pauses)* Always spared. *(Pauses; voice gangster's)* Spared. *(Pauses; voice child's)* Spared. *(Pauses; voice hushed, a whisper)* Spared.

   (The lights fade to black)

The Play Is Over

Olwen Wymark

LUNCHTIME CONCERT

Olwen Wymark

With Olwen Wymark's introduction as a playwright—in 1966 at the Close Theatre, Glasgow, and subsequently at the Edinburgh Festival and abroad—most critics perceived a new writer of considerable power and originality. A consensus of opinion that has continued unabatingly, it reached new heights with the 1969 premiere of *Stay Where You Are* at the Traverse Theatre, Edinburgh. (The play appeared in *The Best Short Plays 1972.*)

Members of the Scottish press cited it as "the best new play produced in Scotland in 1969," one that again vividly demonstrates that "Mrs. Wymark's way with words and ideas is indeed rather like a firecracker: but there are feelings behind them and powers of organization at work upon them that provide not only intellectual stimulants but a profound dramatic satisfaction."

B. A. Young, the influential reviewer for London's *The Financial Times* has written of the author: "Olwen Wymark not only has a remarkable, vivid and original imagination, she has an immaculate sense of what is effective on the stage. Many writers today seem to be writing for themselves alone: if we can't follow them, so much the worse for us. Mrs. Wymark's writing is always theatrical, full of humor, tension and poetry that are *shared* with the audience. She is a writer of unusual merit."

Lunchtime Concert, published for the first time in the United States in *The Best Short Plays 1975,* is a play of great universality, the embarrassment and the conflict that is always present between our "civilized" veneer of reality and the darker passions beneath. The characters are a bird-watcher and an odd couple, a teen-ager and a genteel old woman, whose mutual needs and affections drastically affect the sensibilities of the former, the proverbial "normal" man.

Olwen Wymark was born in Oakland, California, in 1929, and grew up in Palo Alto, where her father was a professor at Stanford University. Her mother is English and the daughter of the noted writer, W. W. Jacobs, who with Louis N. Parker wrote *The Monkey's Paw,* one of the theatre's most popular short plays.

Mrs. Wymark spent two and a half years at Pomona College, then went to England to complete her education at University College, London, where she met her husband, Patrick Wymark, a distinguished British actor who died in 1970.

After their marriage, the couple "lived in stimulating poverty in South London" while he was a drama student at the Old Vic School. In 1954, he was engaged by the Royal Shakespeare Company and the Wymarks moved to Stratford-on-Avon where they remained for five years. Upon their return to London, they took a house on the edge of Hampstead Heath where Mrs. Wymark now lives with her children, three cats and a dog.

The author readily admits, "I started writing at about the age of seven and began the Great American Novel nine or ten times but never finished it. I also wrote a great many rather tiring short stories and quite a lot of intense and bad poetry. In 1956, I wrote three radio plays, all of which were produced on the B.B.C., and immediately had two more babies in order not to have to write any more. But when all the children were in school, I ran out of excuses and wrote my first short play which had its premiere in 1966 at the Close Theatre."

Among her other works for the theatre are: *The Inhabitants; Coda; The Technicians; Jack the Giant-Killer; Neither Here Nor There;* and *The Committee,* produced in London in 1971.

In recent months, Mrs. Wymark has been writing for British television and also was the recipient of a bursary by The Arts Council of Great Britain to act as consultant and to write several children's plays for the Unicorn Theatre, London.

In addition to an active writing career and running a large household, Olwen Wymark does a good deal of voluntary work in the field of mental health, mainly for the Richmond Fellowship, an independent charity which sets up therapeutic communities for people who have suffered mental or emotional breakdowns.

Characters:

MAN
BOY
OLD WOMAN

Scene:

The stage is empty except for a tree. On the cyclorama is projected a picture of a wood in spring. The light on the stage should evoke this and be beautiful. As the lights go up, there is a certain amount of sound—rooks in the distance, twittering birds, etc. This fades as the bird watcher comes on. A middle-aged, slightly anxious, somewhat (but not too much) comic looking man, he is hung over with equipment—binoculars, a portable tape-recorder, notebooks, a satchel, etc.

A minute or so of gentle comic biz to get him and his stuff up into the tree. There is a brief pause after he is settled and then the Boy walks on, scuffing his feet, head down, smoking. He is about seventeen, rather loutish, possibly in grubby mod gear. A few steps behind him is the Old Woman. She is probably about seventy, rather fat and bizarre to look at. She has a kind of madly strong face, quite a lot of inept make-up, big features, rather wild eyes. She wears sort of layers of what look like wrappers or kimonos which have been unevenly cut off and crookedly hemmed and over them she wears sweaters or cardigans and scarves. She doesn't look destitute; she just looks odd. She is carrying a picnic basket.

SHE: Why can't you walk with me? Why can't you take my arm and walk with me? I'm an old lady.

HE: Who'd want to walk with you?

SHE: Then why did you come?

HE: I had to come. You know damn well I had to come.

SHE: I know no such thing. This picnic was not my

idea. I didn't want to come traipsing out into the woods. I would have been perfectly satisfied to spend the day in my own home.

HE: Your own home, ha! Who pays the rent? Who bought all the stuff in it?

SHE: Who lives in it, eh? Who lives in it?

HE: I do. It's my house.

SHE: You'll forgive me contradicting you but I think you'll agree that to live in a place means habitually to reside there. I hardly think your arrangements vis-a-vis that house fulfill that definition.

HE: Why don't you belt up? If you could just listen to yourself when you start talking like that, you'd never speak again for shame. *(Enunciating clearly)* It's very boring to listen to and you might just as well save your breath.

SHE: Well, of course we can't all be brilliant conversationalists like you.

HE: Oh, shut up, will you!

SHE: I sometimes wonder why you do bother to pay the rent.

HE: Just to keep you quiet, believe me.

SHE: *(Walks over to him and speaks in a friendly collected way)* I've said this before but I think perhaps it is worth going into again. There is no need for you to provide me with a house. You are in no way responsible for me and there is not the slightest reason for you to maintain me or even to see me. If you *want* to do it, the exercise is justified. If you do not want to and it causes you only irritation and pain, then you need...not...do...it.

HE: Belt up! Belt up! Belt up! Will you stop yammering at me. Talk, talk...on and on and on.

SHE: *(Angry and jangled)* I have hundreds of friends, you know. I would not be destitute. Oh, no. Don't think I depend on your charity. The entire Fabian Society of the country would rush to my aid if I lifted my little finger. They remember me. They know my worth. You say I'm old, you think I'm ugly. Believe me, there are dozens and dozens of people who remember my beauty, who value my conversation, enjoy my company. Do you think I have to be dependent on a scruffy little lout like you?

HE: *(Delighted that she has entered the arena)* Your great beauty! Your conversation! Don't make me laugh. Look at you. Look at your crappy old clothes. Look at that crazy make-up you put on. The Fabian Society! You're really funny, you know that. Hundreds of friends, my foot! If the dustman says good morning to you, you go weak at the knees for an hour. You haven't got any friends. The only ones who care for your bloody so-called conversation are your bloody cats and you know it. If I didn't pay the rent for that house and keep you there, they'd throw you out in the street like the old rubbish you are.

SHE: Don't speak to me like that. I don't have to take insults from a stupid working-class dolt. Who do you think you are? Where do you come from? Who were your parents, answer me that? You're nothing. Nobody. An empty, ill-mannered ludicrous lout.

HE: *(Dancing up and down with real pleasure)* Go on! Go on!

(There is a pause. She looks at him and then puts her hands on either side of her head deliberately and carefully. She takes a deep breath)

SHE: I will not go on. I do not wish to go on.

HE: *(Urgent)* Come on. Come on. Be a sport for once.

SHE: *(Singing it slightly)* I will not. I will not.

HE: *(Throws down his cigarette and grinds it out)* We always have to do everything your way, don't we? Madame bleeding chairman. *(He lights another cigarette)*

SHE: I wish you wouldn't smoke so much. You're too young to smoke like that. Especially without any breakfast. You'll ulcerate your entire system, mark my words.

HE: For God's sake, leave me alone and mind your own business. Just because you're old, you think you know everything.

SHE: Sorry I spoke, I'm sure. *(He shrugs indifferently and turns his back on her. After a moment she goes to him*

*and puts her hand on his shoulder and with her other hand
turns his face to her. He is unwilling to look at her and tries to
free himself but then does look and lets her look)* I really am
sorry. *(Importing sadness, tears)*

HE: *(Very gently)* I know. It's all right. Don't cry
now. It doesn't matter. Look, I'll put my fag out and we'll
put the basket down and you can tell me a story, okay?

SHE: Oh, yes!

*(They put the basket down and she sits on it in a very
formal attitude, retying a scarf or two and then putting
on a very odd hat which she has been carrying. He
kneels like a small child at her feet. There is a pause
while they look at each other and smile)*

SHE: *(Lucidly and really nicely)* Once upon a time
there were three gifted but suffering men. One had eyesight
so powerful and so brilliant that if he looked at the rocks
they flew apart before his eyes. The second could hear all
sounds. The delicate tissue of his typanums vibrated and
hummed to the sound of buds rustling and opening in the
spring, and the noise of surf breaking on a shore hundreds of
miles away crashed and boomed in his ears with fearful violence. The third had a stride so powerful that if he took a
step, he sprang halfway across the world. *(They rise slowly
looking at each other and as she continues the story they take
hands as for a minuet and execute slow simple steps walking up
and down)* The man with the brilliant eyes had to be blind-
fold always, the man with the exquisite ears had to bind
them with layers and layers of linen, and the man of the
great stride walked always with his ankles bound together
with heavy lengths of chain. And one day...

HE: One day...

SHE: The King came to the men.

HE: Yes...yes.

SHE: And the King said, "I need your great eyes. I
need your wonderful ears. I need your powerful stride. The
time has come."

HE: The time has come. *(Lovingly he puts his arm
around her and rests his forehead gratefully against her shoulder)*

SHE: "The time has come" the King said. "I need you." *(They recommence the slow dance and she is smiling slightly and gazing into the distance)* Yes, now I need you. I want you to...I want you...*(She falters and stumbles in the dance)*

HE: *(Seizing her wrist and trying to make her go on with the dance)* I want you to what? The King said "I want you to..."

SHE: *(She can't move. She is frightened and her hand goes nervously to her mouth, fumbles with her lips)* I want you to...I want you to...*(Whispers)* I can't remember the end.

HE: *(Tearing her hat off her, pushing her roughly away and then stamping and stamping on the hat)* You bitch! You lousy rotten old hag! You can't remember the end! You can never never remember the end. What are you trying to do to me? My God, what are you trying to do to me?

SHE: *(Goes back fearfully from him, exaggeratedly pathetic)* Don't touch me! It's not my fault. Wait. Wait for a moment, I'll remember it. I'm old. I forget things. Wait.

HE: You lie! You lie! *(He is moving after her and weeping with rage)* It's not because you're old. Don't give me that. It's because you like to do it, that's why you do it. You don't care about me. I don't matter. *(He leaps forward and seizes her around the throat and shakes her)* If you ever do that to me again, I'll kill you. I'll squeeze your skinny old neck till you're dead.

SHE: Help! Help! Help! *(But her voice is a deliberate whisper)*

HE: *(Pushing her away)* You'd like it, wouldn't you? You'd really like it.

SHE: *(Tidying herself up)* On the contrary, I assure you I have no wish to die.

HE: Oh, I don't mean die. Not all the way. It's not that. But you get a big kick out of it, don't you? Me beating up on you. *(Advances on her)* You'd like me to knock you about a bit, eh? Give you a few punches? A couple of kicks? You'd love that, would you?

SHE: Quite the little Freudian, aren't we? Because you are a sadist does not necessarily mean that I am a masochist.

HE: You'd wrap up everything in words, wouldn't you? It's all talk with you. God, if you knew how boring you are.

SHE: The incomprehensible is bound to be boring to the uncomprehending. I'm afraid you simply don't have the equipment for any kind of intelligent analytic discussion and if you did you wouldn't use it.

HE: Not if it meant I was going to get like you.

SHE: Well, I think I'll go now.

HE: What do you mean go? You can't just walk out like that. What about the picnic?

SHE: I've lost interest in the picnic. As a matter of fact, I've lost interest in you. You're always at great pains to tell me how much I bore you, but I don't think I have ever succeeded in making clear to you how infinitely tedious you are to me.

HE: Oh, we've heard this so many times. Can't you think of anything new? Whenever you think you've lost a bit of ground, you fall back on this swanky talk. "Infinitely tedious," ha! You don't find me tedious. You wouldn't dare. You'd be lost without me and you know it.

SHE: I'm going to go now, but before I go I want you to listen to me very carefully. I haven't said any of this before because I was sorry for you.

HE: You sorry for me!

SHE: Yes. I'm sorry for you because you're young, because you're stupid and because you're lonely. You do not interest me as a person because you're not a person at all. You're really rather grotesque.

HE: That's great coming from you, Mata Hari.

SHE: There was a time when I thought that with a little patience, a little affection, I might be able to help you bring some kind of pattern to your life. But that's all used up now. I have no patience left for you. I've run out. And as for affection... none! None! I feel nothing for you, do you hear? Nothing at all. I am free. I am absolutely free and I can do what I like with my life.

HE: What's left of it.

SHE: I thank God that there is less of it left for me than there is for you. You have all the time in the world to get lost in. I know where I've been, I know where I may go and I know where I am going. And I'm going now. Goodbye.

HE: Go then. Do you think I want you to stay? This is a big relief to me I can tell you. Maybe now I'll get a bit of peace and quiet.

SHE: Maybe you will. I doubt it. *(Starts off)*

HE: Are you coming back, or aren't you?

SHE: I'm not coming back.

HE: This is your last chance you know. I won't give you another one. No use coming crawling back on your hands and knees "Take me back" *(Parody voice)* "Take me back. I can't get on without you."

SHE: *Stupid boy.* Do you think I did all that for myself? I always did it for you and I'm not going to do it anymore.

HE: You did not. You did not! You did not! Listen to me. Listen. You've got one more chance. Just one more and then that's it. Finish. Kaput.

SHE: I'm going.

HE: That's right. Go. Self, self, self, that's all you think about. *(Runs quickly round to face her and prevent her going)* Do you think I want you to stay? Do you think I want to be tied to an old bag like you? You smell, do you know that? You smell of cats and mould and cabbage, did you know that, eh? And look at the clothes you wear. You're a walking jumble sale. Do you think I like being seen in public with you? All my friends laughing at me?

SHE: All your what? *(Amused, contemptuous)*

HE: My friends. I've got a lot of friends, don't you worry about that.

SHE: Good. Then give me my hat and let me go.

HE: Oh, no. Oh, no. It's not your hat, it's mine. I paid for it. You can take your smelly old clothes and your cats but you certainly do not get this hat.

SHE: All right. Keep it.

HE: I will. I mean it. I really will. I'm warning you.

SHE: Keep it. Keep it. I'm going.

HE: And how far do you think you'll get without it?

My God, I can just see you staggering along without this hat. You won't get ten yards, you old fool. Go on, go. I'm sick of you. *(She continues to walk off and again he runs wildly around to confront her)* There's just one thing more. I just want you to think about this one thing. You do realize, don't you, that the whole thing is based on jealousy. I'm young. I work. People admire me. And you're old and you're ugly and you're jealous. You...you want to be out in the middle of the stage, don't you—out in the middle of the stage in black net tights cracking the whip. That's all you ever really wanted. Oh God, yes. Don't think I haven't known this all along. I can read you like a bloody book!

SHE: *(Bored, superior)* Lay it on. Go on! And the money. Don't forget about the money.

HE: I'm not forgetting about the money. And you can't make me forget it by using that lady muck voice either. It's what you've always wanted—to get hold of my money. Oh, yes! That's your dream. Do you think I don't know that? Do you think I fell off a Christmas Tree? You bloody black widow spider...*(He sinks to his knees and buries his face in her skirts)* You disgust me. You sicken me.

SHE: *(Twisting her head about, wringing her hands)* Let me go. I want to go. Let me go!

HE: *(Holding her tighter)* Go then! Go! For God's sake, leave me!

SHE: I want to. I want to. Heaven knows I... Who are you? *(Looking up distractedly she has seen the man)*

HE: *(Letting her go and looking up too)* What the hell are you doing up there?

MAN: I...I...forgive me, I couldn't...

(The woman and the boy get up and walk over to the tree together rather menacingly)

SHE: I think you had better come down.

HE: If you don't, I'll bloody well drag you down. *(Makes a jump for the man's leg who pulls it up quickly)* What are you spying on us for?

MAN: No, wait! I'm coming down. *(Swings from a branch and drops. The boy advances on him and the man speaks as he backs away)* Believe me, I wasn't spying on you. I often come here, you see, to do a bit of bird-watching.

HE: Do you expect me to believe that? You were spying.

SHE: Stop. Leave him alone.

HE: *(Surprised)* He was watching us.

SHE: Nonsense. What makes you think anyone would want to spy on you? *(To the man)* You must forgive him. He gets carried away.

MAN: Not at all. Quite understandable, but I assure you I had no intention...I do hope you will forgive me. It was rather an awkward position, you see...

SHE: Of course, of course, I quite understand.

HE: Well, I don't.

SHE: *(Sweetly)* You wouldn't. *(To man)* So you're a bird watcher.

MAN: Well, not by profession of course, but it is a very great hobby of mine. I often come to these woods. I see some very interesting birds here.

HE: *(Suggestively)* I'll bet you do.

SHE: Please don't take any notice of him. His sense of humor is not refined.

HE: That's right. Run me down to a perfect stranger. You really love showing me up, don't you?

SHE: *(Ignoring him)* And this is a tape recorder, is it?

MAN: Yes, it's a bit difficult to manage in the tree as you can imagine but I'm getting the hang of it.

(The boy has wandered over to the tree and is examining the bird whistles. He blows one)

MAN: *(Seizes his binoculars. Very excited)* What? What? My goodness, it's a nuthatch. How extraordinary at this time of year! Where can it be? Don't go. Don't go. *(He is looking all over the place through his lookers and finally swings round and focuses on the boy who puts the whistle down and smiles at him and flaps his arms like wings)* Oh. Ha. Ha.

HE: *(With great cordiality)* We were about to have a story. Do join us.

SHE: Do. We'd be delighted to have you.

MAN: Really I don't think...

HE: Oh, come on. She wants you to. She may be an old bird but she's worth watching.

SHE: *(Good humored)* This is a watchbird watching you! *(She makes pretend binoculars out of her hands and waltzes over to the boy looking at him)* Did you brush your teeth last night?

HE: *(Striking attitude with toes out and hands behind back. Smiles broadly)* Yes!

SHE: And did you brush your teeth this morning?

HE: *(Attitude of despair. Covers face with his hands)* No.

SHE: Ah ha! Got you! *(Makes machine gun noise and pretends to shoot him down)*

(He clutches his stomach and "dies." They both laugh and then he jumps up and puts his hands up to his eyes)

HE: This is a watchbird watching *you!* *(She is delighted and takes up the child pose)* Did you tidy up all your toys this morning?

SHE: Yes!

HE: And did you take a bath this month you smelly old boot?

SHE: *(Pettishly)* There now. You've spoiled it. You're always spoiling it.

(The boy is still laughing at his own joke and pretends to shoot them both down)

SHE: Stop it. That's enough.

HE: Ooooh, if I only had a real gun, eh? Pow! Got him in the leg. Pow! In the stomach.

SHE: *(Playing up again and standing in front of the man to shield him with her arms outstretched)* Don't shoot!

HE: You can't save him now. You're both doomed. You can leave me for another man but not alive. *(He dances about trying to shoot at the man)*

SHE: That'll do now. That's quite enough. You're embarrassing the gentleman.

HE: Who cares about him?

SHE: I do. He is our guest. Now come along, you

said we were to have a story. *(To the man)* You'd like to hear a story, would you?

SHE: *(Muttering)* Yes of course. Very much indeed.

SHE: You see? Put on the hat.

HE: What me? I'm not telling it.

SHE: Of course you are. It's your turn.

HE: I can't. You know I can't. You're just trying to show me up again.

SHE: Don't be a silly little juggins. Certainly you can. Put on the hat.

HE: *(Puts on the hat)* All right. All right. But it won't be my fault if...don't blame me...*(He starts to walk up and down rapidly and talks very fast to start with)* There was this country, a little one, I don't know where it was. And it had a King. An old bloke who wasn't much cop...one of those geezers that thought if he had a crown on his head he was God Almighty, know what I mean? Nothing ever happened in this country. I mean, no wars or anything. Nothing changed. It just went on and on. And then all of a sudden one day this young chap comes along. Big chap. Very strong. Uh...uh...uh...he didn't have any parents, he was brought up by wolves in a cave in the mountains. He could talk animal language and all. Big strong handsome chap. He had this sword and he killed the King. I mean everybody wanted him to really but they just hadn't said. And then he took over the country. And then, my God, things began to happen. He raided all the border countries and got all their gold and everything and he killed off all the old deadbeats that had been running the place...ministers and that. And then he built fountains and casinos and dance halls and he closed all the schools.

MAN: What about public transport?

HE: What?

MAN: What about public transport? Buses and trains and trolleys. Did they go on running?

HE: Oh, no. He didn't bother about that.

MAN: Well, how did people get to work in the morning?

HE: They didn't have to. Don't you see? There wasn't any work to do. I mean there was all this gold and treasure. Plenty of it. He'd got it for everybody, not just himself. He wasn't a selfish chap. He was more a hero, you know, like Robin Hood or somebody.

MAN: Yes, but how was the gold administered to the general public? Who was in charge? You did say that the entire governing body had been wiped out. The Post Office for example, what became of that?

SHE: Are all these interruptions necessary? We are present as an audience, you know, not as inquisitors. It's only a story, after all.

HE: Only a story! That's just what you'd say. It's more than that...

MAN: Does it have an ending?

HE: If you could just shut up for a minute, we could find out, couldn't we?

MAN: You mean you don't know if its got an ending or not?

SHE: Why should he? He's telling it...he hasn't told it.

MAN: What is the reason for beginning a story if you don't know the end.

HE: Look, don't bother with him. He's a real hack type. Whodunits is what he wants. We don't need you, you know, mate.

SHE: Let him stay. He's not doing any harm. Go on with the story.

HE: If he'll shut up nagging about the ending.

MAN: But there will *be* an ending, isn't that so?

SHE: Probably not. His stories never do have endings.

HE: You dare say that to me! What about your rotten stories, hey? When do we ever hear the endings to those, hey? My God, what a bloody cheek!

SHE: All my stories have endings.

HE: *(In passionate rage)* You lie! You lie!

SHE: *(Calm. Raising her voice slightly but not looking*

at him) All my stories have endings. It does not always seem judicious to tell them to you.

HE: You cheat...that's a get-out and you know it. You're scared stiff of the endings...you always are.

SHE: Not on my own account.

HE: I'll kill you. I swear to God, this time I will kill you!

MAN: *(Coming between them)* Stop! Please. Please. Do finish your story. I really am most interested.

HE: Get her to tell you one. *(Turns away...then back)* With an ending.

MAN: Would you?

SHE: Certainly. Only a short one, mind.

HE: Don't think I'm going to give you the hat.

SHE: I don't need it.

HE: Ha!

SHE: *(Walks to the center stage and sits on basket)* There was once a very beautiful young girl...

HE: Of seventy-seven!

SHE: Who's entire life was spent swinging on the end of a rope. A heavy gold chain was wrapped round her wrists, not painfully, and she held the rope above the chain with both hands and swung back and forth in great sweeping arcs.

HE: Wearing black net tights.

SHE: Wearing black net tights of course. *(Smiles with real friendliness at him. He shrugs this off and turns away)* Below her and facing her on the ground stood a young man with his arms always upraised. Whenever she reached him on her swing forward, so that for an instant she was hanging immediately above him in the air, he would turn his face up to her and call her to come down into his arms.

HE: Oh, *very* romantic.

SHE: And one day she decided that she would come down and on her backward swing away from him she began to unwind the chain from her wrists and on her swing back she slipped her hands free and dropped down into his waiting arms.

HE: Knock him down?

SHE: *(Surprised but not offended)* Oh, no. He was very strong. He held her tightly in his arms and they kissed. And then the rope on its return journey, swung back and the heavy hanging chain struck her on the temple and she fell dead.

(There is a pause. The boy is standing stock still, facing upstage. The man leans forward still in a listening attitude. She looks placidly down at her hands)

MAN: And that's the end?

SHE: Oh, yes.

HE: *(Not turning)* How could you?

SHE: You spoke?

HE: *(Coming down to her, bends over her)* You'd stop at nothing, would you? You'd do anything at all to get at me, isn't that right? My God, what are you trying to do to me?

SHE: *(Stands and faces him speaking gently but rather impersonally)* Are you aware that those are the exact words you used earlier when I couldn't finish the other story?

HE: Not couldn't. Wouldn't.

SHE: Exactly. And what makes you think I am trying to do *anything* to you?

HE: Think! I know. My God, I've lived with you long enough to know what you're doing to me.

SHE: If you know, why do you continue to ask?

HE: Because you pretend you don't know, that's why. Because you won't say it.

SHE: Say what?

HE: That you want to do for me. Just say it. You're trying to destroy me.

SHE: You're trying to destroy me.

HE: No! No! No!

SHE: *(To the man)* You see how difficult he is.

HE: That's right. You side with him against me. He's much more your type isn't he with his little whistles and his posh hat. Look I'll just buzz off, right? You stay with him and have a nice little chat. The old folks at home. I'm off.

SHE: If that's what you want to do.

HE: What I want to do doesn't come into it. It never has and you know bloody well it never will! Listen, even this gink here who doesn't know anything about anything...even he can see perfectly well that you're throwing me out.

MAN: Oh, surely...pardon me, but it was you and not this lady here who suggested going.

HE AND SHE: That's not the point.

(They stop then and turn and smile at one another)

HE: *(Going to her and standing right in front of her, close but not touching and looking into her eyes)* You were, weren't you, throwing me out?

SHE: Yes.

(He leans his forehead on her shoulder and she puts up her hand and lovingly strokes him)

HE: Do you want me to go?

SHE: *(Crooningly)* No. No.

MAN: *(Suddenly blustering)* Look here!

(They turn and look at him surprised but amiable)

SHE: Yes?

MAN: I'd just like to...I mean, if I could get a word in edgewise...after all, I didn't wish to be involved in this at all. It wasn't my idea. I was invited.

HE: *(With great charm)* Of course you were invited, old man. We're delighted to have you. Have a sandwich.

SHE: Have some lemonade.

HE: Or a bun. The buns are very nice buns. We always bring buns and they do tend to be the high point of the picnic, don't they?

SHE: Well, you know, I always like the apple at the end the best. Have an apple.

MAN: I do not wish to have anything to eat. I would simply like to say a few words...

SHE: But by all means.

(She and the boy look at the man with interest and anticipation)

HE: Is it a story?

MAN: No, it's not a story. I don't tell stories, and

neither do any of my friends. In fact it is my opinion that all this storytelling is something of a waste of time.

HE: And sitting up in a tree like a monkey and blowing whistles isn't, eh?

MAN: It's a different thing. It's a recognized hobby, even, in some cases, a vocation.

HE: Vocation! The priest of the pee wits.

SHE: Hold your tongue! *(To the man)* He has no breeding, no background. You can understand it is often very hard on me, very difficult to put up with him. I am used to a certain graciousness, a sophistication... many of my friends were in the Arts, you know, the theatre, music, literature.

HE: That's right. I mean you just have to look at her to tell she moves in the very best circles. She's got wonderful taste in clothes, you know. Expensive mind, but after all if you're going to spend money on clothes why not buy the really good stuff. Real county, you can tell. She's got blue blood in those baggy old varicose veins, you know. *(He turns her round and pulls up her skirts to show her legs)* What legs, eh? Who's Marlene Dietrich? I mean, just take a look at those lovely gams.

SHE: *(Flattered and looking down at her legs)* I always did have pretty legs.

HE: Come on, do us a little dance. Show the gentleman the way you do the Highland fling why don't you? He'd like that, wouldn't you?

MAN: *(Flustered, takes out his binoculars and looks out toward the audience)* Was that a blue tit?

HE: Blue *tits!* I never said that. Let's not have any of that filthy talk here.

SHE: *(Laughing)* Silly boy! Oh, you are naughty.

HE: Course I am. That's what you love, isn't it? *(Pats her suggestively on the bottom)* Come on, curvaceous, give us a dance and drive us all mad.

SHE: Well, all right, if you really want me to.

(The boy starts to clap and she picks up her skirts and

executes a fairly skillful Highland fling. He claps faster and faster and her dance gets wilder and wilder. She is whirling about)

HE: *(Seizing the man round the waist)* Come on, Bishop, do the tango with me. Let's get in on the act.

(He drags the man across the stage doing a very exaggerated tango. The man is beside himself with embarrassment. The boy spins him round and sends him into the woman's arms. She has stopped dancing and has been clapping. She embraces the man and kisses him on the lips)

HE: *(After a sharp pause strides over to her in a murderous rage. He flings the man aside and grabs her by the shoulders)* You go too far! You whore, you go too far. What do you think you're trying to do? God, you filthy bitch! Who do you belong to, tell me that? Who keeps you?

SHE: *(Pulls away from him and walks away straightening her clothes)* No one. No one keeps me and I belong to no one.

HE: You belong to me and when you're out with me you'll behave yourself.

SHE: *(Over her shoulder. Rather coquettish)* Who's jealous?

HE: Jealous! Are you out of your mind? Who'd want you? Who else would ever put up with you? You ought to be down on your knees every day thanking God that I do take care of you.

SHE: I take care of *you.* Because I choose to. Out of the goodness of my heart. I'm sorry for you... you're just like any other stray animal as far as I'm concerned.

HE: Animals. That's what you like. That's what you're really after. Well, how would you like it if I told you that the reason I never touch you... like an *animal*... is because I'm funny. I'm a bit odd. *(Lisping, camp talk and walk)* I prefer the gentlemen and I always have. I'm a nice boy, aren't I? *(Goes over to the man and strokes his arm)* Would you like me to come home with you? We could have fun.

(The man throws off his hand and walks distractedly over

to the tree and starts picking up his whistles and things)

HE: Don't go, saucy. I know you like it.

SHE: It's not true! You're lying!

HE: What do you care anyway? You find me "infinitely tedious," remember? But the nice gentleman doesn't find me a bit tedious. We're going to have a lovely time together, aren't we?

SHE: *(Pulling the man away from the boy)* Leave him alone, do you hear me? He's only a child.

MAN: Madame! What do you mean? I assure you I have absolutely no interest...

SHE: Don't palter with me. I know him well enough to know that he would never make any advances unless he'd had some encouragement. Oh, we know your sort.

HE: We certainly do. Oh, come on. We can't fool her. She's been around a long time, you know. She knows the seamy side backwards, forwards and sideways. Come clean now. Go on. Tell her what you said to me behind the tree. *(Hugs and nuzzles the man)*

MAN: Don't! Leave me alone...

SHE: I knew! I knew! You filthy beast! Bird-watching indeed! You've met each other before, haven't you? Where? When? How many times?

HE: *(Seizing the man's muffler and putting it on as a priest's stole. Steps back and makes sign of the cross)* Come, my child. Confess. How many times?

SHE: Don't try to put me off with your jokes. I want to know the facts. I have a right to know. I'm going to call a policeman. It's against the law you know, corrupting the young. How dare you? He's a good boy. He's not one of your cheap little street corner tarts.

HE: Gracious, what a thing to say. This is a real gentleman; he's a real high class type. He wants to educate me...teach me all about art and music and all that. Oh, we've had some lovely talks.

MAN: Wait! Stop! What are you saying?

SHE: *(Drawing the boy to her)* Can't you see what he's doing to you? Oh, you're too innocent, too trusting. All this talk is just a front. He wants to get you in his clutches.

HE: *(Outraged)* Is that your game? All those things you said about how sensitive and intelligent I was. All lies? Call a policeman. Call Lord Wolfenden. Call the Press. We'll blow this story sky high. "Respectable Birdwatcher Ensnares Innocent Lad."

SHE: "Vulture revealed."

HE: "Apple-cheeked Working Boy Tells All."

MAN: *Stop!*

(There is a pause. They all stand still)

MAN: *(Walks over to the woman. Speaks with quiet intensity)* I will not be involved in this. *(To boy)* I will not be involved.

SHE: Not a very sporting type, your friend.

HE: Dead loss, really.

MAN: You mean it was only a game?

HE: I don't know. *(To her)* Was it only a game?

SHE: I expect so. Yes, I should think so.

MAN: You ought to *know*. It's important to know. I've been watching you...

HE: He's been watching us.

SHE: He's the Watch Committee, can't you tell?

HE: He's a watchbird watching us.

MAN: Please! You must listen to me.

HE: You got something to say?

MAN: Yes, I have. Yes.

HE: Right.

MAN: The funny thing is...I know it's none of my business. I mean, I've never really spoken to strangers before.

SHE: Oh, you're not a stranger, surely. We have met. We are friends. We are concerned with each other.

MAN: Concern. Yes. Yes, that's it. I *am* concerned ...well, worried. You see, I don't understand you.

SHE: And you feel that you should?

MAN: Well, what I mean is...for one thing, I can't quite see how it comes about that you are...uh...*(Hastily)* together if you see what I mean.

HE: Well, we live in the same house, see?

MAN: *(Hopefully)* At first I thought... I wondered if you might be related. An aunt and nephew... oh, well, a great aunt of course...

SHE: Oh...

HE: Nitto, mate. Don't say that. I mean that really hurts her when you say she's old. Don't do that.

MAN: I'm so sorry. Forgive me. I didn't...

SHE: Please. It's quite all right. I am old.

HE: So what?

(They smile at each other)

SHE: So what.

MAN: Not related?

(They laugh)

SHE: No. Really not.

MAN: When I asked you if all that was a game just now, neither of you seemed to know. Well, *(To boy)* was it a game before when you were going to kill her?

HE: Oh, I don't think so. I was really narked, you know. She goes too far a lot of the time.

SHE: So do you.

HE: All right, all right. We don't need all that. The gentleman's talking to me just at the moment.

MAN: *Would* you have killed her?

HE: Oh, no. I couldn't kill her. I love her.

MAN: But how can you?... I mean, you can't... not this way... what I mean is... don't you see it's not suitable ... it's, well, it's bizarre!

HE: Now look, what is all this? You said you had something to say. Well, if it's only insults...

SHE: *(Judiciously)* Bizarre. It's really a very *nice* word. Don't be cross with him. Let's hear him out.

HE: All right, but what's it all about?

MAN: It's about life. About the way of leading life. *(He pauses and looks a little surprised)* My goodness, that sounds very pretentious. *(To woman)* Believe me, I don't make a habit of preaching to people. I live my own life; I expect other people to live theirs. But don't you see... surely *you* must see how reckless all this is.

SHE: Reckless...?

MAN: What I mean to say is life *isn't* a game, is it? I mean if everyone went around doing exactly as they felt...not *bothering*...well, I mean, where would we be? What would happen?

HE: I don't know what you mean, not bothering. I bother about her. And she bothers about her flaming cats. And sometimes when she's not drunk with power, she bothers about me.

SHE: I trust you are not speaking seriously. You know perfectly well that every hour of my day is taken up with bothering about you. My poor little cats get very short shrift I assure you.

HE: Oh, come on. You've got those bloody lights boiling on the stove all day. I've seen you spend hours at a time trying to teach one of them how to catch a mouse.

SHE: And a great deal more rewarding it is than trying to teach you how to speak proper English. The poor little dear can't help it if it was born without the correct instincts.

MAN: That's just what I mean!

(They pause and look at him)

MAN: Uh...instinct.

SHE: Yes?

MAN: If we allow ourselves...if we simply follow our instincts. Instinct is very powerful. Don't you see, we would all be doing...all sorts of...letting ourselves go. Well, jumping off roofs, tearing off all our clothes...yes, killing people.

SHE: I'm not sure that I follow you. For one thing the climate in this country is not at all suitable.

HE: And for another thing it would take her two and a half hours to tear that lot off.

MAN: You misunderstand me. I am talking about order. There must be a pattern. Just as there is a pattern in the universe, an order and design in our natural world so we, too, if you follow me, must find the design, arrange the pattern of our own lives. If not, then, as the Bard puts it "Chaos is come again."

SHE: *(Gently)* The whole of the line is "And when I love her not, chaos is come again."

MAN: *(A little testy)* I was not discussing the play. I was only using the line as a pointer.

HE: Well, go on, mate. You point at it and we'll look at it.

SHE: Would it perhaps be easier if you had the hat?

MAN: Thank you, no. I am not a superstitious man.

HE: It's not a superstitious hat. You just put it on when you want to tell something. I mean, you must admit, old man, you're not getting on very brilliantly without it.

SHE: He could get on a great deal better without these irrelevant interruptions from you.

HE: I like that. I haven't interrupted nearly as many times as you.

SHE: Ah, but my interruptions, you see, are relevant.

MAN: *(Raising his voice and overriding them)* Let us look for a moment at electricity.

SHE: *(Affably)* By all means.

(The man's voice has become rather crisp and authoritative and it is this that makes the woman and the boy move over to the basket where the woman sits and the boy sits beside her on the ground. With docile attention they follow the man with their eyes as he paces up and down in a measured way and continues:)

MAN: As you know, electricity is a tremendously powerful force—the Life Force, as it were, of the elemental world. The atom itself is held together by positive and negative charges of electricity—electrons, neutrons, protons—and if one electron is drawn or struck from its orbit in the tiny universe of the atom, at once the chain reaction releases a blast of fantastic power. A mass of matter that was, but a heartbeat ago, millions of little ordered worlds is now a flash, a roar, a flame of terrible destruction, and then…a huge, silent, towering cloud of death.

SHE: *(Clapping)* Very nice. Beautifully put.

HE: *(Joins clapping)* Lovely, mate. Very good.

MAN: *(Modestly)* Thank you.

SHE: Do you ever do any acting? You have a wonderful delivery.

MAN: As a matter of fact, I once played Macbeth in an amateur production.

SHE: I'm sure you were splendid.

HE: You should come along one day and join us in charades.

SHE: That *would* be nice. We often have charades on a rainy day. You would be a very good influence. He *(Indicating the boy)* is always confusing what is real with what is make-believe. We had the police in once...

HE: Wait a minute. That wasn't my fault. Who was screaming like a banshee out of the scullery window?

SHE: That was acting. *(With dignity)* It was certainly not my fault that those officers...

MAN: Oh, please...stop...I don't think...

HE: Look, he's got something he wants to tell us. He doesn't want to hear a lot of stories about your horrible past. I mean, nobody would believe half of them. What about the time they nearly took you off to the bin...that time you started singing them Leeds in the public library.

SHE: Lieder. German Lieder. I had been deeply moved by a work of Heine I was reading at the time.

HE: Well, you would have been moved for good and all if I hadn't said you were me mum and having one of your poorly turns. Remember that doctor and all the pills he gave me for you? "You are in charge, my boy! You must help your mother."

SHE: And what did you do with them, you vicious little monster? Fed them to my pussycats. I thought they were dead. I haven't cried so much since I was a child.

HE: They were all right. Just passed out like a lot of drunks. Laugh? They were really comic, they really were.

SHE: *(Giggling)* It really was very funny. We laid them all out in the front garden and strewed them with flowers and you turned your collar round...

(The man has been watching them with increasing anx-

iety and now with a wild look on his face has his hands over his ears)

HE: Look at him. You got him all upset again. Why can't you shut up and let him get on? *(Reaches over and touches the man who takes his hands from his ears and looks down at him)* You go on, my friend. Go on with what you were saying. We're listening.

MAN: I don't know if I can. *(Pauses and straightens ...takes a deep breath)* But I must. I will. Everything you say, all the things you tell me show so clearly that neither of you has any real respect for the dreadful power of life.

SHE: Dreadful?

MAN: Anarchy is dreadful. Order is beautiful. If we could return to electricity: I often see it as a great giant whom we have made our slave. But a dangerous slave. We must take great care. There is no room for frivolity. We cannot take risks. We conduct this giant into our buildings and our machines and force him to work for us. Imagine the giant made captive in our ridiculous little houses, humming and straining to find a way out—rushing to every possible outlet—is this the way?—and each time finding himself ignominiously trapped. The rage! The anger! You know yourselves what a dazzling blaze there is if we relax our guard for an instant. *(Then musingly to himself)* If a child, a soft creeping baby, puts its little fingers into the holes of the electric point, how the prisoned giant will seize him! The savage bite...the terrible scream of pain... *(He breaks off and is silent, smiling slightly. The woman and the boy continue to listen expectantly but then look at each other in uneasy perplexity. The woman pats the boy briskly on the knee, clears her throat and rises)*

SHE: Prisoned giant. What an interesting metaphor. Like Prometheus.

MAN: *(Blankly)* Prometheus?

SHE: The giant bound to the rock. The bringer of fire.

HE: Go on. Tell us that one. *(To man)* It's a very good story this. Not a made-up one...it's out of a book.

She's very good on this one. Come on. You come and sit with me. Take a little break.

(The man obediently sits on the basket)

HE: Like a smoke?

MAN: What? Oh, no. No, thanks.

HE: You don't mind if I do? Go on. Get on. We're listening.

SHE: *(Sweetly)* You do realize that that is the eleventh cigarette you have had this morning. I cannot think you have so much as glanced at that copy of the Lancet that I put under your pillow.

(The boy makes a move at her and she hastily continues. The story is almost chanted and she should sketch or suggest the incantatory feeling and the movements of a Greek chorus. The boy is all smiling and pleased attention throughout. The man looks a little mesmerised and sways slightly to her rhythms)

SHE: Here is the story of Prometheus son of the Titan Iapetus and Clymene, brother of Atlas, Menoetius and Epimetheus and sometimes called the Father of Mankind as it was related Prometheus had created man out of earth and water.

HE: *(Sotto)* Lovely, in'it? You like it?

(The man just looks at him distractedly and then returns his attention to the woman)

SHE: Atlas and Menoetius joined in battle with Cronus against Zeus who killed Menoetius with a thunderbolt and condemned Atlas to support Heaven on his shoulders for all eternity. Prometheus, wisest of his race, had been taught by Athene architecture, astronomy, mathematics, medicine and all useful arts which he had passed on to mankind. Athene then admitted him secretly to Olympus where he lighted a torch at the fiery chariot of the Sun and presently broke from it a fragment of glowing charcoal which he thrust into the hollow of a giant fennel stalk. Then, extinguishing his torch, he stole away undiscovered and gave fire to mankind. Zeus swore revenge. He had Prometheus chained naked to a pillar on Mount Caucasus where an eagle tore at his liver all day, year in, year out; and there was no end to the pain because every night his liver grew whole again. Hercules killed the eagle and delivered the sufferer with the consent of Zeus who in this way had an opportunity of allowing his son to gain immortal fame.

MAN: *(Sitting quite still on basket, staring ahead of him)* Not an eagle. It wouldn't be an eagle.

SHE: You think not?

HE: Why shouldn't it be? Why does it say eagle if it doesn't mean it?

MAN: *(Rising and speaking eagerly)* Well, it stands to reason, doesn't it? It wouldn't be a bird at all—it would be a pterodactyl.

HE: A terry who?

MAN: *(Impatiently)* Pterodactyl. Pterodactyl. A prehistoric bird. Well, not a bird, technically. A sort of vast flying lizard. Huge scaly wings. *(He flaps his arms in large movements and begins walking very slowly about)* The nearest thing we get to it in modern times is a vulture. You know, the long skinny neck...a sharp hooked beak. I don't know if you've noticed but the eyes are always rather large and brilliant...piercing. Oh, yes, definitely, yes, yes, yes, it would be a pterodactyl. *(He has stopped walking and flapping and is rubbing his hands together. He walks over to the boy, takes him by the arm and leads him to the tree)* It's quite easy to conjure up the scene. Imagine it. Dawn, I should think, when it came, wouldn't you? The bird...the Thing, I mean; Prometheus chained to the rock, like this. *(He pushes the boy back against the tree and takes his arms and puts them round the tree. The boy is puzzled but smiles a little, clasps his hands high up so that his face is upturned)*

MAN: He is exhausted but apprehensive because he can smell the dawn, there is a faint glimmer of gray light in the sky. He turns his head this way and that. *(The man turns the boy's head from side to side)* Straining to see that awful familiar shape flapping toward him through the gloom. Ah! He sees it! He twists and turns his body against the cold hard rocks, straining against his chains. He knows what is coming. He twitches in his nakedness.

(Suddenly the man rips the boy's shirt open. The boy tries to get away but the man fiercely pushes his hands up again behind the tree)

HE: Hey! Cut it out. What are you doing?

MAN: *(Over his shoulder to the woman)* You said charades, didn't you? You like charades. *(Then back to the boy)* It's quite clear in the sky now. Moving much faster. Closer and closer it comes speeding toward him. It is upon him... the brilliant terrible eyes... it swoops! *(He pushes his head down into the boy's bare stomach and butts him savagely. He lifts his head, then butts him again, then lifts as he says the next lines)* The sharp beak plunges into the flesh, the blood spurts out, sickening pain... again... again... again...

(The woman has rushed over and she wrests the boy away from the man who is left crouched in front of the tree still making the movements with his head and muttering and moaning)

SHE: Stop it! Stop it at once! We don't like this game.

(She cradles the boy in her arms, his head against her breast. Then kneels in front of him to button his shirt)

MAN: *(Straightens and turns around sharply to face them)* Game? Game? Game? Listen to me. I see them. I watch them, the birds. I know the things they do. Monstrous, vicious things. Oh, they can chirp and twitter... soft little feathers... hopping, pecking. I have seen a mother robin peck out her babies' eyes! I've seen a rook, a great black shiny rook rape and savage a dove! They can't fool me. I watch. I watch. I see them. Starlings in a pack clawing and tearing a thrush to death. They're afraid of me though. Do you know what I do? Do you know? *(Smiling, triumphant)* I... exterminate... them. I am the Law. They know that. They know I'll punish them. Look. Look here. *(He dashes over to his bag and tears it open. It is full of the dead bodies of birds. He takes them out and hurls them on the ground as he talks)* One moment struggling in the net or the trap... then they are in *my* hands. Sometimes I jab them with my knife. *(Does this)* There! That's what pecking feels like! Sometimes I tear off their vile wings. *(Does this)* I wring their necks or sometimes I stamp them to death. Abominable! Disgusting! You can't get away from me. Law and order. Execution.

(He is quite incoherent and has begun to tear at one of the bodies with his mouth. During all this the woman and the boy, clutching each other, have cowered back and are watching him, terrified)

SHE: What shall we do? We must run away. Quickly! Quickly!

HE: No. No. We can't leave him like this. We got to do something for him.

SHE: What *can* we do?

MAN: *(Lifting his head covered with feathers and blood, whispers)* Tie me up! Tie me up!

HE: That's it. Yes. There's some rope under the tree. *(Runs over to get it)*

SHE: Be careful.

HE: Help me. Grab him! He won't hurt you.

(She runs over and pulls him over to the tree The boy very rapidly ties him up if possible much in the position the man had held him there. He is bound fast, head down, panting. There is a silence. They step back together and look at him. Pause)

SHE: Do you think perhaps a drink of lemonade?

HE: Here. Give us a hanky. *(She takes one out of her sleeve and he takes it over to the man and gently wipes his face)* All right. All right. It's okay now. All over now.

SHE: *(Judiciously)* Well, that's an improvement, I must say. I should put his hat on him. He might catch cold.

HE: No, I tell you what. We'll give him our hat. You'd like that, wouldn't you? Here. Give it to me.

(She hands him the hat and he puts it on the man. She steps back and takes a critical look)

SHE: I don't think, do you? It looks out of place and his stories are not good, I'm afraid.

HE: He's pretty nippy with the surprise endings, though.

SHE: Oh, ripping. *(They both laugh)* But I think the hat might hinder more than help, don't you? I think we'd better keep it. *(Boy takes hat back and puts it in his pocket)* No, but we mustn't be unkind. I think he was really upset. *(To man)* Forgive us. We wouldn't want you to think we were mocking you. It's been most interesting, truly it has, but we really must be running along now.

HE: Listen, that was great all that stuff you told us about electricity and the atoms and all. I mean, we won't forget it, honest.

SHE: It is in our memory locked and you yourself shall keep the key to it.

HE: Do you think you could lay off the quotations just for once? It's only showing off, you know.

SHE: It would naturally appear so to an impoverished mind. This gentleman, unlike you, is extremely cultivated and well read. In conversation with him I am able to draw on that great treasury of human spirit and endeavor that has...

HE: Oh, for God's sake, can it! I want my lunch.

SHE: The mind too, must be fed.

HE: *(Grinning good-naturedly and slapping her on the bottom)* Ah, come on, Mrs. Einstein. Be a sport. I brought you here to enjoy yourself...

BOTH: And enjoy yourself you shall!

SHE: Very well. Get the basket. *(She looks uncertainly at the man)* I suppose he *will* be all right.

HE: He'll be fine. Tell you what? I'll untie this knot at the back for him.

SHE: Well, if you think... It doesn't seem awfully courteous. We did ask him to our picnic.

HE: He wasn't awfully courteous with my shirt, was he? Look, he's not our sort.

SHE: That is true.

HE: Course it's true. He'd spoil everything. Wouldn't he... eh?

SHE: Yes, I'm afraid he would. Well, come along then. *(They start to go out. Bring in softly, sound of birds)*

SHE: Not but what he wasn't very good value, really. A very *original* chap I thought, didn't you?

HE: All right for you to say. He wasn't tearing your clothes to bits, was he?

SHE: That was going too far, I quite agree. "All those buttons to sew on," I thought to myself. As if I hadn't enough to do...

HE: Don't make me laugh. You...sew on buttons?

SHE: Mind you, it was not a thing I was brought up to. A little embroidery, yes, crochet, tapestry work...that sort of thing. Buttons were left to the maid...

HE: Goodness, Duchess, I could listen to your memoirs all day, but do you think you could do me a really big favor?

SHE: What's that?

HE: Shut your big fat cake hole and *let's get on!*

SHE: The expressions you use!

HE: All right. All right. You're you and I'm me.

SHE: *(Pinching his cheek)* And very nice, too, little Lord Fauntleroy.

HE: *(Giving her a smacking kiss on the cheek and starts to run off. Calls back in a posh voice)* Come along, dearest, time for tea and crumpets. *(He goes off)*

SHE: Coming, Ceddy darling. Oh...*(Turns to man)* Goodbye. It's been so nice. *(Goes off but calls genially back over her shoulder)* Don't let the sparrows get you! *(Goes off but we hear her voice fading away)* Wait for me! Will you please wait for *me!*

(The man stands with his eyes closed, oblivious of their departure. The lights begin to go down until the whole stage is nearly dark except for a spotlight on his face. As the lights fade, so the bird sounds begin to get louder and louder and become discordant and threatening; the twitter of finches and blackbirds is transformed into the menacing cries of hawks and ravens and there is the loud fluttering of wings. The man cries out in fear and hunches, cowering, against the tree, twitching and panting)

MAN: It's the trap! I'm in the trap! Help me! Help me!

(Then the lights begin slowly to come up again and the bird sounds dwindle into the woodland sounds of the be-

ginning of the play. He is still. Then slowly he lifts his head, opens his eyes, looks apprehensively about. Nothing. He straightens, relieved, becomes aware of the rope and indignantly wriggles out of it. Affronted and huffy he looks this way and that for the woman and the boy. He walks over in the direction of their exit, makes an angry gesture with his arm and calls after them, but not too loud in case they should hear)

MAN: I shall report this! I shall certainly report this!
(Then back to collect his things, fussy and precise, muttering to himself. Finally, rope coiled over one arm, tape recorder over the other, knapsack on his back, he squares his shoulders and prepares to go. He nearly trips over the bodies of the birds and, for a moment as he looks down at the carnage, a look of fear crosses his face. His knife is lying among the feathers and blood. Without expression and with great care not to touch anything but the knife, he moves it out into a clear space with his foot. He picks it up with quick relief and then looks down fastidiously)

MAN: *(Under his breath)* Litter! Disgusting. I don't know how people can!

(Briskly and self-righteously he goes)

Curtain

Robert Kimmel Smith

A LITTLE DANCING

Robert Kimmel Smith

Robert Kimmel Smith was born in Brooklyn, New York, in 1930, and was educated at Brooklyn College. After serving in the U.S. Army, he obtained work as an advertising copywriter and remained in that field, in advancing positions, with several other companies until 1967 when he formed his own advertising agency, Smith & Toback, which was dissolved in 1969.

He began writing as a full time occupation in 1970. In a reply to a request for biographical data, Mr. Smith reflected: "In 1970, I was going to be forty years old. I had dreamed for a long time of finding out whether or not I had the talent to be a professional writer. Having closed my ad agency in December, 1969, I decided to give writing a shot. I wasn't getting any younger, and I probably wouldn't ever be any richer, so what the hell! My wife's encouragement, as you can imagine, meant a great deal. So, in January of 1970, I began. I wrote *Ransom* (a suspense novel published in 1971) all that year. A publisher bought it on the strength of the first one hundred manuscript pages in September. I finished my rewrite in December."

Ransom was followed in 1972 by a children's novel, *Chocolate Fever;* and in 1973 by *Sadie Shapiro's Knitting Book,* which became one of the year's most popular comic novels.

The author continues: "I wrote the first part of the two plays, *A Little Singing, A Little Dancing,* in 1971. Actually, the play was, for me, an exercise in learning how to write a play. I did it in ten days. When the people at the Eugene O'Neill Memorial Theatre Center in Waterford, Connecticut, took it that year, I became a playwright.

"Apparently, for me, plays come in a rush and a novel is a long grind. *Up In Smoke* (presented at the Berkshire Theatre Workshop, Massachusetts, in 1973) was written in a week. *A Little Dancing* took two weeks. The play is based on a true story I'd heard, in which a mother had her son bring her some marijuana cigarettes because she wanted to know what they were about. The framing of the story, and the consequences (which, to this editor, culminates in some rather candid and surprising revelations) are fictional.

"I live in Brooklyn (with his wife and two children), among the middle-class people I write about. I will continue to live here, hopefully writing funny plays and novels for a long time, God and my wife willing! Comedy is my love, and is all I really want to do. Not just being funny, but, in William Goldman's phrase, funny *about something*. I hate being hemmed in by reality in my work. Human beings are strange people, they do crazy things. They operate on cock-eyed motives to achieve devious ends. With luck, I might get some more of their misadventures on stage."

A Little Dancing (and its companion piece, *A Little Singing)* was presented in 1972 at the Washington Theatre Club and in 1973 at the Manhattan Theatre Club. The play appears in print for the first time anywhere in *The Best Short Plays 1975.*

Characters:

PAUL LEVY, *a young man*
HARRIET LEVY, *his mother*

Scene:

The basement of a one-family row house in Brooklyn.
The room has been decorated in a night club motif, and
not too successfully. There is a small serving bar with
three stools in front of it, a small table and two chairs.
A low vinyl couch is left, front. There are various
framed family pictures adorning the walls, and on the
rear wall is a simple stereo phonograph and a record
rack. The entrance and exit to the room is concealed behind a partition and leads to the steps which take one
upstairs into the kitchen. A top hat design is inset in a
circle in the asphalt tile floor. The room is illuminated
by two brass wall sconces, and by hanging redshaded
fixtures. At the rear end of the bar is a red wallphone.
The overall effect of the room is bowling league modern.

The time is the present. Evening. Paul Levy, a young
man of twenty-five is at the back end of the bar, already
engaged in a conversation on the telephone. He is wearing
a colorful shirt, with the sleeves partly rolled up, and a tie
that he has loosened and pulled partway down.

PAUL: *(On the telephone)* No, no, you go ahead and
eat. I caught a bite on the way over to mother's...all right,
maybe I'll have it cold later...I don't know...*(Looks at
watch)* Not too much longer...How is she? *(Sighs heavily)*
Janet, how is she? She's up to four tranquilizers a day, that's
how she is. I could hear it in her voice—The goddamn *Mil-
town* sound...As soon as I said "Hello" she jumped on me
with the whole medical report, I didn't have a chance to say
two words to Pop...No, her arm is okay. Now it's her leg.
It's been *drawing* for a week...How the hell do I know what
drawing is? Do you know what *drawing* is?...Wait a min-

ute...*(Paul reaches over the bar and finds a bottle of Scotch and a glass. He takes ice out of the bucket on top of the bar and pours himself a drink)* No, I'm down in the basement, she can't hear...I know, Janet, I know. Listen, she's so tranquilized I don't think even *she* knows how she is anymore. If it's not heart palpitations, it's her stomach. Or her lower back spasms or her gall bladder. Arthritis, headaches—do you know she went to Dr. Phillips and had another ECG last week?...No, I'm not kidding. What's that, three in the last year? Yeah, yeah, I'm trying to give her sympathy, Janet, but it's hard. Christ, every time I come over here I can't wait to run away. *(Listens for a moment)* Hypochondria, Janet, what's the cure for that? Listen—I was in the john upstairs before and there was the Reader's Digest—folded back to an article about low blood sugar. Uh uh...Are you ready for *hypoglycemia?* Next week. Guaranteed. Honey, I'm telling you—if they were writing about goddamn *leprosy* somewhere and she read about it, the following week she'd—

MOM: *(Off)* Paulie?

PAUL: *(Looks over his shoulder as his manner changes. Quietly)* Chickee, the cops. *(Up)* Uh-huh. Right, so I won't be too late.

(We hear her footsteps descending the stairs to the basement. She enters on this speech. Harriet Levy is a trim, nervous woman of about fifty. She is wearing a flowered cotton housecoat and flat shoes, with peds barely showing. In her hand she carries a dishtowel)

MOM: Paulie? Are you down here? *(Enters and sees Paul on the phone)* Is that Janet?

PAUL: *(Looking at her, nods)* Right.

MOM: *(Crosses to Paul)* Can I say hello?

PAUL: Wait—Mom wants to talk to you.

MOM: *(As Paul listens for a final second before passing the telephone to her, she can't resist ruffling his hair. At other moments, whenever she is comfortably in range, she will also caress and fondle her son, always idly, naturally and without forethought)* Hello, darling, how's my favorite daughter-in-law? What? Yes, he's fine. The same as ever...So when am I going to see you, huh? I know you're busy. And I know you work, but on a weekend... maybe you'll drop in next weekend with Paulie, the two of you. What do you say? I'll make a pot roast, the way Paul likes it, with pan roasted potatoes... where? No, he didn't tell me... To Tanglewood for the weekend? I see... Well, all right, maybe the weekend after. Okay darling. You too, sweetie. Goodbye. *(She hangs up. Paul has taken his drink and crossed to the table, where he sits)* Is that an angel? That's some girl. *(Discovers she is still holding onto the dishtowel)* Will you look at me. Finished the dishes and I'm walking around with a dishtowel in my hands. Like a nut, right? *(She wipes the bar where Paul might have spilled an imaginary drop of Scotch. Paul takes out a flip-top box of Marlboro cigarettes and lights one. Leaves the box on the table. Mom leaves the towel on the bar. Takes an ashtray from the bar and brings it to Paul. She hesitates for a moment before sitting down)* Berkeley, California.

PAUL: Berkeley, California.

MOM: *(Walks a few steps away)* So is it a good job, at least? Something you'll like?

PAUL: I don't know yet.

MOM: So far away.

PAUL: I'll be going out there in a month. For the interview. Then I'll know more.

MOM: The other end of the world.

PAUL: It sounds good. And the pay is right.

MOM: Berkeley, California.

PAUL: And from what they've told me it sounds like a challenge.

MOM: *(She sits down at the table)* I'm sure. *(Pause)* And what does Janet say?

PAUL: She's excited, of course. But I keep telling her, I don't have the job yet.

MOM: I keep telling myself that, too.

PAUL: Ah, Mom. You never know. I'm a long way from landing that job.

MOM: Of course.

PAUL: But just the thought of living in California

has Janet running around in circles. You know she's always wanted to get out of New York. To live someplace else.

MOM: No, I didn't know.

PAUL: Oh, sure. Those two years we spent in Munich—in the Army—I think they've spoiled her.

MOM: Listen, New Jersey is nice.

PAUL: It was like a two-year honeymoon.

MOM: Or Rockland County.

PAUL: Every weekend we'd jump in the car and take off for a different city. Milan. Geneva. Vienna.

MOM: Englewood. Teaneck. There are a lot of nice places over there, Paulie.

PAUL: We'd just go as far as a weekend pass would take us. Not a care in the world.

MOM: You've been to your Uncle Charlie's house in Montclair. Could you want a nicer place to live?

PAUL: *(Just getting the drift)* Than where?

MOM: Your Uncle Charlie's house in Montclair. New Jersey. Just across the river, maybe forty minutes by car. Not in Berkeley, California, the other end of the world where I'll never see you.

PAUL: *(Shakes his head)* Oh, Mom. Come on.

MOM: Don't give me that come on business. What do you think, Paulie, you're going to move three thousand miles away and I'm supposed to like it? Is that what you think?

PAUL: Wait a minute. The interview is still a month away and who knows what—

MOM: *I* know. You're going to move to California and that's the story.

PAUL: *(There is no coping with this. He raises his glass in a mock toast)* Happy New Year!

MOM: Sure, go ahead, laugh at me. You don't know like I know how these things have a way of working out. All you got to do is think of what you want least in the world and that's what you're sure to get. *(She gets up and begins to pace, her arms wrapped about herself)* What did I do with you, Paulie? Raise you to run away from me? Am I such a terrible person?

PAUL: *(He has been through this old routine many*

times and knows there is no way to avoid it) No, Mom, you're not a terrible person.

MOM: First, it was college. NYU wasn't good enough for you. You had to go to an out-of-town college. Someplace far away.

PAUL: C. W. Post is not far away.

MOM: *(Sarcasm)* Oh, sure, it's just around the corner, right?

PAUL: I could have been home in forty-five minutes.

MOM: *(Whirls to face him) So why didn't you?* Where were you all those weekends...those nights when I walked around here with my heart falling out...looking for a friendly voice...a smile...an ear I could tell my troubles to.

PAUL: Please, Mom, don't start all that again.

MOM: You came home from the Army and I expected a little happiness from you. I thought, maybe, once a week, twice a week—God forbid you should break your heart—you and Janet would come and spend an evening— you would cheer up an old woman who spent her life waiting on you hand and foot. Shows you what kind of idiot I am. To think that you can live to raise a son—and put your whole life into him—and maybe—*maybe*—once in a while he'll have the heart to give a little consideration to what some—*(The television set upstairs begins blaring at full volume: the national anthem, as played in a ball park before a televised game. She stops in mid-speech and exchanges a look with Paul)* Another county heard from. *(She rushes to the stairway and shouts)* Benny! Ben! Will you turn it down! *(Up the stairs she goes, out of sight. Off)* Will you turn it down!

(We hear the kitchen door being closed behind her and her footsteps returning down the staircase. The sound of the anthem is heard no more)

PAUL: It must be eight o'clock. *(Stretches)*

MOM: You can set your watch by him.

PAUL: *(Getting up. Yawns)* I didn't realize it was so late.

MOM: You're going?

PAUL: Um. I was thinking about it.

MOM: What's your hurry? It's early.

PAUL: Eight o'clock.

MOM: So? That's late? You come here once in a blue moon, you're going to run away?

PAUL: All right. I'll stay a little while.

MOM: Good. *(Pause)* You want a cup of coffee?

PAUL: No. *(Yawns again)* Maybe I'll go upstairs ...watch a few innings with Pop. *(Starts for the stairs)*

MOM: Oh, no, you won't!

PAUL: *(Stops moving)* What? *(Grins)* Come on. Maybe you'll watch with us.

MOM: Paulie...

PAUL: You used to be such a fan. Remember?

MOM: Paul. Let's talk.

PAUL: Come on—remember the quiz game we used to play?

MOM: My God, we hardly see each other.

PAUL: *(Going into his fake announcer's voice)* Our contestant is Mrs. Harriet Levy. All right, Mrs. Levy, for two hundred dollars—who made the last unassisted triple play in a World Series game?

MOM: *(Disinterested)* Bill Wambsganss, Cleveland.

PAUL: Absolutely right! For four hundred dollars, tell us—how many home runs did Babe Ruth hit in his lifetime?

MOM: Seven hundred and fourteen.

PAUL: Fantastic! Another winner! All right, for eight hundred dollars—name the player with the highest lifetime batting average.

MOM: Tyrus Raymond Cobb, Detroit Tigers, hit three-sixty-seven lifetime.

PAUL: This woman is amazing, folks, amazing! Okay, Mrs. Levy—for sixteen hundred dollars uh...um...who plays shortstop for the Mets?

MOM: Shortstop...wait a minute...

PAUL: Shortstop for the Mets. Hurry, time is running out.

MOM: Wait! Uh...Pee Wee Reese!

PAUL: Reese? *(Laughs)* Oh, Ma, that was a long time—

MOM: ...Swoboda?

PAUL: *(Laughing)* Swoboda?...

MOM: *(Joining in the laugh)* I didn't even get the Dodgers straight and now we got a whole new team.

PAUL: Pee Wee Reese, wow!

MOM: So who's the shortstop?

PAUL: *Chaim Yankel,* that's who. You just blew sixteen hundred bucks.

MOM: Call me pisher.

PAUL: Pisher.

MOM: Thanks a lot.

PAUL: *(Laughs)* How could you miss Harrelson? My God, you used to be fan number one around here.

MOM: When you were home. Not anymore.

PAUL: You gave it up.

MOM: For Lent.

PAUL: I thought, Purim.

MOM: For Purim I gave up golf.

PAUL: And Yom Kippur?

MOM: Horseback riding.

PAUL: Of course.

MOM: I never go horseback riding on Yom Kippur.

PAUL: It's a sin.

MOM: Mortal. *(He has crossed behind her and bends down to hug Mom. Kissing him)* That's my Paulie.

PAUL: *(Breaks off. Takes his glass and begins to cross to the bar)* The same.

MOM: I could always laugh with you.

PAUL: A regular Milton Berle.

MOM: Do you remember the times we had, Paul?

PAUL: *(Singing)* "Those were the days, my friend..."

MOM: *(Over his song)* When your father was working nights...all the times we had. When I would read to you...remember?

PAUL: Yep. *(Begins making another drink)*

MOM: And then, when you got older, we'd read together...and talk about books...and politics...

PAUL: *(Prompting her)* Remember the beach?

MOM: *(Does a take)* Oh, God, remember!

PAUL: You had that big bag of sandwiches...

MOM: Veal cutlets...

PAUL: And Pop picked up the sandwich bag, *and* the bag of garbage...

MOM: And he dropped one bag in the garbage can on the way to the car and when we got to the beach and opened up the sandwiches—

PAUL and MOM: *(Together) Garbage!*

MOM: He was so ashamed...

PAUL: And so mad.

MOM: Four dollars worth of veal cutlets.

PAUL: In the garbage.

MOM: I thought he'd have a hemorrhage. *(Paul laughs. Is about to take a drink)* And how about the time he caught you with that dirty comic book?

PAUL: *(Almost spills his drink)* Ooooh, yeah.

MOM: My God, that was a filthy book! What was it? Moon Mullins?

PAUL: Popeye.

MOM: Right, Popeye! How could I forget? Olive Oyl without any clothes on.

PAUL: I thought he'd kill me.

MOM: *(Laughs)* And that Popeye. My God, he had a thing on him...

PAUL: You know, for a year I thought you had to eat spinach to grow a *schlong* like that.

MOM: *(Scandalized, but loving it)* Paulie!

PAUL: *(Innocence)* What? What'd I say? What was so terrible?

MOM: *(Goes into hysteria and ends up coughing. She takes out a handkerchief to wipe her eyes as Paul grins at her from behind the bar)* Oh...you are something...

PAUL: A regular Danny Kate.

MOM: *(Looks in her housecoat pocket and can't find her cigarettes)* I left my cigarettes upstairs. *(Reaches for the box of cigarettes Paul has left on the table)* I don't remember...who gave you that comic book?

(*Looking at Paul, she takes out a cigarette and puts it in her mouth. What she doesn't see is that it is not a Marlboro, but a neatly rolled marijuana "joint"*)

PAUL: Jeffrey.

MOM: (*Taking up a match, about to light up*) Cousin Jeffrey?

PAUL: (*Looks up and sees the trouble he is in. A shout*) No!

MOM: (*Startled, she jumps up*) What!

PAUL: (*Rushing madly around the bar*) Wait!

MOM: (*Takes cigarette out of her mouth and holds it in her hand, unaware of the motive behind Paul's madness*) It wasn't Cousin Jeffrey? (*Brings match back up and cigarette back to her mouth*)

PAUL: (*Sees he can't reach her in time*) Don't light that!

MOM: (*Dumbly*) What? (*Now she see it*) Oh, my God!

(*Paul stands before her in shock and blows out the match she is holding in her hand. Mom, frozen. Paul reaches to take the "joint" from her but she turns away, clutching it*)

PAUL: Ma...(*Mom backs away from him*) Mom ...give me...

MOM: (*Shakes her head*) Paulie...is this...? (*Paul nods*) And you...? (*Paul nods*) Marijuana? You mean you ...really...? (*Paul nods*) Oh, my God! (*Collapses into a chair*)

PAUL: (*Sits down at the table with her*) Mom... let me—

MOM: Paulie!

PAUL: Ma, let me explain.

MOM: Wait...I'm shaking like a leaf.

PAUL: Ma...

MOM: Marijuana. Marijuana. Now I *really* need a cigarette. (*Paul reaches for the flip-top box, but Mom catches his hand. She opens the pack and shakes out three more "joints"*) Aren't there any real cigarettes in here?

PAUL: Yes, if you'll let me—(*Reaches out again*)

MOM: (*Snatches the box away. Takes out a Marlboro.*

Begins to light it, then stops. Can she trust it?) Is this thing all right?

PAUL: Mom—

MOM: I don't know whether to smoke the damn thing or not.

PAUL: It's all right. *(Mom eyes him curiously. Slowly, she lights up, anticipating disaster. Only after she exhales does she trust it)* Mom, I think I better—

MOM: Wait! Let me calm down. I swear, my heart is beating like a trip-hammer.

(Paul sighs. Gets up and starts walking back to the bar to get his drink. Mom examines the four "joints," spreading them out on the table) So this is what everyone's afraid of . . . and this is what my son is smoking. *(Picks up one "joint")* A pot.

PAUL: A "joint."

MOM: A "joint?" Ahah! And what's pot?

PAUL: Mom—

MOM: Answer me!

PAUL: *(Takes a sip of his drink)* Pot is grass and grass is marijuana. Same thing. When you roll a cigarette, it's called a "joint."

MOM: *(Nods sagely)* Sure, big shot, you would know everything. *(Pause)* And how long are you smoking these?

PAUL: Mom, look—let's make believe you never opened that pack of cigarettes and none of this happened. All right?

MOM: Not all right. What do you think—I'm gonna find out my son is walking around, hooked on marijuana—and I'm going to forget about it?

PAUL: I'm not hooked, Ma. You don't get hooked on grass.

MOM: Sure, sure. I'm supposed to believe that?

PAUL: Mom, I mean it. Look—

MOM: Then why do you have so many? Answer that—*(Sudden thought)* Paulie, you're not a pusher!

PAUL: Oh, for Christ's sake! Ma—will you listen to me. I smoke marijuana! Grass! Mary Jane! Okay, now you know. I'm not a head and I'm not a pusher. I smoke it because I like it—and I'm going to go on smoking it as long as I can get it, understand? So you can just save all your lectures and your wringing hands because, believe me, you don't know a damn thing about it.

MOM: Paul—

PAUL: All right? What else do you want to know? *(Advances on her from the bar)*

MOM: Paul, calm down.

PAUL: You wanted to know how long, right? Okay. I started smoking it in college. Plus two years in the Army, right? And I'm home almost a year. So what's that? Four, five years? *That's* how long. Now, you got any more questions?

MOM: Paulie, wait a minute. How did I become the wrong one here?

PAUL: Nobody's right and nobody's wrong.

MOM: Then why are you so angry?

PAUL: *(Pauses, then slowly smiles)* Who's angry? *(Sits down. Pause)* Can I have a cigarette?

MOM: Which kind?

PAUL: A Marlboro.

MOM: *(She passes him a cigarette and he lights up)* Paul, can we talk?

PAUL: I'm listening.

MOM: All right. First of all, you know I'm not the kind of a mother who's going to yell and scream and carry on just because she found out her son is a marijuana fiend. Okay? And you already told me that you're not going to stop no matter what I say, so I'm not going to say. But, Paulie, tell me why you want to smoke these things when the whole world is up in arms against it, and everyone knows how bad it is? Why, Paul?

PAUL: Because the whole world is full of shit, Mom!

MOM: Just like that.

PAUL: Exactly.

MOM: The whole world is wrong, but you're right, huh?

PAUL: Why do you smoke Pall Malls when you know they're going to kill you?

MOM: I'm switching to King Sano.

PAUL: That's just a slower death.

MOM: Paulie, smoking cigarettes is different.

PAUL: How?

MOM: Because, when I started smoking, who knew about lung cancer? Who knew that you would get hooked? Or it was hazardous to your health, they should drop dead with their advertising altogether. When Lucky Strike green went to war—and your father started working nights at the garage—I started smoking.

PAUL: But don't you see—

MOM: No, I don't. All I know is, you knew it was bad, but you did it anyway.

PAUL: It's not bad.

MOM: Paulie, you don't know what's going on with these things. Everyone's kid is smoking them, and every parent you talk to is going crazy. *(Paul laughs)* I mean it. In the beauty parlor, when you play mah-jongg, it's the number one topic of conversation. Everyone is frightened to death. Afraid their kid is smoking this stuff behind their backs—and doing bad knows what else—and they'll wind up in jail, and not get into college. You hear horror stories every day.

PAUL: And no one knows a damn thing about it!

MOM: *(Nods)* True. *(She picks up a "joint" and looks at it closely)* Look at this thing. What's so terrific about it? Tell me.

PAUL: You want to find out? Smoke one.

MOM: Paul, talk sense.

PAUL: I am. Just get off one time and you'll know everything.

MOM: Now you're being ridiculous.

PAUL: Of course. You see, you're like everyone else. *(He gets up and begins to pace. Mom sits holding the "joint")* Mom, if it wasn't illegal, half of frigging America would go ape on it every day. That's how beautiful it is. It's...it's another world...where you can say anything and do anything without being afraid. Where you can float...relaxed, free. And sometimes...in the dark, with just a few colored lights...and maybe some rock playing softly...you can lay back in the dark and you touch...and... *(Stops himself)*

MOM: And what?

PAUL: And nothing.

MOM: Tell me.

PAUL: There are things I don't want to talk about.

MOM: Like what?

PAUL: *(Looks her in the eye)* Like sex. All right?

MOM: *(Gasps)* You mean...Janet smokes it, too?

PAUL: Look, Mom—there are just some things—

MOM: Oh, my God!...the both of you!

PAUL: *(Sits down)* All right. You tell me. Tell me what sex is like. Go on, describe it for me.

MOM: *(Half smile)* I don't remember.

PAUL: *(Smiles)* Tell me what it's like to get high on Scotch. How does it make you feel?

MOM: Is it like that?

PAUL: Yes. Only different. Better.

MOM: And Janet smokes it with you?

PAUL: Yes. It's better when you smoke it with someone. Especially someone you love.

MOM: *(We can see her mind changing as she fingers the "joints" on the table)* Listen, Paulie—can you leave me one?

PAUL: Two, if you like.

MOM: Just one.

PAUL: *(Delighted)* You're really going to try it?

MOM: Yes...I think so.

PAUL: *(Leans over and kisses her on the cheek)* Mom, you're beautiful!

MOM: I'm also crazy. But listen—maybe you're right and the whole world is wrong. I got to find out, right?

PAUL: Right.

MOM: And maybe then I'll know something, right?

PAUL: Right.

MOM: Look—I already found out a lot.

PAUL: Like what?

MOM: Like you and Janet have been smoking it for five years.

PAUL: Four.

MOM: It doesn't affect you? I mean, in your work?

PAUL: No. I'm not a head.

MOM: A "head." *(Shrugs)* It's a whole new world. *(Paul gathers the three "joints" and puts them back into his Marlboro pack, leaving the one Mom is holding)* All right, soon I'm going to know. *(Pause)* Paulie, your father will never smoke it with me. In fact, if he knew what was going on down here, he'd kill the two of us.

PAUL: Absolutely.

MOM: So I smoke it alone then, right?

PAUL: Look—it's not so bad. Tonight, after he goes to bed, put on your pajamas, come down here...maybe turn the lights down, put on the stereo, stretch out on the couch...

MOM: When I smoke it, Paulie, what's going to happen to me?

PAUL: It's different for everybody.

MOM: Like being drunk, you said.

PAUL: Yes. Only different.

MOM: *(Grins)* Terrific. *(Pauses)* Paulie, I'll tell you right now. I'd feel better if I smoked it with somebody.

PAUL: *(Considers)* Maybe you can...isn't there someone?

MOM: Who? Are you kidding?

PAUL: There has to be someone.

MOM: My friends would think I'm crazy if I asked them to smoke grasses.

PAUL: Grass. You smoke grass, plural, and you share a "joint," singular.

MOM: See? I don't even know how to say it right, where am I going to find someone to smoke it with?

(A whole new problem for both to consider. It takes a moment)

PAUL: Aunt Louise and Uncle Harry? *(Mom: cackling laughter)* What's so funny?

MOM: *(Still laughing)* Uncle Harry...

PAUL: *(Slightly offended)* It was only a suggestion. *(Mom: more laughter. When she stops)* Why not Uncle Harry...? He and Louise always struck me as being—I don't know—a little more hip than the rest of the family.

MOM: Only on the outside.

PAUL: I mean, he always said he's in publishing...

MOM: Distributing *The Sheetmetal Worker's Journal* is not being in publishing.

PAUL: All right. *(Thinks again)* The Sterns? Next door?

MOM: Hah! They'd turn me right in to the police.

PAUL: Come on. They're nice.

MOM: That was years ago. You wouldn't know them.

PAUL: They've changed?

MOM: And how. He's got a hunting rifle in the basement and an American flag decal on his car. The whole *shtick*.

PAUL: No! I'm really surprised.

MOM: You've been away a long time, Paul. Everything changes.

PAUL: I guess so *(Thinks again. Mom begins laughing again)* What?

MOM: Uncle Harry...

PAUL: Hey! *(He's got it)* How about Cousin Sarah?

MOM: Oh, Paul! How could you say that? Her Larry got in trouble at Cornell for smoking it. Everyone knows that.

PAUL: Gee—I didn't know.

MOM: They kept it very quiet.

PAUL: Look—there has to be someone who'll share a "joint" with you.

MOM: Yes. Alvin.

PAUL: Alvin?

MOM: From the beauty parlor. You want me to ask him over?

PAUL: *(Offended again)* The hell with it. Forget it, then. Or smoke it alone. It's not that important.

MOM: Oh, no you don't. You can't get me all excited and then just walk away. I mean it, Paul.

PAUL: *(He smells something coming. Looks at his watch)* Mom, I better be going. Janet must be wondering what's keeping me.

MOM: Paulie...maybe the next time you and Janet...

PAUL: *(Shaking his head)* Uh-uh.

MOM: I mean...I could leave Dad home and sleep over...

PAUL: No. That's private.

MOM: I only asked. *(Pause)* Maybe...just you and me?

PAUL: Wrong.

MOM: Now, I mean, tonight.

PAUL: Mother, no!

MOM: What's so terrible? You could watch me, show me what to do. I'd feel better about it if you were here.

PAUL: I don't sit around and watch people get stoned. It's a bad scene.

MOM: So smoke it *with* me.

PAUL: Out of the question.

MOM: *(Leans over and pats his arm. Coaxing)* Come on, Paulie. Baby...How many times do I ask you to do something for me?

PAUL: I've got to get home.

MOM: Please, Paulie...Listen—I'll call Janet and tell her.

PAUL: *(Quickly)* Tell her what?

MOM: *(Smiling)* Anything you want. She's a good girl. She'll understand. *(Studies Paul's hesitant uncomfortable look. Short laugh)* You should see your face. What a picture. Are you afraid of something?

PAUL: I don't know.

MOM: Come on.

PAUL: *(Nodding toward upstairs)* What about Pop? Upstairs.

MOM: You heard the ball game. That's it for the night.

PAUL: Mom—

MOM: Until after the news. Then he'll ask me to make

him a cup of Sanka. *(She's on her feet)* You can call Janet if you like. I'm going to make sure the door is locked. *(Away she goes upstairs)*

PAUL: *(Very undetermined, he walks to the phone. Reaches for the phone, then stops)* Jesus! I don't know if I could explain it to her.

MOM: *(We hear her footsteps. As she enters, she is alight with excitement and animation)* Snug as a bug. We're all set. You're not calling Janet?

PAUL: No.

MOM: All right. Whatever you say. *(Sudden thought)* But you better take the phone off the hook. *(He does it)* All I need is for Cousin Gussie to phone when we're in the middle. Although, maybe I'd be better off talking to her looped.

PAUL: Stoned.

MOM: Whatever. *(She pushes up her sleeves and seems about to burst out of her skin. She picks up a "joint" and walks toward Paul at the bar)* Wow, Paulie. I'm so excited I'm jumping up and down inside.

PAUL: Well, calm down.

MOM: I can't.

PAUL: Sit down.

MOM: *(She seats herself on a bar stool)* Oh, boy! Look—goose pimples!

PAUL: Will you take it easy? Just relax.

MOM: Relax? I'm afraid I'm about to die, how the hell am I going to relax?

PAUL: There's nothing to be afraid of. *(Begins walking away)*

MOM: *(Concerned)* Where are you going?

PAUL: *(Walking toward record rack)* To put on some music. Sometimes it helps. *(Looks through record rack)* Don't you have anything but Mantovani?

MOM: Why? Won't that work?

PAUL: *(Looks at her. Puts on the Mantovani. Soft, syrupy, and low)* Mantovani is fine. *(He starts back, stops, turns the lights lower, accentuating the red lighting)* There, that's better.

MOM: *(After Paul seats himself beside her at the bar)* Do you feel crazy?

PAUL: *(Nodding)* Weird. *(Pause)* Turning my own mother on.

MOM: *(After a moment of thought)* Whatever happens, tell them it was my idea.

PAUL: Nothing may happen. It doesn't work with everybody.

MOM: With me it's going to work.

PAUL: *(Looks at her)* I'll bet it will.

MOM: *(Stretches nervously)* All right, I'm ready. *(Bravely picks up the "joint" and puts it in her mouth. Reaches for the matches)*

PAUL: Just a minute. Let me tell you how to smoke it. You've got to drag as long as you can and hold the smoke inside. Don't exhale—just hold it all in.

MOM: I'll probably choke. *(She puts the "joint" in her mouth again)*

PAUL: Stop. You've got to wet it first.

MOM: Wet It?

PAUL: To make it burn slowly. Just wet it with your saliva.

MOM: *(Making a face)* That's disgusting.

PAUL: Wet it.

MOM: *(Licks the joint and looks at it)* Ecchh!

PAUL: Light up.

MOM: *(Hesitates)* You sure you don't want to...

PAUL: *(Cocks a finger)* Go! *(With great trepidation she succeeds in making herself light the "joint." She takes a deep drag and holds it)* You're doing fine.

MOM: *(Holds it until she can't, then inhales with a great noise)* I don't feel anything.

PAUL: It takes time.

MOM: *(Repeats the action, holding the smoke. This time she inhales and begins to cough)* Paulie...this stuff is strong. *(Paul nods. Offers the "joint" to Paul)* Horseshit and splinters, I swear to God.

PAUL: No. You go ahead. *(Mom takes another hefty*

drag) You take a few more. I don't need very much.

MOM: *(She's an old hand now. Inhales. Takes another)* Nothing. A big fat zero.

PAUL: *(Takes the "joint" and pulls a quick one. Hands it back and it's Mom's turn again)* Oh, man...that is wonder grass.

MOM: *(Passes Paul the "joint" again)* So? What's taking so long?

PAUL: *(Passes it back and watches as she inhales)* Easy. Take your time. *(He rubs his nose and blinks his eyes a few times. It has already hit him)*

MOM: Is anything happening to you? *(Offers "joint" to Paul, who gestures—"No"—with his hand)*

PAUL: *(Slowly)* Uh—huh. How you doing?

MOM: I'll tell you what it's doing, it's making me sick. *(Takes another)*

PAUL: Never hurt you. *(A beatific smile)*

MOM: What are you smiling at?...You're starting to feel good.

PAUL: *(Winks at her and nods)* Beautiful...

MOM: *(Goes back to work, puffing furiously and holding it in twice more)* Nothing is happening. Absolutely nothing. *(Oh, yes it is!)* Abso—Oh—wo-wo-wee-wee-wow-wo. *(Shakes her head)*

PAUL: You're there.

MOM: I'm fine. I'm perfect. I'm okay. I'm—wo-wo-wee-wo-wo. *(Paul giggles. A crazy smile on her face)* Hey ...Paul...you know what?

PAUL: What?

MOM: *(She has a great message, but doesn't know what it is)* Um...*(The hell with it! She rests her head on her arms on top of the bar. And slowly begins sliding sideways off the bar stool. The sight of his mother falling off the stool is very interesting, and so Paul watches until she's about to drop off and then he reaches out to stop her. Mom reacts violently to his touch. Stands on the floor. Yells)* Aaaaagh! Oh! *(Removes his arm)* Next time you touch me, give me a warning. *(Rubs her arms)* Your hand is like ice. *(Rocks on her feet. Paul gives her support again. Walks her over toward the couch)*

PAUL: Easy. Just sit down.

(She sits, but only for a moment. Then she plops down lengthwise on the couch, her legs dangling over the edge)

MOM: Dynamite. Wow-wow-wee! Dynamite! *(Paul looks at her, sits down on the floor beside the couch)*

MOM: I'm as high as a treetop. *(Paul giggles)* Oh, boy, Paulie... I am really flying away.

PAUL: If Uncle Harry could see you now...

MOM: Never mind Uncle Harry—how about if your father could see me?

PAUL: Oh, wow! *(They laugh again)*

MOM: *(After a short silence)* Moon calling earth ...moon calling earth...come in, earth...

PAUL: Hello, Mr. Moonie...

MOM: Hello, Mr. Earth...

PAUL: How the hell are you, Mr. Moonie?

MOM: I'm terrific, Paulie, I'm fantastic. Wow, I never felt better in my life. In fact...I think I'm going to throw up. *(She sits up quickly, holding her head)*

PAUL: Easy.

MOM: My whole head is spinning like a top.

PAUL: It'll stop soon. Relax.

MOM: Did you ever get the feeling that your entire body is straight but your head is on backwards?

PAUL: Lie down, but keep your eyes open this time.

MOM: *(She stretches out. After a pause)* My God!—this stuff can turn you into a maniac in two seconds flat ...Paul? *(Face turned upward, eyes closed, He doesn't answer)* Paulie?...Are you there?

PAUL: Uh-huh.

MOM: Listen...I think I can feel the hair in my nose growing...

PAUL: What?

MOM: It's getting very curly in there...

PAUL: Far out.

MOM: Extremely curly and very long.

PAUL: That's nice...

MOM: It must be from the sun, right? *(She raises a hand to shield her eyes from the light)* Because the sun is very strong in here today. *(Paul looks at her curiously)* Remind me, when I get done on this side, to turn over.

PAUL: *(Turns his face upward to take the "sun." After a pause)* You know...my whole life I've hated these red lights.

MOM: I know.

PAUL: Where the hell did you ever find them?

MOM: In an Italian funeral parlor.

PAUL: Ug-*lee!*

MOM: Your father brought them home one day.

PAUL: Well, I hate them. I meant to tell you that for a long time.

MOM: You did. Before. A long time ago.

PAUL: Why the hell don't you get rid of them?

MOM: Why, he says. You know why. Because lights are red and money is green. *(Paul giggles)* You know something? Your father is in love with those crappy lights. *(Paul giggles harder)* What are you laughing? Your father happens to have terrific taste. *(A short laugh)* Although, I'd hate to tell you where... But it's a well-known fact—Your father is a patron of the arts. You didn't know that, did you?

PAUL: *(Laughing)* No...

MOM: Oh, sure...Listen—Leonard Bernstein doesn't make a move without checking with your father. Calls him up wherever he is. All the time. *(Pause)* Not to mention Ben Shahn...and Norman Mailer. Guess who called him yesterday? Mike Nichols, that's who! I mean, your father doesn't fool around with shnooks—I'm talking *giants.*

PAUL: *(Amused)* That's beautiful.

MOM: Nothing to it, your father happens to be a very big man. You ought to hear the calls he gets.

PAUL: You really are flying...

MOM: Like a kike in a high wind. Ooops! Did I say "kike?" I meant to say "kite." Sorry...I must be out of my mind, huh, Paulie?...Listen—this stuff is terrific...Wow!

...Remind me to recommend it to your father, maybe he'll lay off the booze.

PAUL: What are you talking about?

MOM: Your father and his booze.

PAUL: *(Focusing more clearly) What* booze?

MOM: Hmmm, that is a very good question. Lemme see...there's vodka...and rye...and bourbon—that's mainly the booze, but if you got anything else he probably wouldn't say no, either.

PAUL: Jeez, you are really stoned. Pop doesn't drink that much.

MOM: *(Laughs)* Are you nuts? Doesn't drink much? You must have seen him drunk a hundred times.

PAUL: Like when?

MOM: Like a hundred times. Lots of times. *(Laughs)*

PAUL: Name ten times.

MOM: Like, any time...Paulie, you mean you don't know your father is always half in the bag?

PAUL: *My* father?

MOM: No, the iceman!...Pop. Daddy-o. The man upstairs.

PAUL: Pop drinks?

MOM: No, he drunks. Past tense. You mean you never noticed, right?

PAUL: You're making it up.

MOM: You really see only what you want to see, Paulie. God, how could you miss it?

PAUL: I don't believe you.

MOM: All right, I won't get sore...Listen—in the morning, when I'm still in bed, he's already had a couple of quick ones. And in the garage all day, plenty.

PAUL: Hey, Ma—come on.

MOM: And then he walks in and marches straight to the cabinet. "I think I'll have one little drink," he says. Bushwa! *(She laughs without humor)* Dumbhead...you never saw anything, right?...You never noticed sometimes when you talk to him, he doesn't answer you? Or you'll ask him a question, a simple question, and he'll say something that

doesn't fit? *(Paul isn't looking at her and doesn't answer)*
Paulie, you never noticed that? *(She sits up, looks at Paul)*

PAUL: ...Yes...I noticed that...

MOM: So?

PAUL: *(Long pause as she watches him)* Well, I just
thought he was...you know...a little deaf. *(Mom whoops
with laughter. Over her laugh)* Or he was just a...a very
quiet man. *(Sets her off again. Lets her laugh end as he absorbs
the information)* My father...Jesus Christ!

MOM: Well, I wouldn't exactly call him that.

*(There is a long pause in which Mom and Paul contem-
plate each other and then look away, lost in private
thoughts. The record has ended and we hear the stereo
hum as the needle goes round and round on the inner
portion of the disk. The sound becomes intrusive. Paul
becomes aware of the stereo and slowly gets up. He
walks to the stereo and looks back at his mother before
shutting it)*

PAUL: *(With false gaiety)* Are there any more
requests?

MOM: *(In fake drunk voice)* Play "Temptation."

PAUL: *(Almost to himself)* I already did. *(He switches
off stereo)*

MOM: Hey, what kind of party is this? Come on, put
on Harry James. *(When Paul does not react she rises and joins
him at the stereo)* Come on, we're just getting started. *(She
finds a record in the rack)* Here you go—"Favorites of the
Forties." A hundred songs for five bucks, how can you go
wrong? *(She puts the record on. Paul looks at her and walks
back to the bar)* Now you're gonna hear something. Glenn
Miller. Woody Herman. *(The record comes up on the speaker:
Charlie Barnett's "Cherokee")* Charlie Barnett! *(She begins to
dance a musical number for an audience of one. It is a Lindy
Hop and she is fairly good at it, doing turns and twists and
always looking to Paul for approval. He sits at the rear bar
stool, his face and manner contemplative)* Hey, hey! Ooooh—
get hot! *(She kicks off her shoes)* Some stuff—eh, kid? *(She
twirls with abandon)* Wheee! Oh, baby, you should have seen

me when I was in my prime...*(Another "break")* "Chicky," the dancing fool, they called me...was I hot stuff...*(The music grabs her again and she transports herself into a series of wilder and wilder turns)* Loose as a goose...beat me daddy, eight to the bar...*(She turns to Paul and gestures with her arms)* Come on, Paulie...*(Paul shakes his head. Still dancing)* Come on, I'll show you how...*(Dances toward him and takes his arm. He is unwilling, but she is insistent and drags him away from the bar and onto "The Floor." "Cherokee" has ended and "In the Mood" comes up)*

PAUL: Ma, no...I don't want to...

MOM: Whaddya mean, no? I didn't get started yet. *(As Paul stands still, Mom begins to use him as her Lindy partner, going off on breaks and twirling back, holding onto his hand. Paul shows his disinclination to participate in this ritual by standing still, a look of displeasure on his face. Singing)* "In the mood...de da de da da"...*(Twirls)* That's how you dance? That's dancing? Like a piece of wood? *(Slows down and finally stops dancing. Shakes her head as she looks at Paul)* Go ahead, expect pleasure from children...

PAUL: Have you had enough?

MOM: *(Gasping as she begins to feel winded)* Enough...

(Paul goes to stereo and shuts it. Mom stands for a moment catching her breath, then walks to the table and sits down)

MOM: *(Ruefully)* Chicky, the dancing fool...

PAUL: *(Crossing to join her. Mockingly)* How's your heart?

MOM: Terrific. Knock wood.

PAUL: And your leg? *(Sits down)*

MOM: Also fine.

PAUL: It's not *drawing* anymore?

MOM: *(Catches his mockery)* What are you taking? An inventory?

PAUL: For a sick woman, you're a terrific dancer.

MOM: For a kid who's never around, you got a big mouth.

PAUL: You never like it when I tell you the truth.

MOM: If you knew the truth, you'd be entitled to talk.

PAUL: *(Looks at her)* We were talking about Pop. About drinking.

MOM: *(Makes a small gesture)* Oh, that.

PAUL: Yes, that. I don't believe you.

MOM: So don't.

PAUL: You're making it up.

MOM: I'm making it up.

PAUL: If he was a drunk, why wouldn't I know about it?

MOM: Do you ever open your eyes? Do you ever see anything?

PAUL: Why haven't I smelled it on his breath?

MOM: He's always chewing something, that's why.

PAUL: Then why—

MOM: *(Cuts him off)* And don't tell me you never noticed *that*, either. The Juicy Fruit King, the great white mouth. If it's not chewing a mile a minute it's wide open, catching flies...And I'll give you another reason: he's very careful. *(A bitter laugh)* Oh, boy, is he careful...*(She reaches out and grasps Paul's arm)* Dumbhead...you still don't believe me. Do you?

PAUL: No.

MOM: I don't think you'd know the truth if it fell on you.

PAUL: I know this—you're always dumping on him, always running him down in my eyes. As long as I can remember.

MOM: And I'm always the wrong one with you, and he's a saint.

PAUL: Not a saint...but not a dummy, Ma.

MOM: Not a saint...oh, boy, if you only knew how right you were...

(She gets up and begins walking toward the bar)

PAUL: There's nothing to know.

MOM: *(She stops and looks back at Paul)* Don't push me, Paul, or you'll hear something you'll wish you didn't hear.

PAUL: When did you ever hold anything back?

MOM: *(A stab in the back)* All right, kiddo, the ball game is over. *(She lights a cigarette, looking sidewise at Paul)* What do you think, I'm gonna go on protecting him so you can think *I'm* the bad one? No more of that jazz, sonny boy. All right, where do I start? How about...a little abortion? How does that one grab you, for openers? *(Paul, silent, stares at her)* What's the matter, Silent Sam, you don't know what to say? Is that a little too much for you, huh?...You were four years old, how the hell would you know about it? A neat little abortion, right on the kitchen table—on Gerry Street—I can remember it to this day. A little *shtoonk* doctor—a refugee—recommended by your father. Always had good taste, your father, and I screamed my head off it hurt so much and I bled like an animal...a wonder I didn't die right then ...How do you like that, Paul? *(Pause)* What's the matter, cat got your tongue?...First I tell him to be careful and he won't listen, and then he's telling me we've got to get rid of it. *It,* Paul, *it*...the brother or sister that would have been four years younger than you. Only we were too poor then, and I let him talk me into it. Dumb...so dumb...

PAUL: *(Quietly)* Ma, that's enough...

MOM: Yeah, I thought it was enough too, but it was only the beginning, Paulie...only the beginning. *(Crosses behind him)* Remember when you were seven and you went to live with Aunt Sarah for two weeks? Would you like to know why, Paulie?

PAUL: You were sick...in the hospital.

MOM: I wasn't sick and I wasn't in the hospital. I was with my mother, let her rest, because I walked out on him, Paulie. I left him. And I wasn't coming back. And everyone, the whole family, came down on my head to come home, to take him back...and on his hands and knees he came crawling to me, pleading and begging, to take him back...he wouldn't do it again...he swore up and down until he was blue in the face I should only forgive him ...*(Pause)* I can even tell you her name...*Marie*...that skinny blonde *courvah* bitch...May God strike her dead if she's still alive that no-good bastard...Marie...And then your grandfather, Rueben, that good, sweet man, came to my mother's house and we sat in the kitchen and I made him a cup of tea and he drank it and he looked at me with those soft brown eyes he had...and he held my hand and said "Chicky...my little Chicky...*fegele*...you got a man that's a bum and a boy that's an angel...*fegele*...for the boy...for his sake...go back and bring him up..." And I looked in his eyes and I saw that no matter what else, I couldn't hurt that man...*(She is now behind Paul, holding his shoulder)* So for you...Paulie...for you, I went back to him. And for you, we tried again to live like people. And for twenty years I've put up with it...the drinking...and the other women...and the not talking to each other...all of it...just so you could grow up the way you are...*(She sighs and walks around the table)* And now you're going to run away from me...right, Paul? Because I'm the bad one...the old lady who's always complaining...and always sick...and interferes, and only cares about herself...*(She picks up the ashtray and stubs out her cigarette. Turning, she walks to the wastebasket behind the bar and dumps the ashtray. She finds the dishtowel and gives the bar a wipe, then the ashtray. Carefully, she puts the ashtray in its proper place on the bar, stares off into space for a moment, and looks at her watch)* All of a sudden it got late. Dollars to doughnuts he must have fallen asleep in the club chair again...*(She starts toward the stairs, stops and turns to Paul)* I'm going to make him a cup of Sanka, do you want some? *(Paul, not looking at her, shakes his head, "No." Stares out front. Shrugs)* All right. *(Walks toward the stairs, stops)* Listen...before you come up, you'll turn out the lights? *(Waits for a second, but Paul doesn't move. Shouts)* Ben! Benny! *(Exits, we hear her going upstairs. Off)* Benny, wake up! Turn off the TV, Ben, I'll make a cup of coffee.

> *(We continue to hear her voice from above, as she rouses her husband and gets him to come to the kitchen.*
> *Paul rubs his face and slowly rises. Crosses to the bar and retrieves his cigarettes. He is shaken, clearly, and*

trying to make sense of it all. He reaches for the telephone and slowly dials a number)

PAUL: Hello...yeah, I'll be leaving soon...I'll tell you when I get home...What? No, she didn't take it well, Janet...In fact...In fact...*(He's convinced himself of something)* In fact, you won't believe what she pulled on me tonight...Unbelievable, honey...I tell you the old actress was in rare form...Uh-uh...Listen, I'm going to call Thompson tomorrow afternoon...Right ...I'll start as soon as they'll have me...Uh-uh... *(Laughs)* They can have the rent till the end of the month...Who cares? No, it never rains in California...you know that...

Slow Curtain

Mark Medoff

DOING A GOOD ONE
FOR THE RED MAN

Mark Medoff

Mark Medoff came to national prominence with his drama, *When You Comin' Back, Red Ryder?* which recently concluded a tremendously successful engagement at the Eastside Playhouse in Manhattan. Clive Barnes of *The New York Times* described it as "a fascinating and commanding play" and added that "Mr. Medoff writes superbly." The drama originally was presented in the fall of 1973 by the Off-Off-Broadway Circle Repertory Theatre Company where it received much acclaim and in December it was transferred to Off-Broadway for a regular commercial engagement. The author was honored with The Outer Critics' Circle Award for Best Playwriting and an "Obie" award for Distinguished Playwriting for *Red Ryder*. The play also was named one of the "ten best plays of the New York theatre season, 1973-74" by Otis L. Guernsey, Jr., editor of the theatre yearbook.

Mr. Medoff was born in a small town in Southern Illinois. His father was a doctor and his mother was a psychologist. At the age of nine, because of an asthma condition, the family pulled up stakes and moved to Miami Beach, Florida, where his writing started. As he recently explained to an interviewer: "As an assignment in high school I wrote a short story and got an A plus for it. So I sent it off to *Collier's* magazine and immediately got a rejection slip back. I was puzzled how *Collier's* could not accept an A plus story? The *Collier's* turndown made me become a closet writer."

Nevertheless, he kept on writing. There were lots more A plus stories and in college some prize winners, one of which was included in *The Best College Short Stories of 1963*. As he wrote, Mr. Medoff began to notice that all of his stories had copious lines of dialogue and just a couple of lines of prose. "My mother always said I had a good ear for dialogue, but it took me twenty-seven years to find out that she was right." And thus the stories turned into plays, written in longhand, a pattern he developed at the University of Miami and Stanford, where he went for graduate work.

A current Guggenheim Fellow in Playwriting, Mr. Medoff is an Associate Professor of English at New Mexico State University, from which he received the Westhafer

Award this past spring, the highest accolade the university has to bestow on one of its faculty.

In addition to his teaching and playwriting, the author also upon occasion acts and directs. As a matter of fact, he stepped into the New York cast of *Red Ryder* during the summer of 1974 after playing in the Chicago production for six weeks. His performance there received unanimous critical acclaim as well as a Joseph Jefferson Award nomination for Best Actor.

Mr. Medoff's other works for the theatre include *The Kramer,* presented by the American Conservatory Theatre in San Francisco and at the Mark Taper Forum in Los Angeles. His most recent play, *The Wager,* was presented at the Manhattan Theatre Club early in 1974 and at this writing is scheduled to open in October at the Off-Broadway Eastside Playhouse under the direction of Anthony Perkins.

Doing a Good One for the Red Man, described by its author as "a red farce," deals with the exploitation of an American Indian who is encountered by a newly-wedded couple. Humorous and pertinent, it arrives at a surprising yet pointed climax. The comedy is published in an anthology for the first time in *The Best Short Plays 1975.*

His other published short plays include: *The Froegle Dictum; The Ultimate Grammar of Life;* and *The War on Tatem.* At the moment, he is at work on two new plays, an original screenplay, and a film adaptation of a novel. He lives in Las Cruces, New Mexico, with his wife and daughter, and a large, companionable dog.

Characters:

INDIAN
GRACE
LEONARD

Scene:

The desert just east of the Grand Canyon in Holly-
wood, Arizona.
    An Indian sits cross-legged on an old packing crate
before his rancid looking mud hut. He is dressed in
worn and dirty Navajo clothing and holds a toy tom-
tom. He stares fixedly before him. About him are vari-
ous haphazard displays of pottery and turquoise beads
and rings.
    A young couple enters. They are Grace and Leonard.
They are dressed in white with the exception of the cam-
era on Grace's wrist, the hand mirror she bears before
her, the lenses of her sunglasses, and the bag of golf clubs
slung across Leonard's shoulder. Following their en-
trance, Leonard takes out his putter and begins to prac-
tice his stroke.

    GRACE: *(Flowing in on a cloud of narcissism)* It *is* an
Indian, Leonard. I told you it was an Indian. Say something
to it.
    LEONARD: *(Following slowly and without interest)*
Hi-ho. *(No response from the Indian)* Looks like a wooden
job. Could be an ambush.
    GRACE: Oh, Leonard!
    LEONARD: Yes, Grace?
    GRACE: *(To the Indian)* Hello, I'm Grace and this is
Leonard. We're on our honeymoon. *(No response)* We saw
you sitting here and we thought we'd stop and chat and perhaps learn something about our heritage and such.
    LEONARD: We just saw the Grand Canyon. *(No re-*

sponse) It's a pretty big hole, isn't it? *(No response)* Could you picture it as a cesspool?

GRACE: Leonard!

LEONARD: Yes, Grace?

GRACE: *(To the Indian)* Then we left there and we were driving and we kept seeing Indians in colorful garb and I said they were real and Leonard said they were hired extras in a travelogue about the picturesque Southwest.

INDIAN: *(Speaking simply, yet deliberately)* Beads, pottery, rings.

GRACE: Oh, Leonard, he spoke! *(To the Indian)* I'm going to do a silly thing now. I hope you won't mind. I've always wanted to say "How!" to a real Indian...How!

INDIAN: Take picture with me—cheap.

GRACE: Oh, yes! Stand over there, Leonard. These can be our Christmas cards this year.

LEONARD: *(Moving without interest "over there," to Grace)* What do you want me to do?

INDIAN: Got three choice: Can take picture of me tied to stake, you holding burning torch to pile of twigs—one quarter and one nickel.

GRACE: I'm not crazy about that one.

LEONARD: What else?

INDIAN: Picture of me circling your car on crummy old tricycle waving tomahawk—one quarter and one dime.

GRACE: Nooo, I don't think so. Leonard?

LEONARD: Ixnay.

INDIAN: Last one picture of me and you on horses— me in full Navajo chief outfit, you in cavalry colonel outfit; we smoking peace pipe and exchanging tokens of friendship. Cost one half buck.

GRACE: Oh, yes—that's it!

LEONARD: *(Simultaneous with Grace's line)* Great! We'll take that one.

INDIAN: Tough luck. Can no do. Horses die last winter.

GRACE: Oh, I'm sorry.

LEONARD: That's too bad. I really wanted that picture. *(Drifting off into fastasyland)* It's funny, you know—but I always kind of pictured myself as a cavalry man...even if it was only a colonel.

GRACE: Could I just have a picture of you and Leonard shaking hands or something?

INDIAN: Cost one quarter.

GRACE: Go ahead, Leonard. Shake hands.

LEONARD: No—listen! *(Ramming his putter down the back of the Indian's shirt)* He sits there and I do some flexing off his shoulder here. *(To the Indian)* I been workin' out like a maniac since two weeks ago.

(Leonard works into a tentative flex)

GRACE: Smile, boys.

(Neither Leonard nor the Indian smiles. Leonard searches for the right flex)

LEONARD: Specializing on my upper arms. You think it's easy, you're crazy.

GRACE: Ready?

LEONARD: *(Working finally into a tricep-bicep layout)* I'd like to show you my workout chart so you could see what it takes to build upper arms.

GRACE: *(Snapping the picture)* There.

INDIAN: That be one quarter. You pay now?

LEONARD: *(Retrieving the putter)* Are you kidding? I keep a running tab wherever I go.

GRACE: *(To the Indian)* You know something? Your face is a veritable map of America. It's just like Leonard's old wallet. *(Making the association)* Do you have any leather goods?

INDIAN: Beads, pottery, rings.

(Grace begins to look over the goods)

LEONARD: How's business?

INDIAN: Not so good.

LEONARD: *(Moving in for a confab)* Gee, that's tough. But then this is your slack season, I guess. I'll bet in the summer you really rake in the dough, huh? If you don't mind me asking, how much does a guy like you rake in during the year?

INDIAN: Hundred seventy-five dollar.

LEONARD: Holy cats! A hundred and seventy-five simoleans a week?

INDIAN: Year.

LEONARD: A year! Get out.

GRACE: Leonard, look at these darling beads.

LEONARD: Hold it—lemme get this straight here. You tryin' to tell me you only make a hundred and seventy-five bills a year in the location you got, and with the merchandise you're pushin'? Why you lyin' redskin! *(Pause)* Oh Jesus, I didn't mean that, it just slipped out. *(To Grace)* I didn't mean that.

GRACE: Of course you didn't. *(To the Indian)* I can assure you he didn't mean that. Why, Leonard was vice-president of Concerned Students on the Near Left last year.

LEONARD: Oh, my God, why did I say that?

GRACE: We've been wearing African and Indian shirts to parties for almost a month now.

LEONARD: I feel sick.

INDIAN: Not matter.

LEONARD: Of course it matters.

INDIAN: Not matter.

GRACE: Let it matter!

INDIAN: Not.

GRACE: You mean you forgive him? *(The Indian nods simply, once.)* My God, he forgives you.

LEONARD: He forgives me.

GRACE: He's a saint! Leonard, he's a saint!

INDIAN: You buy authentic souvenirs?

LEONARD: Are you kidding? We'll buy plenty. *(To Grace, turning her loose to help him do penance)* Buy!

GRACE: Leonard, look at these pots—

LEONARD: Buy!

GRACE: *(A miracle)* They're clay! Look—Arizona Indian clay!

LEONARD: Oh, my God! *(Then suddenly sober)* Wait a second. All of the sudden now I'm really concerned. My compassion for this suffering saint has exploded in the aftermath of my no-no. Okay, let's say you only make a hundred and seventy-five a year sellin' this line...What do you got goin' in oil?

INDIAN: No oil.

LEONARD: Why you son of a...What do you mean, no oil?

GRACE: All Indians are in oil, aren't they? Isn't that part of the deal?

LEONARD: Sure it is. *(Squinting into the distance)* What do you call that out there?

INDIAN: Desert.

LEONARD: Leonard means that derrick out there on the horizon. What do you call that derrick?

INDIAN: Cactus. Want cactus candy? Give to friends. They go upchuck.

GRACE: Oh, yes, Leonard! Evelyn and Jay would get such a kick out of cactus candy.

LEONARD: Give us a crate.

GRACE: Not quite so fast, darling. *(To the Indian)* May I sample a piece first, please.

INDIAN: No sample.

GRACE: *(Offended)* Well!

LEONARD: No sample, no buy.

INDIAN: No buy. Make go upchuck.

GRACE: What is he saying?

LEONARD: What do you mean, make go upchuck?

INDIAN: Cactus candy. No buy. Make you puke. Plenty bad stuff.

LEONARD: *(A big condescending smile)* Can I give you a little piece of advice? Now I just got my master's degree in Business Administration so I think we'll both agree that I know from whence I speak. You're never gonna get outta the hundred and seventy-five bracket goin' about this selling thing like you are. Know what I mean?

INDIAN: Not know.

(Bored with Leonard's speech, Grace has returned to the goods)

GRACE: I'm picking some things out. Very nice.

LEONARD: I mean—look. Okay now, I'm you, right? Now I'm in business. I got a little roadside jobby here in Arizona, right? And I'm sellin'...uh...beads and...rings ...and pottery. All right now—

GRACE: And cactus candy. Don't forget that. I love these rings—

LEONARD: He said it makes you puke, Grace, didn't you hear him say about puking? I really don't foresee it as a biggie seller.

GRACE: *(Bringing Leonard in close for a private remark)* He was merely being charitable because you wouldn't buy any. Pay attention, darling.

LEONARD: Okay. Whatever.

GRACE: And stand up straight.

(She helps him stand up straight. Leonard heads back to the Indian, Grace back to the goods)

LEONARD: So beads and rings and pottery and cactus candy. Now—

INDIAN: You want buy me?

LEONARD: What?—Wait a sec. Okay now...*(The Indian's line registers)* What'd you say?

INDIAN: You want buy me?

GRACE: *(On whom the line registered immediately)* Oh, Leonard, let's!

LEONARD: What do you mean, buy you?

INDIAN: You buy me. Good deal.

GRACE: *(To Leonard)* Pretty please.

LEONARD: Now lemme get this straight a minute. You're offering yourself to us for sale. Have I got that straight?

GRACE: *(To the horizon)* Think of it—our very own human!

INDIAN: I live in your house, eat three square ones a day.

LEONARD: Listen, I don't think you know from whence you're giving me this crap. Don't you realize the deal you've got here?

INDIAN: Me starving.

LEONARD: Who you kiddin?

INDIAN: Things really rotten.

LEONARD: What? You mean the competition is too keen?

INDIAN: Hungry all goddamn time.

GRACE: Here now—let's watch our language.

LEONARD: I don't see any other shops around. Looks to me like you control the territory.

GRACE: *(Grabbing Leonard and moving him away from the Indian)* Maybe we could buy him and rent him to Frontierland.

LEONARD: Huh?

GRACE: We might even become an agency.

LEONARD: *(To himself)* Leonard and Grace Rent-an-Indian.

GRACE: *(To the Indian, calculatingly)* We were at Disneyland. I think we neglected to mention that.

LEONARD: *(Follows Grace's lead)* Quite a bit of fun. Been there?

INDIAN: No been.

LEONARD: Damn cute actually.

GRACE: You'll be interested to know that they've got this authentic Indian show. With real Indians, you know, and they come out into the little friendship circle—right out of this darling little teepee, and they're just kids—teenagers—and they dance their crazy little heinies off to the wanton rhythm of the tom-tom.

LEONARD: Every hour on the hour. In between shows I'll bet they're in that teepee stowin' away those hot fudgers, boy.

GRACE: It's quite nice.

LEONARD: The old chief, you know, he makes this speech about how the red brothers are happy that the white brothers have come to...uh—

GRACE: Integrate.

LEONARD: *(Competitively)* —assimilate, as it were, the red man's traditions. Then he brings out the first dancer who does this thing about brotherly—

GRACE: *(Dropping out of the sell)* Except, you know

something, Leonard—they look so...bored or—

LEONARD: Bored!

GRACE: —or resentful.

LEONARD: Resentful! What are you— With the money they're rakin' in and the assimilation that's goin' on.

INDIAN: *(Simply)* Atrocity.

LEONARD: What do they got to be resentful about? Are you— *(To the Indian)* What'd you say?

INDIAN: Beads, pottery, rings, me.

LEONARD: What'd he say, Grace? Did he say—

GRACE: Atrocity. He said atrocity.

LEONARD: Atrocity. *(Angrily)* Atrocity what?

GRACE: Not in that tone of voice, Leonard.

LEONARD: *(Moving in with a wagon load of righteous indignation)* You know what's wrong with you? Your whole self-concept is screwed up. With your mercantile heritage and colorful traditions, you oughta be an ego-maniac, for chrissake!

INDIAN: Me die before go Disneyland.

LEONARD: They wear those fancy headdresses and everything!

GRACE: *(A shocking thought)* Maybe it's all an act.

INDIAN: They hate.

LEONARD: Hate? Hate who? Who hates?

INDIAN: Indian hate.

GRACE: *(Jolted)* Don't you see, Leonard—it's all an act. Why those dirty little fakers!

LEONARD: At Disneyland! Are you crazy? There's brotherhood oozin' outta the woodwork. Those Indians love it. The ole choo-choo goes right by the ole teepee. *(Train whistle)* Whooo-whooo! Oh sure, maybe they haven't got the kind of deal you got goin' for you—oil and a chain of shops and all—but at least—

INDIAN: All Indian hate all white man. *(Begins beating tom-tom and chanting)*

GRACE: *(Moving to Leonard)* Leonard, perhaps we ought to get out of here. I think you've done something.

LEONARD: Done what? Hey, lay off the drum routine, will ya? *(To Grace)* I'm trying to help this schmoe and he's pounding his stupid drum and talking about hating ...Listen—Tonto!

(The Indian intensifies the beat at the mention of Tonto's name)

GRACE: Leonard, are you listening to me? I said let's get out of here before—

LEONARD: Okay, look—we'll buy you.

(Drumming and chanting stop)

INDIAN: You buy?

LEONARD: Yeah.

GRACE: Leonard...

INDIAN: Okay, you got new ball game

GRACE: At least find out how much first, Leonard.

LEONARD: What's your price tag? And don't give me any west coast mark up.

INDIAN: Thirty dollar.

LEONARD: Thirty dollars! Christ, I can buy a slightly defective toy poodle for that.

GRACE: Maybe we should get a dog first. I'm really starting to wonder about this whole thing. Maybe just a souvenir or two—

INDIAN: I be son.

LEONARD: Son! You're old enough to be my grand-father. Just how old are you, Gramps? Don't tell me, Eighty...*six.*

INDIAN: Be thirty-one next Friday.

LEONARD: Bulldork! Don't gimme that crap—

GRACE: May I see you alone, Leonard. *(Reluctantly, Leonard moves away with Grace)* I honestly think a dog first, darling, and then we'll see about an Indian. Now, I'm choosing some trinkets and then we're—

INDIAN: I get car.

LEONARD: *(Swinging back to the Indian)* Your own? Hell no! You'll borrow on the weekend.

GRACE: Leonard, what are you saying?

LEONARD: What *am* I saying? You're not going to be our son.

INDIAN: Be brother then.

GRACE: Well now, aren't we all brothers in the sense of men loving one another? *(Sings)* Let freedom ring...

LEONARD: Yeah, like that—that's fine. But not brother brother—like you just hang around the house and hit the refrigerator kind of thing.

INDIAN: What I be to you?

LEONARD: You'll be my...man.

GRACE: His valet.

LEONARD: Yeah...My guy.

GRACE: Yes.

INDIAN: Kemosabe?

LEONARD: Yeah—kemosabe.

INDIAN: In other word, I be maid.

GRACE: Maid? No, silly. Ladies are maids. Men are—

INDIAN: Niggers.

GRACE: Well...yes. No! What are you talking about?

INDIAN: Maid nigger.

GRACE: No!

LEONARD: No! I mean a lot of them are...uh—

GRACE: Mexicans.

LEONARD: Sure. Mexicans, Puerto Ricans—

GRACE: What are we saying, Leonard?

LEONARD: What *are* we saying?

GRACE: Here: A lot of maids are white niggers—that's what we're trying to say.

LEONARD: Right. Plenty of maids are white niggers. What do you mean white niggers? Who started all this nigger stuff?

INDIAN: Indian and Nigger and Mexican get together.

LEONARD: *(Fearfully, but low key)* What for? *(The Indian starts beating the tom-tom and chanting again. Leonard, to Grace)* What's he pullin' the drum routine again for?

GRACE: *(Heading for some goods)* I'm making some definite souvenir commitments. We haven't given him any money yet. That could be the—

LEONARD: *(To the Indian)* What do you mean the Indians and the Niggers and the Mexicans're gonna get together? *Could you lay off that, hey!* You've givin' me some headache. *(The Indian stops drumming and chanting. Leonard, all business and quiet reason)* Now what do you mean about this getting together?

INDIAN: What you think I mean?

LEONARD: I think you mean the three of you are gonna get together and...uhm...don't tell me...uhm...get the *Jews* 'cause they—

INDIAN: Not.

LEONARD: Not, huh?...How 'bout...uhm...you're gonna get together and...uhm...get the *Catholics* 'cause they—

INDIAN: Not.

LEONARD: Not again. Uhm...I give up.

GRACE: *(Moving in)* I don't give up. You're going to get together with the Negroes and the Mexican-Americans and you're going to build an army and you're going to wipe the white man off this continent.

LEONARD: *(Laughing)* Don't be ridiculous. Jesus, Grace, you got some imagination—

GRACE: Aren't you?

INDIAN: First we torture his rotten white ass! *(Begins to drum and chant again)*

LEONARD: First you're...Oh, no, you don't! Now listen, I'm tired of listening to this crap. *Cut that out!*

(Leonard grabs the tom-tom and destroys it maniacally. The Indian is stoic. Silence)

GRACE: Do you have a broom? I apologize for Leonard's childish behavior.

LEONARD: *(Pulling himself together)* Okay, look I'm sorry, but I get so goddamn tired of hearing all this stuff about...Look, pal, I'm on your side. I'm—

INDIAN: You white son of a bitch.

(The Indian gets off his crate and disappears behind the hut)

LEONARD: Where's he going? *(Calling)* Where you goin'?

(There is no response from the Indian, so Leonard sets himself defensively at the corner of the hut, his putter raised like a club over his head)

GRACE: I'm not sure how that's going to work against an arrow, Leonard.

(The Indian returns from the opposite side with another tom-tom. Grace warns Leonard with a gesture and Leonard turns frantically and leaps at the Indian with an offensive yell which the Indian totally ignores)

INDIAN: *(Taking his seat again)* You owe me for one General Custer tom-tom. This Warrior-of-Navajo-Nation model. How you like?

LEONARD: *(Takes up drum, looks it over, beats it a time or two)* Nice. Gotta helluva tone. *(Leonard turns away and has a go at imitating some authentic beating and chanting; stops abruptly, little embarrassed)* I've always wanted to do that one for a real Indian—you know, just to get some authentic criticism. What'd you think? *(Returning the tom-tom)* Never mind—you'll tell me later; maybe you can teach me a coupla solo numbers. Okay, now listen, getting back to this other thing—

GRACE: Pardon me, but do you have a toidey?

LEONARD: Grace, for chrissake, I'm trying to—

GRACE: I'm sorry, Leonard. *(To the Indian)* Excuse me, but do you have a—

LEONARD: Uh...Grace, maybe you didn't—

GRACE: Leonard, I have to tinkle.

INDIAN: You need urinate?

(Leonard and Grace do a slow take)

GRACE: Why you disgusting savage! Did you hear what he said to me, Leonard?

LEONARD: You wanna watch your language, fella, or am I gonna have to take you downtown?

INDIAN: Take downtown, buy burger and order of fries.

LEONARD: Later. Now, I wanna clear up this miscon—

GRACE: Leonard!

LEONARD: Oh, for chrissake! *(To the Indian)* You got a toilet?

INDIAN: Have dumping grounds. Down in gully. Big hole. *(Points offstage)* There.

LEONARD: *(To Grace)* Go.

GRACE: *(Quietly offended)* It's time to leave, Leonard. We'll take these few trinkets—

LEONARD: Are you outta your mind? You think I'm leavin' with this kinda misunderstanding between us?

GRACE: I don't think you under—

LEONARD: *Use the hole, Grace!* I gotta straighten this son of a bitch out.

GRACE: I...am...not...going...to—

LEONARD: *(To the Indian)* You wanna do me a favor? Just ignore her. Can we get together on that? *(Leonard ignores her. The Indian continues as before. After a moment, Grace exits haughtily to the hole)* Now look, you gotta understand that just because I'm a white guy doesn't mean I'm not sympathetic to you people. Let's be—

INDIAN: Cram sympathy up ass.

LEONARD: No, now look, I'm not kidding about this. You can't make all white men guilty for the...uhm...you know...of a few.

INDIAN: Many.

LEONARD: Okay—many, few, what's the difference? The point is you can't just lump all of us together.

INDIAN: Indian lump.

LEONARD: Don't be ridiculous. See, that's just the point. Can I blame you for Custer's Last Stand? No, of course not. Well, in the same light, you—

INDIAN: You owe me two hundred million dollar.

LEONARD: For what?

INDIAN: New York.

LEONARD: Oh, no, you don't! Okay, so maybe twenty-four bills was a bit of a screwing, but a deal's a deal. See, that's part of what makes the democratic system run.

INDIAN: Screwing.

LEONARD: Deals!

INDIAN: How come no Indian ever President?

LEONARD: Oh, that's cute. I haven't been waiting for that one, right? Has a colored guy ever—

INDIAN: What about Jim Thorpe?

LEONARD: *(Fond memories of Burt Lancaster as Jim Thorpe)* Hey—could that guy punt the pigskin!

INDIAN: You screw his brains out.

LEONARD: Are you kidding me? We made a movie about him and everything.

INDIAN: How many Indians star of tv?

LEONARD: *(Laughing)* This is funny, you know that? You are just—Ahha! Tonto! What about ole Tonto?

INDIAN: Him Uncle Tom Indian. Disgrace to Indian nation.

LEONARD: *(Threatened; low key)* What Indian nation?

INDIAN: *(Rhetorically, with the same intonation as Leonard)* What Indian nation?

GRACE: *(Entering with enormous disdain)* That's some hole. You want to hear about a hole, Leonard?

LEONARD: *(Fretting about the Indian nation business, distracted)* No.

GRACE: *That's* a hole.

INDIAN: Big smelly hole.

GRACE: *(Moving in to remonstrate with the Indian)* Smelly! Why that's . . . Just go down there, Leonard, and take a whiff of that hole. Do yourself a favor. *(To the Indian)* That's disgraceful. Do you know that? Disgraceful. Can't you . . . can't you control yourself until you get home at night?

INDIAN: Home where?

GRACE: To your house or ranch or whatever you live on.

INDIAN: You funny lady. Ha ha! Me live here.

GRACE: You don't live here.

LEONARD: Of course you don't.

INDIAN: Hmm. That funny. All this time, think me live here. No wonder so unhappy: this not my home. If me not live here, where me live?

GRACE: That's what we're asking you. We're not saying you have to have us over or anything. We're just curious as to where you live.

INDIAN: Live here then.

GRACE: Now stop it!

INDIAN: Not live here, huh?

GRACE: No.

INDIAN: Hmm. *(Pointing)* Live over there?

LEONARD: Listen. See: You tell us; we not tell you.

GRACE: *(Trying to speak his language; helpfully)* We not know where you live; that be why we ask you where you live so you tell us and then we know, too.

INDIAN: Live here. In this hut.

LEONARD: *(Coming in to the Indian's ear and speaking the first sentence very softly)* You're about the dumbest bastard I ever met.... Now look! This isn't your house. This is your ... office.

GRACE: Your stand.

LEONARD: Your store.

INDIAN: Ah—my store.

LEONARD: Right.

GRACE: Yes. Now ... when you leave your store at night, where do you go?

INDIAN: Ah!

GRACE: He's got it.

INDIAN: Go to hole.

LEONARD: He hasn't got it.

GRACE: Let's try this: Where is your family? Squaw and pa-poopsies? Where them?

INDIAN: No family. Have Uncle Harry; him on road.

LEONARD: So that's how you rake it in, you crafty son of a gun, you. Pushing it on the road. Clever.

INDIAN: White man clever. Him screw ass off Indian. Pay Indian fifty cent for authentic moccasins, sell to niggers for eight bucks and to white man for buck-fifty. Him clever, boy. Really drag dumb ass Indian over proverbial coals. When we get you, we gonna bury one helluva lotta hatchets in your white head, boy. *(Here the Indian smiles, changing his expression for the first and only time in the play)*

LEONARD: You're talking crazy, you crazy bastard.

GRACE: *(Suddenly going over to see the Indian's side)*
No. No, Leonard, don't you see—

*(During the next speech, Leonard is looking around for
something to subdue the Indian with, motioning Grace
to stay clear)*

LEONARD: You're lying through your rotten teeth.
Christ, why don't you see a dentist. Your personal habits
stink. Look at your nails, ya slob. You look like a mechanic,
for chrissake. You think settin' the family up in a fleet of
... what's—What're they drivin'? Caddies?—You think settin'
'em up in a fleet of Caddies and rollin' in dough doesn't
mean ya gotta take care of your teeth and nails?

*(Leonard has found a lasso on the side of the hut. He
tries a cowboy throw at the Indian but misses, so he steps
behind the Indian, puts the loop around his shoulders
and madly ties him up. The Indian puts up no resist-
ance whatever)*

GRACE: Leonard, what are you doing?

LEONARD: I'm tying this—

GRACE: Don't you see, Leonard?

LEONARD: Don't I see what?

GRACE: That we are merely lending ourselves to the
perpetuation of the bitterness that this man feels toward the
white man. My god, I suddenly see.

LEONARD: Oh, not your sensitivity routine, Grace.

GRACE: *(To the Indian)* Do you understand? I'm no
longer blind to your plight.

LEONARD: *(To the Indian)* Don't get your hopes up.
It's only a routine.

GRACE: Oh, Leonard, how little you understand me,
and how little I've understood our red brothers.

LEONARD: I don't know, Grace, you did this bit a lot
better at our Chitlins and Collard Greens Festival last fall.
(To the Indian) All right now, for a coupla grand, we can
turn this stand into a stunner. Got a minute? I'll just unfurl a

coupla ideas here and we'll run 'em up the flagpole and see who salutes 'em.

(Leonard begins looking over the place, making notes on a small pad)

GRACE: *(Intimately, to the Indian)* You've...you've opened my eyes. Do you understand? Oh, I know how silly this must sound, but I'm going to gain you a measure of retribution.

LEONARD: *(Calling from behind the hut)* What are these walls—cement or cinder block?

INDIAN: Mud.

LEONARD: Mud...What kinda mud is what I mean? Cement or cinder block?

INDIAN: Mud.

LEONARD: *(Coming into view)* If you're not gonna be serious, you can't expect the top results. What kinda beams you got? *(No response)* Supports? You know, what holdee up roofee?

GRACE: That's Chinese, Leonard.

INDIAN: Grass and mud.

LEONARD: You got a real cute sense of humor.

INDIAN: And twigs.

LEONARD: Uh-huh. *(Wanders out of sight again)*

GRACE: *(Intimately)* He never has understood me now that I think of it. *(Pause)* And now that I think of it, this is a hell of a time to be thinking of it. *(Pause, dreamily)* You know how when you're young you think about the person you want to marry?

INDIAN: No.

GRACE: *(Oblivious of his answer)* I was the same way—dreaming all the time. And, you know, I never wanted to marry a schmoe like Leonard. I always dreamed about marrying a poet or a professional golfer. That's why Leonard plays golf; I made him take it up...God, he's lousy. *(Pause)* Really a poet, though. That's really what I wanted. And we'd have a big old house in Vermont and every afternoon I'd take lemonade and fudge to his study, and he'd write sonnets to me and make me immortal...What did you dream of? *The Indian stares blankly at her, then resumes his position)* Oh, God, you're really touching me now.

LEONARD: *(Coming into view with a tom-tom)* You ever thought of going the All-the-orange-juice-you-can-drink-for-a-dime route?

INDIAN: Never thought of.

LEONARD: *(Holding up the tom-tom)* What do you get for this model?

INDIAN: Sitting Bull model. Plenty extras. Rawhide binding, fur-tipped drumstick—a steal at buck-sixty.

LEONARD: *(Laughing)* A buck-sixty! You gotta be joshing. No wonder you're still in the Caddy bracket. Christ, with any kind of sound advice you'd have been driving Silver Clouds years ago. Now, if this were my business, I'd up this model to four-fifty. If she turned out to be the top of my tom-tom line, I'd tack on another buck and label her "Special Today Only." *(Puts tom-tom down beside the Indian; to Grace)* You know what I could do with a place like this. Huh?

GRACE: Do it.

LEONARD: I could pull down maybe fifteen-twenty grand in this place with a coupla alterations.

GRACE: Do it, I said.

LEONARD: Do what? Buy him out, you mean, and we'll settle here?

GRACE: No. You buy him out and *you* settle here.

LEONARD: I don't get it.

GRACE: I'm leaving you, Leonard.

LEONARD: What about the wedding presents?

GRACE: Take them.

LEONARD: That's not fair. I want to be fair in this. I'll just take the waffle iron an' what I think I can pass off as authentic Indian stuff.

GRACE: Untie him, Leonard. After nearly five hundred years, it's time he had his freedom.

LEONARD: Are you kidding? Not till I make a deal.

GRACE: *(To the Indian)* My husband...my *ex*-husband would like to make a deal with you for your business.

Let him have it. I can help you start a new life. I'll take you to Albuquerque.. I have an uncle there who owns a cigar store. I know he'll give you a job.

LEONARD: Okay, what do you want for the building and your total inventory?

GRACE: *(To the Indian)* Don't let him cheat you. And be sure to get his golf clubs in the deal.

LEONARD: I heard that! *(Guarding his golf clubs)* One of the first things I'm putting in here is an authentic Indian miniature golf course.

GRACE: *(To the Indian)* When we get to Albuquerque I'll give you our Volkswagen.

INDIAN: Me not touch German car with ten foot pole.

GRACE: Why not? It has a sunroof.

INDIAN: Father, three brothers killed in World War II.

GRACE: World War II... I'm afraid I'm not familiar with that one. Well, I'll give you everything in the U-Haul trailer.

LEONARD: Sounds fair to me.

GRACE: Untie him, Leonard, and let us be on our way. I'm sure you're as anxious to begin your new life as we are.

LEONARD: *(To the Indian)* No funny business: my upper arms are like cast iron clubs. *(Unties the Indian, then to Grace)* I want you to know, Grace, I appreciate what you did for me there.

GRACE: We've shared a lot, Leonard.

LEONARD: It was the least you could do.

GRACE: What will you do now, Leonard?

LEONARD: Not Leonard anymore—that's the first thing.

GRACE: Oh?

LEONARD: Uh-uh. Leaping Jolly Deer.

GRACE: Oh—very nice. Leaping Jolly Deer. What else?

(As Leonard goes on, Grace begins to look over the Indian, wondering how he might look cleaned up and "whitened")

LEONARD: Well, I figure between Williams and Flagstaff I'll throw up maybe ten billboards and hit 'em with the ole pooh-pooh the competition routine. Tired-of-the-same-old-Indian-souvenirs... That one.

GRACE: I suspect that with all our Jewish brothers getting ready to send their children off to summer camp you'll do a fierce business in moccasins.

LEONARD: You think you're telling me something, Grace?... Now, on either side of the teepee, I put up in all caps: LEAPING JOLLY DEER'S—DIZ IS DE PLAZE. Huh?

GRACE: Oh, yes.

LEONARD: Now—ready for this? You listening, Grace?

GRACE: Yes, Leonard.

LEONARD: Gas. *(No response from Grace who is looking at herself and the Indian in her hand mirror to see what kind of portrait they make)* You're stunned, right?

GRACE: Automobile gas?

LEONARD: No, Grace, intestinal. Yeah, automobile! And hold onto your jock, Grace. I'm puttin' in a car wash out back. *(No response from Grace who is doing a little work on the Indian's hair)* Again stunned, huh? Get the picture, Grace: You're on the road to or from the Grand Canyon.

GRACE: And the car is filthy.

LEONARD: You got the picture. Bugs all over the windshield, maybe a bird in the radiator, a skunk squashed into your tire treads. And here you are coming from or going to one of the eight wonders of the world. You're feeling patriotic as hell, see? But here you are in this pig pen of a car. Suddenly—

GRACE: Suddenly...out there on that vast open desert...out there amidst the emptiness of this uncivilized land...it's LEAPING JOLLY DEER'S!

LEONARD: Yeah! FREE CAR WASH WITH FILL UP! The whole approach'll be to hit 'em in their Clean. If they're goin', they'll feel like they won't be despoiling the grandeur of the Grand Can. If they're leaving, the car wash'll act as a purging or somethin.'

GRACE: Oh, Leonard.

LEONARD: What do you think, Grace?

GRACE: It's brilliant.

LEONARD: Oh yeah, well it's not completely formulated yet, ya know.

GRACE: But what a beginning for you.

LEONARD: I mean I know I'm gonna have to put in a coupla crappers and level some of those damn hills and dales out there for parking but— *(Pause)* I wish to hell I could divert some of the truck crowd out this way, but I'm afraid that's hopeless. Unless I put in one damn good takeout burrito stand or something. Well, what say we chow down some pimento cheeses and sign the papers. *(To the Indian)* You got a mortgage on this place? Get the picnic stuff, Grace.

GRACE: Yes, Leonard. *(She exits)*

LEONARD: *(To the Indian)* All right, pal, let's go inside and get this spelled out on paper. I know you probably couldn't care less about contracts and all, but I like everything legal and above board. *(The Indian starts beating a tom-tom and chanting)* Not now, man. You're gonna be big time, then grow up, will ya. *(The beating and chanting intensify. Leonard grabs the tom-tom and destroys it. The Indian takes up the other tom-tom and begins beating it. Leonard grabs this one and destroys it with careful fury. The Indian exits behind the hut)* No more tom-toms! I'll look at all your goods in a minute. Oh, hell!

GRACE: *(Entering with a picnic basket)* I brought some jams, too.

LEONARD: You know what I'm thinking might go in a place like this? Specialized items. You know, the kind of thing that's in big demand on a trip, but where do you get it? Like...uh...the rubber vomit, rubber dog turd line.

GRACE: Do you know what *I'm* thinking, Leonard?

LEONARD: Uh-uh.

GRACE: I'm thinking. Look at us, Grace Paul and Leonard Forsyth—doing a good one for the red man.

(They do a humble take on each other and enter the hut. We hear Leonard's voice, don't see them anymore)

LEONARD: Turn on the light, will ya. Oh, Christ, he doesn't have any electricity here. That's carrying the authenticity thing too far, if ya ask me. *(The Indian comes into view slowly. He's carrying a beaten shotgun. The lights fade to darkness but for a low illumination on the door of the hut)*Hey, ya crazy redskin, throw some light on the subject, will ya!

(The Indian pushes the door open and there is a blaze of shotgun fire into the hut, then sudden darkness)

Curtain

Stanley Richards

Since the publication of his first collection in 1968, Stanley Richards has become one of our leading editors and play anthologists, earning rare encomiums from the nation's press (the *Writers Guild of America News* described him as "Easily the best anthologist of plays in America"), and the admiration of a multitude of devoted readers.

Mr. Richards has edited the following anthologies and series: *The Best Short Plays 1975; The Best Short Plays 1974; The Best Short Plays 1973; The Best Short Plays 1972; The Best Short Plays 1971; The Best Short Plays 1970; The Best Short Plays 1969; The Best Short Plays 1968; Ten Great Musicals of the American Theatre; Best Mystery and Suspense Plays of the Modern Theatre; 10 Classic Mystery and Suspense Plays of the Modern Theatre; Best Plays of the Sixties* (the latter four, *The Fireside Theatre-Literary Guild* selections); *Best Short Plays of the World Theatre: 1968-1973; Best Short Plays of the World Theatre: 1958-1967; Modern Short Comedies from Broadway and London;* and *Canada on Stage.*

An established playwright as well, he has written twenty-five plays, twelve of which (including *Through a Glass, Darkly; Tunnel of Love; August Heat; Sun Deck; O Distant Land;* and *District of Columbia)* were originally published in earlier volumes of *The Best One-Act Plays* and *The Best Short Plays* annuals.

Journey to Bahia, which he adapted from a prize-winning Brazilian play and film, *O Pagador de Promessas,* premiered at The Berkshire Playhouse, Massachusetts, and later was produced in Washington, D.C., under the auspices of the Brazilian Ambassador and the Brazilian American Cultural Institute. The play also had a successful engagement Off-Broadway during the 1970-1971 season; and in September 1972, it was performed in a Spanish translation at Lincoln Center.

Mr. Richards' plays have been translated for production and publication abroad into Portuguese, Afrikaans, Dutch, Tagalog, French, German, Korean, Italian and Spanish.

He also has been the New York theatre critic for

Players Magazine and a frequent contributor to *Playbill, Theatre Arts, The Theatre* and *Actors' Equity Magazine,* among other periodicals.

As an American theatre specialist, Mr. Richards was awarded three successive grants by the U.S. Department of State's International Cultural Exchange Program to teach playwriting and directing in Chile and Brazil. He taught playwriting in Canada for over ten years and in 1966 was appointed Visiting Professor of Drama at the University of Guelph, Ontario. He has produced and directed plays and has lectured extensively on theatre at universities in the United States, Canada and South America.

Mr. Richards, a New York City resident, is now at work on *The Best Short Plays 1976* and the second volume of his very popular and nationally acclaimed series, *Ten Great Musicals of the American Theatre.*